Praise for *J2EE 1.4: Th*

"Need to learn J2EE? *J2EE 1.4: The Big Picture* is a must-have guide that is both enjoyable and educational. I highly recommend it."

Peter van der Linden, software consultant and author of Expert C Programming, Not Just Java, *and* Just Java

"Anyone working with J2EE needs this book. You can get the details and the code examples from a lot of other places, but this book provides the essential understanding of all the parts and how they work together."

Simon Roberts, author of the Sun Certified Enterprise Architect for J2EE Technology *certification exam and study guide*

"I've ordered copies of *J2EE 1.4: The Big Picture* for everyone in my department. Not only because it's the most understandable technical book I've ever read, but because my review copy keeps disappearing from my office."

Larissa Carroll, manager, BEA Systems

"If you're tired of technical books that are all about the details and don't tell you how the whole thing works, you want this book. There's absolutely nothing else like it."

Patricia Parkhill, managing editor, Sun Microsystems

"I like it very much. It definitely paints a clear picture of the whole J2EE thing. It's a book I'd recommend to J2EE developers of any skill level."

Dirk Schreckmann, JavaRanch Journal Editor and Sheriff in the JavaRanch Big Moose Saloon

"This book gives me a headache, because on just about every page I'd slap myself in the head and say 'That's it?!? That's what all the mystery is about?!' Now I feel like I'm in the know. I might not be able to code this stuff yet, but I sure get what's going on now."

Floyd Jones, senior technical writer, BEA Systems

"This book makes J2EE seem so easy. The informal, friendly tone of the book is extremely helpful. It made me understand the beans stuff, CMP and BMP, without any effort at all. In fact, it is frighteningly perfect and uncomplicated. I think the book is also just the right one for managers, project managers, and other non-techies who interact with J2EE developers."

Manish Hatwalne, Software Consultant, Circus Software LLC

"I love *J2EE 1.4: The Big Picture*. I love how it breaks down a big thing, like J2EE services and architecture, into smaller digestible chunks. And once in the micro topic, the explanations are so easy to absorb. The explanations do build on top of each other, making—dare I say it—a big picture. And I FINALLY GET TRANSACTIONS!"

Jeannie Saur, documentation specialist, Trimble Navigation Limited

"I would recommend this as a good beginner's reference for J2EE, or for anyone looking for a supplement for an advanced J2EE course."

—College Java instructor

J2EE 1.4

The Big Picture

Solveig Haugland
Mark Cade
Anthony Orapallo

Prentice Hall PTR, Upper Saddle River, NJ 07458
www.phptr.com

Library of Congress Cataloging-in-Publication Data

A catalog record for this book can be obtained from the Library of Congress.

Editorial/production supervision: *Nicholas Radhuber*
Acquisitions editor: *Gregory D. Doench*
Cover design director: *Jerry Votta*
Cover design: *Anthony Gemmellaro*
Manufacturing manager: *Alexis R. Heydt-Long*
Interior design: *Solveig Haugland*
Marketing manager: *Chris Guzikowski*

PRENTICE HALL PTR
Published by Prentice Hall Professional Technical Reference
Pearson Education, Inc.
Upper Saddle River, New Jersey 07458

Prentice Hall books are widely used by corporations and government agencies for training, marketing, and resale.

Prentice Hall offers excellent discounts on this book when ordered in quantity for bulk purchases or special sales. For more information, please contact:
U.S. Corporate and Government Sales
1-800-382-3419
corpsales@pearsontechgroup.com

For sales outside of the U.S., please contact:
International Sales
1-317-581-3793
international@pearsontechgroup.com

Printed in the United States of America

1st Printing

ISBN 0-13-148010-3

Pearson Education LTD.
Pearson Education Australia PTY, Limited
Pearson Education Singapore, Pte. Ltd.
Pearson Education North Asia Ltd.
Pearson Education Canada, Ltd.
Pearson Educación de Mexico, S.A. de C.V.
Pearson Education — Japan
Pearson Education Malaysia, Pte. Ltd.

Acknowledgments

Thanks to Greg Doench for riding the wacky route of this particular project, and for not minding when we used the word "wacky." Thanks to Tom Post for reading my mind and drawing the cutest EJB container I've ever seen.

Thanks to Jeannie Saur, Floyd "Velvet" Jones, Patricia Parkhill, Dirk Schreckmann, James Chegwidden, Manish Hatwalne, Tonia Sharp, Larissa Carroll, and Paul Wheaton for reviewing and providing thoughts on the book. Thanks to Olav Maassen for going above and beyond. Thanks to Dan Johnsson of OmegaPoint for the reminder that state is not evil. Thanks to Simon Roberts for his insight.

A Different Kind of Technical Book

Here's a little information on what the book's about, who it's for, how the book came to be, and who we are. We're doing this because *The Big Picture* isn't like most books out there. We want to make sure you know what you're getting.

What This Book Is and Isn't

This book is a big picture look at J2EE. What it's made of, how the parts work together, what the heck a container is, what entity beans are for. Occasionally we'll also touch on things like when J2EE and its parts might or might not be the right choice for a particular project.

This book will help you understand how things work so that not only do you know but you can explain the J2EE big picture to others. It will help you feel comfortable asking questions in meetings, and give you a great foundation if you're going on to learn how to do J2EE programming or system administration. You'll also learn the *point* of the technologies. Not just what message-driven beans are, not just what an EJB container is, not just what Web services are, but *why* they're around.

This book is the paperback version of getting that J2EE wizard down the hall from you to sit down over lunch or a few beers and explain things to you. Reading this book is like sitting in a bar with your co-workers after work, not falling asleep in your fourth session of the day at JavaOne.

This book is *not* going to teach you how to *do* J2EE. Don't look for a lot of painstakingly annotated code examples. There are a few bits of code but they're not the focus.

We believe in using a relaxed, casual approach to teaching and to just how we write. For instance, the three main categories of J2EE services are analogous to Brain, Courage, and Heart from The Wizard of Oz, so we use that analogy. And we sometimes say things like "clearly, that would suck" or "stateless session beans are flaky but good at heart."

We do take accuracy seriously. Very seriously. We're just not concerned with writing this book in a way that will get us to the finals of the "Pompous Technical People" competition.

Absolute Technical Completeness Versus Being Easy to Understand

When was the last time you read a big book with lots of information that went into painful detail about exactly what the topic was about?

And was this book *also* easy to understand, easy to read, and a good way for a beginner to get acquainted with the topic?

Probably not. We've never come across a book like that, and we're going to bet that very few of you have, either. Absolute completeness and technical accuracy, and being easy to understand, rarely coexist. When we wrote this book, we knew we were going for being easy to understand.

The way we provide the understanding is to leave out a lot of technical details, and blur some of the details to make the concepts understandable. And we use analogies, which are great for the initial "aha!" moment, but break down eventually if you take them too far. The rmiregistry does not have all the same attributes as a post office or a phone book. We know this. But the analogy is a good way to get the gist of the concept.

This does *not* mean we're not concerned with accuracy. Learning something easily but wrong doesn't do anyone any good. We're just emphasizing that this is a different kind of book you've got here, so you'll need a different set of expectations.

Gus the Ultra-Detail-Oriented Programmer Who Loves to Read Specifications is not going to be happy reading this. People who blanche at the idea of contractions or conversational tone in a book aren't going to like it, either. However, if you want something that will quickly and clearly give you the big picture, though, we're pretty sure you're holding the right book.

Who This Book Is For

This book is for anyone who doesn't fully understand how the whole J2EE thing works. Whether you're a techwriter, a new member of the marketing team trying not to be intimidated by the engineers, a straight-up Java programmer switching to the enterprise stuff, or a senior architect who wants to review a few things, we think you'll find this book useful.

This is also a book for anyone who was turned off reading *J2EE in 36 Months of Intense Boredom*.

That sounds like a fairly wide audience, and it is. The breadth is based on what we found out in reviews, though, not just conceited authors thinking that anything that falls from our lips is valuable to the whole darned world. Here's what happened. Just to be thorough, we asked a wide variety of people to read through the book, and found that pretty much everyone, from an entry level technical marketing person through programmers and architects, found value in it.

- A Web component developer told us he loved the clear explanations of Enterprise JavaBeans, which he hadn't worked with yet.
- A scripter who had worked primarily writing macros liked the book's 10,000-foot approach. (More detailed than the 30,000-foot view but not deep into the code.)
- A technical reviewer took it on vacation (yes, on vacation) and read parts aloud to her nontechnical friend, who claimed that she actually understood portions of it.
- A college-level Java instructor said he would recommend it as an introductory text or as a supplement to an advanced J2EE course.
- An architect for a consulting firm told us he would recommend it to all the architects on his staff.
- Several technical writers appreciated that it provided important information that helped them do their jobs better, but without being overwhelming and confusing.

How *The Big Picture* Came About

It's not often that dancing leads to J2EE books, but that's kind of what happened with this one. Two dance lessons in particular.

Solveig Haugland, one of the coauthors on this book, took a merengue dance lesson a couple of years ago. She came away dazed and confused, feeling like the clumsiest, stupidest person alive, and convinced she'd never be able to do it.

She somehow found the courage to go back to dance lessons recently where she discovered that, in fact, *merengue is the simplest dance there is.* You just step around the floor on the beat and occasionally twirl. OK, there's some fancy hip stuff that's hard to do but it's not essential.

A lot of technical stuff is like merengue. If you don't know the point, and you've got some expert at the front of the room waving their hands and talking about how to move your hips just right when you don't even know where to put your feet yet, you're doomed. Even on something as simple as stepping around the floor in time to the music. And certainly on something like Java, patterns, J2EE, and, well, pretty much any other technical topic.

You might be a godlike J2EE genius in the rough, but you won't know it if you're reading *J2EE: We Aim to Confuse.*

Here's the second dance anecdote. At a Lindy for Beginners class in Boulder, Solveig found that there were a lot of expert dancers there. When queried, they said that they were there just to brush up on their basic steps. These people had been dancing for years, but they came back to the beginner lessons periodically to focus on the basic steps. Without a good basic steps, you tend to screw up the more complicated moves, plus nobody wants to dance with you.

Polishing and reviewing the basics is valuable in dance, and valuable in any profession, especially software.

Book Web Site

The Web site for the book is http://www.bigpicture-books.com.

About the Authors

We've put together a triumvirate of different types of experience on our author team, all heavily dosed with real world experience.

- Solveig Haugland is a technical writer and instructor. She knows what it's like to sit through hours of tech gibberish that make absolutely no sense. She would sooner drink a vial of really vile poison than put stuff into this book like "session beans reify the enduring business processes of your enterprise." Without a suitable explanation, at least.
- Mark Cade is a member of Sun Professional Services. This is the same group that brought you John Crupi, Deepak Alur, and Dan Malks of *Core J2EE Patterns* fame. Mark's been with Java since the beginning and works on big J2EE projects for a living. He's also the coauthor of the Sun J2EE architect exam and the architect exam study guide.
- Anthony Orapallo's a technical instructor and has taught a variety of Java topics, including Sun's Enterprise JavaBeans course. He knows what it's like to be up there in front of a class explaining just what the Home interface is, so he knows how to *teach.*

We check and balance each other to make sure that the book is clear, accurate, and applicable. We've created a book that's accurate and to the point, but simple and clear, that you can actually enjoy reading.

quick contents

detailed contents

Grandfather: "This is a special book. It was the book my father used to read to me when I was sick, and I used to read it to your father...and today, I'm going read it to you."

Grandson: "Does it got any sports in it?"

Grandfather: "Are you kidding? Fencing, fighting, torture, revenge, giants, monsters, chases, escapes, true love, miracles..."

Grandson: "It doesn't sound too bad. I'll try and stay awake."

Grandfather: "Oh, well, thank you very much. That's very nice of you. Your vote of confidence is overwhelming."

The Princess Bride

part I

Introduction to J2EE

"Hello.
I'm the guy who sits next to you
And reads the newspaper over your shoulder.
Wait.
Don't turn the page. I'm not finished."

Lyle Lovett, Here I Am

Part I explains the stuff that no one ever seems to talk about—first of all, what J2EE is for, in plain English. Plus what the parts of the J2EE download are, what the marketing spiel from Sun means (again, just in plain English), and what all those services are all about. We also present situations where you can see clearly that getting J2EE would clearly be a good idea, and situations where it wouldn't.

Part I also introduces you *slowly* to the technologies. As fun as it would be for you to read 50 straight pages on Enterprise JavaBeans, we decided to do it more gradually. We created a small trail of beans in Part I for you to follow through the J2EE forest, so you don't get indigestion or worse. Part II expands on the technologies.

When you're done with Part I, you should know the names of all the players and generally how the whole system works.

Here's what you'll read about in Part I:

chapter 1

High-Level View of J2EE

"Here is Edward Bear, coming downstairs now, bump, bump, bump, on the back of his head, behind Christopher Robin...here he is at the bottom, and ready to be introduced to you."

A. A. Milne, Winnie-the-Pooh

Let's get down to the essence of J2EE. What is it? People talk about using it a lot. The marketing people say it's powerful and complex and don't forget robust. But so is your morning mochachino. So that's not really useful information.

We're going to go beyond the buzzwords in this chapter to explain J2EE in plain English. Plus we'll talk about not just what it is but, more importantly, why. Why do you care about J2EE? What does it do for you as a manager, developer, customer, or D) other?

The Chapter in Brief

Here's the trailer for this chapter, so you know what you're getting into.

Some applications are distributed, which means they're online, or the code for the applications is spread out over a bunch of different machines because they're so big or are in heavy demand. These applications have to deal with special challenges because of being distributed: the application developers need to worry about security, data integrity, and resource management. These are difficult things to handle. So application servers were created to provide these services so application developers could concentrate on the application instead. J2EE is one standard for creating application servers and the applications that hook up to them to take advantage of those services.

Here's what we cover in this chapter.

- *Who's Afraid of Building a Big Distributed Application?*
- *Application Servers Are There For You and Your Distributed Application*
- *The J2EE Application Server Standard*
- *An Application Server Is Like a Factory*
- *Where J2EE Came From*
- *Example: Antoine's Online Pizza Business*
- *Tools Sun Provides*
- *The Chapter in Review*

Note: As you might well have gathered, this is not your typical technical book. Gus the Ultra-Detail-Oriented Programmer Who Loves to Read Specifications is not going to be happy reading this. If you want something that will quickly and clearly give you the big picture, though, we're pretty sure you're holding the right book. For more information, see *A Different Kind of Technical Book* on page vii.

Who's Afraid of Building a Big Distributed Application?

Think about your text editor.

Now think about how you'd write code for a text editor.

We'll start small, then start exploring what happens when you have to deal with different environments.

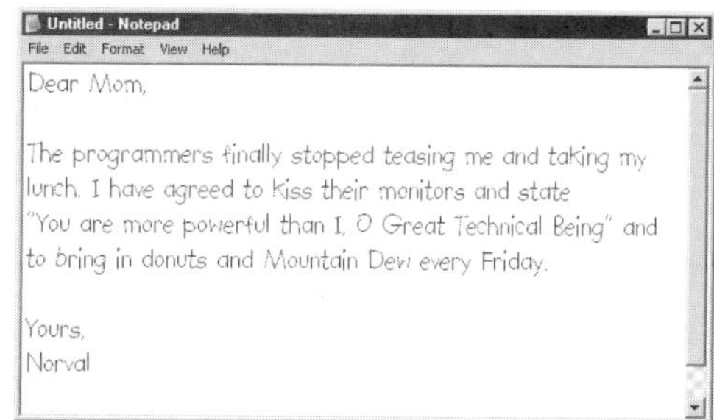

Dear Mom,

The programmers finally stopped teasing me and taking my lunch. I have agreed to kiss their monitors and state "You are more powerful than I, O Great Technical Being" and to bring in donuts and Mountain Dew every Friday.

Yours,
Norval

Writing a Nice Little Application That Never Leaves Home

Imagine trying to write code for that nice little text editor program. Not something you can code in a day by any means, but its functions are fairly clear and limited.

The application has to handle what you type or click, translate that into the standard ASCII system for figuring out what character the typist wants, display it, enable cut and paste, etc. All on the same computer. So all in all this programming project is relatively manageable and focused in scope.

Writing an Online Application With a Lot of Users

Now think about trying to write a different kind of word processing application. Something that lots of people can access at the same time. They just go to www.multiuser-wordprocessing.com and just start the application there. Hundreds of thousands of people are going to be trying to use this. They'll be typing up their theses and shopping lists and letters to customers. And retrieving other documents they've already created and printing the documents. See Figure 1-1 for a representation of all those people getting at the application.

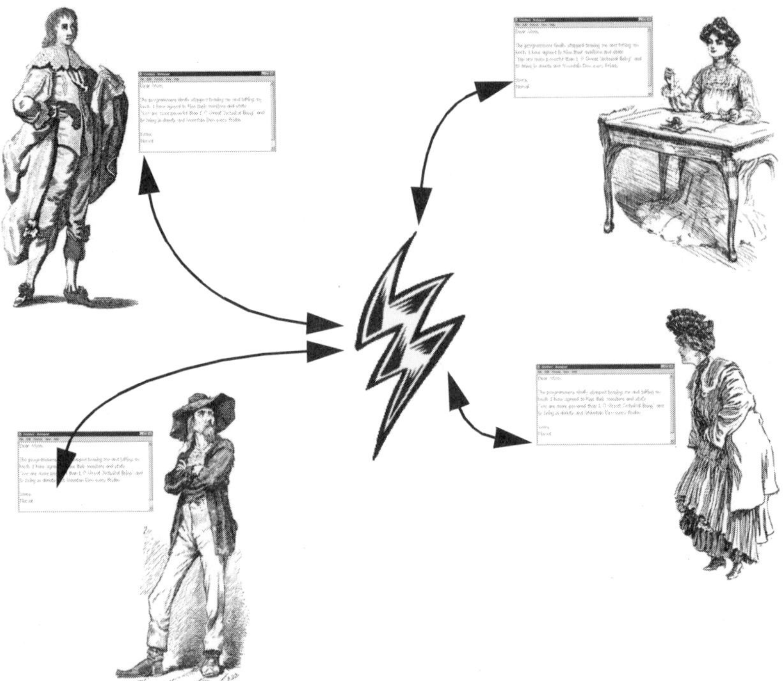

Figure 1-1 Multi-user online word processing application

This is a *distributed application*, since the code that makes the application run, and the application data like people's preferences and documents, are distributed on different computers.

How do you make sure the distributed application will work well with lots of people, from all over the world potentially, using it at the same time?

- What about resource management? What if everyone's trying to use it during the holidays to write holiday letters? How do you make sure that the program isn't really slow with all those people using it?
- What about data integrity? If you're in Oslo and you make some changes to your shopping list, will that text for sure be saved in the right document, or will "Remember to buy reindeer" show up in the annual report of some very confused guy in Fargo?
- What about security? Can Olav in San Jose find out everyone who's using the word processing application, and spam them with a list of hot sexy COBOL programmers with their own webcams?

These are all issues you really don't have to worry about when you're writing a normal safe single-user application. These are all issues that companies like Amazon have to deal with every day. And Amazon is just the beginning. Imagine applications that are even more important than text processing or Amazon, like aircraft control systems. If your order for that Hello Kitty TV gets goofed up, no big deal. If two planes try to land in the same spot, that's a big problem.

So making distributed applications run well with security, data integrity, and resource management is important. We get that. But normal software development is hard enough, and making software work when there are pieces of code on different computers and multiple users trying to access it, is even harder. Orders of magnitude harder.

Hmm. Wouldn't it be nice if you could just find something that would help out with all these issues? Software that you could connect your application to and boom, your distributed application is running safe and sound?

Application Servers Are There For You and Your Distributed Application

With all that buildup, there'd better be such a piece of software. And there is.

A distributed application, like the big online or critical ones we talked about in the last section, can be hooked up to the Special Powers of an *application server.* Then the distributed application can be up and running safely and efficiently without your having to write the code to deal with all those problems yourself. When your application is hooked up to an application server, you've got services that deal with all those problems we mentioned in the last section.

An application server is kind of like an empty factory. You move your business into and boom, you've got a security system and assembly lines and all sorts of cool tools that you didn't have to build yourself.

An application server is software that doesn't do regular stuff like sell you socks or let you write documents. A server's users aren't people; the server's users are other applications. Application servers provide services to distributed applications. These services include security, data integrity, and resource management (making sure there's enough memory to go around). These services are already written up and ready for you the application developer to take advantage of. All you have to do is write your application to hook up to an application server, and boom, your system is up and running and lookin' good.

J2EE Is One Standard for Application Servers

There are lots of different kinds of application servers. J2EE is one kind of application server. CICS and Tuxedo are other types of application servers. The one that comes in .NET is another.

But we're not talking about them in this book. Let's take a closer look at what's actually in a system using a *J2EE* application server.

The J2EE Application Server Services in Brief

A J2EE application server gives you three main categories of services:

- **Security** The J2EE application server takes care of *security*, a marvelously complex issue we'll get into later in a bit more detail. Security makes sure people who aren't authorized to get at the application, or to do things that aren't authorized, can't do stuff they shouldn't. It keeps a list around of what each part of the application can and can't be asked to do, and by whom. And more.
- **Data integrity** The server manages transactions, meaning that if a customer's order comes along in three different steps and the power goes out just before the third part is completed, that the other two are cancelled and it's as if nothing ever happened. The programmer still has to do some brain work, however, since if you don't plan well you can still screw up your data, but the application server gives you tools for the mundane, repetitive stuff that's so easy to get wrong if you're a human rather than a computer. We're also using this category to cover the capability of the container to help the application get information in and out of the database without screwing up the data.
- **Resource management** The server takes care of *resource management*. One aspect of this is ensuring that memory used by one part of the application gets freed up and available for use by other parts. The container can also create ready-made connections to the database to make database access quicker and cheaper.

What Do You Have If You Have J2EE?

The term "J2EE" is tossed around an awful lot, and it's hard to tell just what it is (partly because some of the people talking about it, including your boss, don't quite know what it is). "Have you got J2EE? Are you J2EE compliant? Is that J2EE or are you just happy to see me?" Etc.

People Who've Got J2EE Applications

When people say "Hey, my application is J2EE," they mean that:

- They're running a J2EE application server

And that the application they run their business on is:

- A J2EE application, written specifically to work with a J2EE application server

People Who Sell J2EE Application Servers

If you're talking to people whose nametags say "Hi, I sell J2EE application servers!" they mean that:

- They and their team of fairly brainy programmers have written a J2EE application server. They've followed Sun's rules for how to make a J2EE application server, and have probably looked at the blueprints (coding guidelines), patterns (design guidelines), and reference implementation (sample J2EE application server) that Sun provides to help people like them make application servers.

And they also mean that:

- You or anyone can write a J2EE application that will hook up to their server and get J2EE services.

And if they have any marketing skills at all, they also are subtly reminding you that:

- You or anyone can take a J2EE application that's already hooked up to a different company's J2EE application server, and just switch over to *their* J2EE application server instead. More on that shortly.

Who Uses J2EE?

People who have big applications use J2EE. This seems a little too simple but it's a start. We'll explain that a little more. The official term for the applications that need J2EE is, as we mentioned, *distributed enterprise system*. Distributed means that the application, including the data, is two or more different computers. (There are other ways to be distributed but we'll leave it at that for now.)

Two basic things create the need to be distributed:

- Being online means you're distributed, automatically. Someone with their browser can be anywhere, your code is in Poughkeepsie or wherever. Not all online applications need to use J2EE, but being online does mean you're distributed.
- Having a lot of users means you probably want to be distributed. The more different computers you can use, the more computer power you have to run your application, and you'll need a lot in order to make the application run fast enough for all those users. The more users you have, the more storage space you'll need for user data, as well. If you have 10 users and each requires 2 MB for their data, that's not a big deal. If you're a bank or a credit card company or Amazon and you have millions of users, you're going to need a lot of machines to store all that data.

We talk about who might use J2EE, and what's a good fit, in Chapter 7, "Does a Cup of J2EE in the Morning Always Smell Like Victory?," on page 79.

You could use J2EE with small applications but that would be like using the space shuttle to go grocery shopping. A lot of work and complexity you don't need when a Subaru, Vespa, or bicycle would work just fine.

The J2EE Application Server Standard

We mentioned previously that someone selling you a J2EE application server might want to remind potential customers that it's easy to move an application from one J2EE application server to another. Here's why that's true.

J2EE Is a Standard for Application Servers

J2EE isn't a specific application server product. It's a standard, a type, rather than a specific server product. You can't go to a Web site or a store and say "I'd like the J2EE Application Server, please." And if you did, the clerk or error message would pop up and say "Which one?"

J2EE is a *standard* for creating servers. A standard is just a set of rules people follow to make things easier and more consistent.

When you buy downhill skis, for instance, you know that no matter what brand of downhill boots you buy, they'll fit into the downhill ski bindings because everyone uses the same *standard* for creating downhill boots and bindings so they'll fit together. (Your cross-country ski boots wouldn't fit into downhill bindings, of course, since cross-country bindings are created using a different standard.)

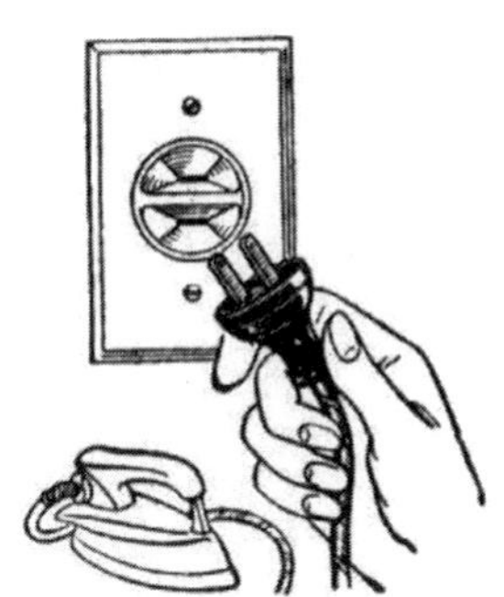

American companies making appliances all adhere to the same electrical *standard* of 110 volts, and multiple companies in Europe adhere to the 230 volt standard.

Having a standard is nice because you can buy a bunch of different irons, or hair dryers, and they'll fit into your outlet. Just as the 110 volt hair dryer fits into any 110 volt outlet, a J2EE application fits into any J2EE application server.

Note: More or less. Slight tweaks might be involved. For now, let's say that all J2EE applications fit all J2EE application servers, period.

If you tried to hook a J2EE application up to a non-J2EE application server, it wouldn't work because they use different standards.

J2EE Is an *Open* Standard

J2EE is an open standard. Sun gives people instructions for how to write servers, and applications, to the J2EE standard. Not only that, but they take suggestions for features to go into J2EE, though it definitely helps if you're a big J2EE-friendly company rather than just Some Guy.

This is unusual because software companies usually like to keep how to make their applications to themselves, but not in this case. Anyone can download the specification and write themselves a J2EE application server. (Well, anyone with the necessary technical expertise and intestinal fortitude. Kind of like how anyone can grow up to be elected president.)

That means two things.

- First, there's a lot of choice when you're shopping for a J2EE application server: BEA WebLogic, IBM WebSphere, Sun's Java Enterprise System, and so on. All those companies have downloaded the information for how to build J2EE application servers, and built'em.
- Second, that you're not stuck. Let's say you've bought a J2EE application server. If you don't like your first pick—maybe the company doesn't give good customer service or they're overpriced—you can go out shopping again for a J2EE application server from a different company.

  Once you get the new application server, switching your application to it goes relatively easily. All the J2EE application servers work fundamentally the same way. You might have to do some tweaking depending on stuff we'll get into later but by and large the switch between J2EE application servers is a great deal easier than switching between types of servers.

An Application Server Is Like a Factory

As we mentioned previously, an application server is like an empty factory where you can set up your business. If you've got a business, you don't have to build your own factory. You can just move your business into it and automatically get all the benefits of that factory. It's got an amazing security system, incredibly fast internet built in, assembly lines for bringing the parts you need in or taking them away, a recycling system, cleaning people, meeting rooms, an office manager, and all sorts of other things that your business needs desperately but which really aren't core to your business, whether it's airplanes or pizzas or financial services.

Now, to be sure there's more to it than just showing up with a few boxes and signing on the dotted line. There are some really complex rules you need to follow in order to use this factory. You need a team of workers that are trained to work in this factory. And the rent isn't cheap. But it's got services you need and over all, it's better for you to do your business in this building than to try to build your own factory from the ground up, or to use a smaller, punier factory. After all, if you're making airplanes or medical equipment, you want a serious place to do it. You can't make good airplanes sitting around in someone's garage. On the other hand, if you're making pot holders, you probably don't need a big complex powerful expensive factory to do it in. (Unless you're making a *lot* of pot holders.)

Another benefit is that it's a standard kind of factory. So if it burns down you can go find another factory of the same kind and move on into that one without retraining your workers and changing processes.

Let's match up the analogy and reality briefly. We talked about the factory providing services; these are analogous to the application server's services of security, data integrity, and resource management.

- Security – In the factory, this could correspond to big security system for the outside, plus those little card recognition things outside all the rooms where important stuff is going on. So someone might be able to get into the factory itself but not into other parts.
- Data integrity – In the factory, this would be like an office manager who sees the people who come in to place orders and makes sure that their orders get sent through correctly. If they just up and leave halfway through the order process, the office manager never places their unfinished order. The office manager also makes sure that pieces of paper from different people's orders don't get mixed together.
- Resource management – In the factory, this would be making sure that everyone has enough tools to do their jobs. If all the workers need hammers to do their jobs but you can't afford to buy them all hammers, then the resource manager scurries around taking the hammers from the workers who are on lunch break or doing riveting, and giving them to the workers who need to do hammering.

Geek Note: J2EE Is a Platform

If you
really want
to know

You've probably heard people going on about whether Java is a platform. And it is. What's a platform, though? A platform is a large collection of features that can be used by a bunch of different applications. The features are administrative things, not central to what the applications do, but still necessary. And the features provided by platforms are generally difficult enough to write that it's nice to just be able to hook up to them rather than to have to write the code for them yourself.

You can think of a grocery store as a platform. If you want to make a cake, you can go there and just get the cake mix. So can all the other people in the world who want to make cakes, or have milk and cereal. So each and every one of us doesn't have to grow our own wheat, grind the flour, cut the sugarcane, grow the cacao plants, raise the chickens for the eggs, and so on. Not only does this make things easier for you and the other grocery store customers, but consider this. You just want to throw a birthday party. You don't want to get into sugar cane and raising chickens. You are perhaps even allergic to chickens. Doing all the things it takes to arrive at the final cake product is so not what you want to do with your time.

As we mentioned before, all analogies break down eventually. Don't take this too far. It does however give a good rough idea of the type of benefit a platform provides.

A platform is not an operating system. An operating system stands between you and your applications, and the hardware and deals very specifically with manipulating the hardware.

Where J2EE Came From

Some say, when asked where J2EE came from, that Ada Lovelace and James Gosling loved each other very much, and then nine months later J2EE came along.

Some will give you another explanation.

Here's that explanation. It probably wasn't lost on most of you that the J in J2EE probably has something to do with Java. So let's go briefly into Java to see where J2EE came from.

Java is a programming language developed by Sun. It does the same general kinds of things as other programming languages, like C++. It has a few key features that distinguish it from other programming languages, which you can read about in *The Gist of Java in General* on page 245.

Once upon a time there was only Java. Just plain Java, not J2EE or J2ME or J2SE or Java 2, Heroes' Edition.

But Java grew, and features got added, and more tools were developed, and people asked for more features. And the marketing people started to get twinkles in their eyes. So in a change that was partly code reorg and partly a marketing-related renaming event, Sun waved its wand, changed the name of Java to *Java 2*, and split the single Java entity into triplets: *J2SE*, *J2ME*, and *J2EE*.

J is for Java, and 2 is for 1.2

If you really want to know

*The J is of course for Java, and you'd think that the 2 would be an indicator of a version. However, that 2 is one of the most confusing numbers in Java. It's been Java 2 since **1.2**. Java **2** is now on version **1.4**, and before that Java 2 was on **1.3**. So if you're confused, that's the right way to feel.*

The splitting of Java resulted in what's shown in Figure 1-2.

J2ME

Java 2, Micro Edition

A different toolset for writing Java applications for **handheld devices** and other items with limited resources

J2EE

Java 2, Enterprise Edition

An additional set of tools that work with J2SE. J2EE is tools for writing **big distributed applications**.

J2SE

Java 2, Standard Edition

The core functionality of the Java programming language, for writing **regular run of the mill applications**.

Figure 1-2 Java became three different types of Java

- **J2SE** – Java 2 Standard Edition. The basics for writing regular programs that probably aren't going to stray too far from their home computer. If you wrote a regular text editor application in Java that just runs on one person's local computer, you'd be using the Standard Edition, J2SE.
- **J2EE** – Java 2, Enterprise Edition. These are the big tools that are used to create servers and the applications that work with them. These are the tools for handling applications that have separate bits working together and distributed all over the world.

  J2EE can't go anywhere without J2SE, but it adds on a whole lot. J2EE is like a big trailer you can hook up to your J2SE SUV and go out and survive in the desert for a year. It doesn't run without J2SE but man, does it add a lot.
- **J2ME** – Java 2 Micro Edition. Java that does stuff that's similar to J2SE, but generally smaller cuter applications and on pagers, PDAs, smart cards, etc. If J2SE is an SUV, J2ME is a Vespa scooter. Don't worry about it for the rest of this book.

Example: Antoine's Online Pizza Business

It helps to learn stuff in context. Here's the scenario we'll be using throughout the book: Antoine and his online pizza business. Antoine starts off with a regular old online application, nothing fancy, and it works fine. As his business grows, though, he has to make changes, and eventually ends up using a J2EE application server with a J2EE application.

The point of this section is to see what happens as a business grows, and the situations that would lead to choosing to go with a J2EE system.

Antoine Starts an Online Pizza Store

Antoine had just quit his job as a program manager in order to fulfill a life-long dream: making and selling gourmet pizzas. He bought a lot of pepperoni, flour, eggs, secret spices, and all the other stuff he'd need to make his pizzas. But he didn't want the expense of setting up a store, so he's got an online business instead. Orders come in over the Web site, Antoine makes the pizza there in his kitchen, he calls his cousin Gus over to deliver it, and boom, people get their pizza. He's not covered in cash but it's a nice little business.

Antoine got Floyd the programmer to make the pizza Web site for him. Floyd was a tough but genial coot with solid experience and he made the Antoine's Pizza application that Antoine's running on.

Antoine's Pizza is a browser-based application, www.antoinespizza.com, with some nice pretty Web pages. It includes *business logic* too. Business logic is just the central part of any program, not the extra bits that control how it looks or how data gets stored. For instance, when Antoine was doing pizza research he discovered that he wasn't allowed to sell more than ten pizzas to any one person (strict Homeland Defense regulations). He also decided to do a little price promotion: anyone who orders three large pizzas gets free wings.

Business Booms and Performance Goes Bust

So what happens when things change? And they will, if time exists in your dimension.

Here's what changed for Antoine. His pizza was reviewed in *Cheese and Bread Monthly* and overnight, his pizza business was ten times bigger. He suddenly needed to be doing business on a much larger scale. So he hired a bunch more people, and got cooks and delivery people set up all around the country. He scaled up his people so he had enough human resources to handle the demand. But his application was still droning along like it only had a few orders each day, and that caused a lot of problems. Everyone who wanted pizzas couldn't get their orders through. People were placing orders and getting billed for them, but the order never came. One of his pizzas, the meat lovers' super supreme, suddenly started showing up in the vegan menu, and priced at $1.79 instead of $17.99.

Antoine had problems with resource management, data integrity, and security. And it's all Floyd's fault. Floyd had neglected to put in any code in Antoine's Pizza application to deal with these problems. You can't really blame him, though. Writing the code to make sure the application does resource management, data integrity, and security, and to do it well, is harder than doing Enron's taxes in Chinese on a hot day.

Antoine Buys the Features Floyd Left Out by Getting an Application Server

Antoine hired Jennifer the Amazing Programmer to look at his system. Jennifer rides a Harley and wears a black leather jacket, but she's not all flash. She knows her stuff and tells Antoine, "Man, you need an *application server.*"

Thinking that this was all he needed from her, he thanked Jennifer and showed her the door, called up Floyd, and got Floyd to pick out and install a nice application server. Not only did the application server give him data integrity, security, and resource management, but Floyd installed the application server a couple more times on some darned powerful computers to increase performance. One might say he installed a cluster of computers. Then he installed the application server on each one and flipped the switch on the server's Load Balancing feature so that the servers, well, shared the load. Balancing all the users comin' in wanting pizzas.

Antoine Experiences the Heartbreak of Vendor Lockin

Soon Antoine's site is running lickety-split again. Life is good. He's considering outsourcing his oregano needs to Croatia, and he's found just the right fresh mozzarella.

Six months pass, each day more filled with cheese discoveries than the last. One morning Antoine happens to read about a little company called ServeIt going out of business. He thinks nothing of it at the time. However, later that day, he checks his site, and there's some really weird stuff going on. He calls the company who makes ServeIt. Hmmm, he thinks, as he listens to the message.

"Hello, this is the CEO of ServeIt, Dewey Cheatham. Sorry, customers, we've gone out of business. And our application is currently obsolete because it doesn't work with the new YNM Web protocol and new version of Sphinx database you're probably running. And lest ye forget, we write our application servers based on our own closed standards and our lead programmer just took off for Bermuda. So you can't find any other application server that your application can work with.

The ServeIt company had ended with a bang, and Antoine began to whimper.

Antoine called up Floyd, fired him again (with a few choice words) for having selected an application server based on closed standards. He left messages at motorcycle conventions all over the country for Jennifer. He begged her to come back and find him an application server that A) was in business, B) worked, and C) he wouldn't need to throw out if the company went out of business.

Antoine Gets a J2EE Application Server

Antoine brought in Jennifer and she rewrote his application to work with a J2EE application server. Sun, Jennifer told him, publishes all the rules for how to make a J2EE application server and how to make your applications work with one, and there are lots of different companies that sell J2EE application servers. So if WebLogic, the application server he chose, goes out of business or if he doesn't like it anymore at some point in the future, he can switch over to WebSphere (another J2EE application server) without much fuss. Or JBoss, which is free. All this verbage can be summarized by saying that J2EE is based on *open standards*.

Switching to an open standard server was the final key step that switched him from an awfully good system with one fatal flaw (a Vendor Lockin Sword of Damocles hanging over his head) to a full J2EE system.

A Note About Antoine's Pizza Shop

We're going to be using Antoine's pizza shop as our example throughout the book. When we explain any part of J2EE, whether it's Web services or entity beans or servlets, we're going to say Antoine is using it. Antoine's pizza shop is a nice simple example and we don't want to confuse things by introducing a bunch of different examples adapted for each type of technology.

We therefore want you to be aware that Antoine's pizza shop might not, in real life, be a good choice for implementing everything *in J2EE. He would benefit from a nice J2EE system with JSPs (HTML on steroids) and servlets (Java code that specializes in the Internet) connecting to a database. He might also benefit from using the session beans, which rush around doing complex tasks, but perhaps not from entity beans. It all depends on what Antoine's business is like, what he wants the application to be like, and what kind of development team he has.*

So when you read about Antoine, just look at it as a nice simple example and not a specific instance of when to use every bit of J2EE. For more information on choosing one or more parts of J2EE, see Chapter 7, "Does a Cup of J2EE in the Morning Always Smell Like Victory?," on page 79, and Chapter 19, "Good J2EE Architecture," on page 225.

Tools Sun Provides

We thought it would be a good idea to throw in a few specifics from Sun: exactly what elements compose the J2EE tools you get from Sun, and their info on what J2EE is and our Big Picture translation.

So If I Want to Write J2EE Stuff, What's Available to Help Me?

Let's say you woke up this morning with an intense desire to write a J2EE application server. Or you want more than anything in this life to write a J2EE application. First thing you need to do is go get the free information and tools from Sun. Here's what you would get from http://java.sun.com/j2ee

- The J2EE **specification,** which is a big technical manual all about writing J2EE application servers and applications. It's *very* technical. Print it and put on your bookshelf with sticky notes sticking out of it if you want to intimidate people.
- The J2EE standard **code**, or API, or classes—all those names are used. It's all the classes that developers can bend to their will to turn into J2EE applications. Some of it is for writing J2EE application servers, and some of it for writing J2EE applications.
- The **reference implementation**, which is an obscure way of saying a sample application server. People writing J2EE application servers use it as an example of how things work; people writing sample applications use it as a stopgap, free server. It's not necessarily meant to be used for commercial purposes, and is a bit on the slow side. However, depending on how much hardware you want to throw at it, it can be faster.
- The **J2EE blueprints**, which are the guidelines for how to build your J2EE application from an architectural perspective. This means the 30,000 foot level of how to put the system together, not specific things like exactly how to write code. That's what the specification and the API are about.

  The J2EE blueprints aren't the only guidelines for how to do J2EE application servers and applications; a lot of people worship at the altar of Martin Fowler's books, Floyd Marinescu's *EJB Design Patterns* is well respected, and the *Core J2EE Patterns* book has its followers, as well.

The Official J2EE Description From Sun, and an English Translation

The official description of J2EE from Sun is shown in Table 1-1; we've provided their text in the left column and our interpreted version on the right. We hope the original-and-translation here will also help you translate other techy marketing language elsewhere.

Table 1-1 Sun's J2EE marketing spiel, and what it means in English

Sun's J2EE marketing	***English translation***
Enterprises today need to extend their reach, reduce their costs, and lower their response times by providing easy-to-access services to their customers, partners, employees, and suppliers.	This just means "get online or die," and that it's not just about selling to customers. It's useful to have a system up so the people who buy stuff from you to resell can have that convenience, too.
Typically, applications that provide these services must combine existing enterprise information systems (EIS) with new business functions that deliver services to a broad range of users.	You can't just take your old database and old applications, and slap a Web page http://www.myoldstuff.com/index.htm in front of it. You've got to throw in a little new code and new structure too.
These services need to be: Highly available, to meet the needs of today's global business environment. Secure, to protect the privacy of users and the integrity of enterprise data. Reliable and scalable, to insure that business transactions are accurately and promptly processed.	You're going outside your business's walls, so you have to deal with all the problems you encounter the minute you walk out the door, like the potential of having half a million users trying to access your system all at the same time. It would also be nice if your system could grow to accommodate more users without your having to rewrite it, and if it could take orders without screwing them up if the power goes out.
For a variety of reasons, these services are generally architected as distributed applications consisting of several tiers, including clients on the front end, data resources on the back end, and one or more middle tiers between them where the majority of the application development work is done.	You don't have one big lumpy application doing all this; you separate it into tiers (just separate chunks of code) according to the job the code is doing.
The Java 2 platform, Enterprise Edition, reduces the cost and complexity of developing these multi-tier services, resulting in services that can be rapidly deployed and easily enhanced as the enterprise responds to competitive pressures.	J2EE makes the whole development project simpler because it takes care of things like security, dealing with concurrent requests from lots of customers, and making sure your system is always up and running. You still need to write some code to plug into those J2EE services. When you need more of those services or different ones, it's easy to upgrade.

Table 1-1 Sun's J2EE marketing spiel, and what it means in English (Continued)

Sun's J2EE marketing	***English translation***
During the early `90s, traditional enterprise information system providers began responding to customer needs by shifting from the two-tier, client-server application model to more flexible three-tier and multi-tier application models. The new models separated business logic from both system services and the user interface, placing it in a middle tier between the two.	J2EE and the tier-separation thing are the latest and greatest in the evolution of applications trying to figure out, "how do we write big online and/or distributed applications right."
Within Sun Microsystems, several development efforts pointed us toward what would become J2EE technology. First, the Java servlets technology showed that developers were eager to create CGI-like behaviors that could run on any Web server that supported the Java platform. Second, the JDBC technology gave us a model for marrying the "Write Once, Run Anywhere" features of the Java programming language to existing database management systems. Finally, the success of the Enterprise JavaBeans component architecture demonstrated the usefulness of encapsulating complete sets of behavior into easily configurable, readily reusable components.	You've got different tiers that do different things, so Sun made specific kinds of code that you can write that are specially adapted for those tiers. Servlets let you do processing that gets sent through HTTP to the customer. (Servlets do what CGI code did and still does, which is to let regular applications venture out on the Web, but with some improvements.) It's all operating system-independent, none of this "now we need to compile the Windows version" silliness. (As for the reusable components bit...that's still kind of a fantasy but there's progress.)
The convergence of these three concepts—server-side behaviors written in the Java language, connectors to enable access to existing enterprise systems, and modular, easy to deploy components—led us and our industry partners to the J2EE standard.	J2EE Is Good. Use It. (That's basically the gist. This is just Sun's summary paragraph.)

The Chapter in Review

These are the most important concepts in this chapter.

- An application server is software that provides services like security, data integrity, and resource management, to J2EE applications.
- A J2EE application, which makes or sells things or services, hooks up to a J2EE application server, taking advantage of the services the application server provides.
- A J2EE application server is written according to the J2EE application server standards provided by Sun.
- J2EE is an open standard that a lot of companies like BEA and IBM use to write J2EE application servers.
- Open standards in this context mean that there are multiple J2EE-type servers and you can switch from one to another fairly easily.

chapter 2

More on What J2EE Is All About

"You put your right foot in, you take your right foot out, you put your right foot in, and you shake it all about.
You do the hokey pokey and you turn yourself around, that's what it's all about!

Children's song, "The Hokey Pokey"

So far so good. J2EE is a platform that gives you services. Write your J2EE application to hook up to a J2EE application server, and you can have those services.

Services. That's one of those vague words that marketing people use to make it sound like they've got all sorts of great features without saying anything specific. *Resource management*, for instance. Sounds great, and you certainly wouldn't want resource *mis*management, but what does it mean? What exactly does J2EE do to manage resources and do all those other services? Let's get some more detail on these services, and on just how the whole system really works.

The Chapter in Brief

When you buy a J2EE application server, you get not just the software that gives you these services (the software is actually called a *container*) but other tools; everything together is the application server. The server gives three basic categories of services: security, data integrity, and resource management.

The whole J2EE system is enforced by interfaces, which are sets of code showing the programmers what rules they need to follow when they write for the program. Interfaces also allow programmers the flexibility to write what they need to for that application to run.

Here's what we talk about in this chapter.

- *Components of a J2EE Application Server*
- *More on Application Server Services*
- *How Interfaces Make It All Work*

Components of a J2EE Application Server

A J2EE application server is actually one or more pieces of software that together make the application server product. There are usually a couple *containers*, some deployment tools, a Web server, and so on. Those are the pieces of software; the application server is the product as a whole.

Here's what goes into a J2EE application server, including the *container* which we just introduced but didn't define.

A Container Is What Provides the Services

The heart of an application server is a *container.*

We've been talking about how the application server provides all these services, and it's actually this thing called the container? Well, yes. We were simplifying before. Bear with us.

The container program is what gives you the services we've been talking about so much. The container does all the smart stuff: takes requests from the clients and relays the appropriate messages to the application, takes care of security, sends data to and from the database, and so on.

Application server is a general term that you use for any software providing these types of services, J2EE or not. A *container* is the heart of a specifically J2EE-type of application server.

How the Container Interacts With the Application and the User

The applications never interact directly with the outside world. Requests that come in from customers go through the container, and the container tells the application what to do. The application does it, tells the container, and the container does what's necessary to report back to the customer. It's like quarantine, but more so. A J2EE application actually couldn't run on its own, without the container. It doesn't have the capabilities to interact with the outside world and take care of itself, because it relies on the container for so many things. Kind of like how Mr. Burns from *The Simpsons* can't survive without Smithers.

This Application Server Is Big Enough for the Two of Us Containers

The word *container* applies to any piece of J2EE application server code that does these services, or at least a couple of'em. There are different kinds of containers for different types of J2EE application code.

We wanted to illustrate each type of container in this book. We took out our camera and trained it on the software but the results were pretty boring and of course they all looked pretty much alike.

So to visually represent each container, we're using animals. Powerful, smart animals for the more powerful containers, and focused, less widely skilled for the other kind of software we're going to talk about in just a minute. We've decided on what we think is the "silicon spirit guide" of each of the containers and servers.

There's the Web container, the EJB container, and the *Web server*, which we'll talk about very soon. They're shown in Figure 2-1.

Web server that interacts with **HTML** pages only. Like a bee: good at what it does but not destined for upper management.

Web container that handles the heavy lifting and brainier work for Web code. Very bright but lacking one or two of the services that the EJB container gives.

EJB container that takes care of, well, the Enterprise JavaBeans. Strong, intelligent, *and* good-looking.

Figure 2-1 What we're discussing in this section: the two containers plus the surprise guest, the Web server

The Container That EJBs Run Inside Is an EJB Container

We're going to say the EJB container is kind of like a dolphin: about as smart as it gets.

EJB container

What are EJBs, though? Good question. EJBs is short for *Enterprise JavaBeans.* Enterprise JavaBeans are powerful code that can do business logic for you, and represent your application's objects like customers, products, and so on.

Business logic is the stuff that takes in orders, calculates sales tax, and says "OK, let's take three of those out of the warehouse in Atlanta." There are many ways to make business logic; it's just something you have in your program, whether it's written in BASIC or Java. Business logic is the guts of your application, and the kind of beans that do that are session beans. The kind of beans that represent the main things in your application like customers are called entity beans.

The EJB container provides all three of the services we've discussed: data integrity, security, and resource management. The Web container, by way of contrast, only gives security.

There's a Web Container Too

Note: If you've ever heard of the *servlet engine*, *Web container* is the new name.

As we said, there's more than one kind of container. Here's the Web container. The Web container is kind of like a horse; smart, hardworking, powerful. The horse Web container somewhat different skillset from the dolphin EJB container, since they operate in different environments.

Web container

The Web container also doesn't have the data integrity or resource management features of the EJB container; it just provides security. It also provides some resource management since you get some basics for just being Java, but not the full extent of the services from the EJB container. Not because the Web container is wimpy or lazy and wants to give you less, but just because the code that runs inside the Web container doesn't really need as much from the container.

Here's the code that runs inside the Web container.

- JSPs, or JavaServer pages, are Web pages on little tiny Java steroids; there's bits of special Java code in them.
- Servlets are more like normal Java code that's specially adapted to work out there on the Web. They do work behind the scenes, dealing with stuff on the Web side, and sometimes taking orders from the Web side and asking for stuff to be done on the EJB side or in the database. Sometimes servlets will generate an HTML page on the fly.

JSPs and servlets, since they're tools you use to build J2EE applications, need a container too. They can't function out there in the cold cruel Web world on their own either. And they can't use the EJB container since they can't run in the EJB environment, just as a horse couldn't live in a dolphin's environment.

When you buy an application server, you usually get an EJB container *and* a Web container. So that's another reason for having the term *application server*, and *container*. When you get an application server, you usually get two containers.

The Web container also interacts with the *Web server*.

Just to Confuse Things, There's a Web Server Involved Too

So far we've been talking about the J2EE application server. Here's another kind of server, quite different from an application server. (Server is a really broad, overused word.)

The *Web server* is a simple little program that just knows how to speak HTTP (the protocol, or language, of the Internet). It receives all the requests for things like "that page, pizzaorder.html". It figures out where the pages are and sends'em back to the client. It's like a hardworking little bee; not a lot of different skills but what it does, it does well.

However, sometimes it gets a request for something like "pizzaorder.**jsp**" or "pizzas.**class**" which it recognizes as a JSP or servlet and therefore involving Java code, not just HTML. When that happens the Web server sits up in alarm and says, "Hey, this is complicated stuff that's out of my league. This is a job for the Web container."

How does the server know that the request is for a servlet or JSP? This depends on the server. For example, Apache uses modules that are plugged into the server. The modules are configured to look for certain URL patterns such as .jsp that are handled by that module.

You can get pretty much any Web server you want. Some Web servers, like Apache's, are free. The Web server usually isn't there in the box when you buy an application server since they're so simple and not that unsimilar. However, often the application server you buy will have a special little adapter program so that whatever Web server you pick, it'll be able to talk to that application server. You install your EJB container and Web container, you install your Web server. Then you take the right plugin program, for your Apache Web server or whatever, and install that too. Figure 2-2 shows what might happen if a user simply asked for a plain old unimaginative info.html page.

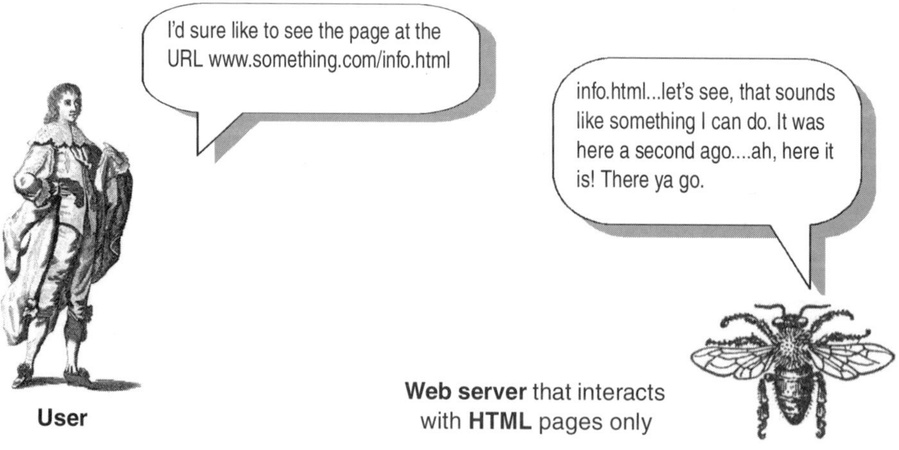

I'd sure like to see the page at the URL www.something.com/info.html
info.html...let's see, that sounds like something I can do. It was here a second ago....ah, here it is! There ya go.
User
Web server that interacts with **HTML** pages only

Figure 2-2 Client, Web server, and a plain ol' HTML page

Note: Sometimes people say *users*, sometimes they say *clients*. Sometimes that means a person, sometimes it means the client application which is usually but not always a browser. Our point here is just that when you hear *client* or *user*, it's pretty much the same functionality.

In Figure 2-3, we show how the scene would play out if the user now wanted a JSP instead of plain HTML. The customer talks to the Web server, who talks to the Web container. And as it turns out, the JSP code needs a session EJB to do some work for it too, so the EJB container gets involved, as well.

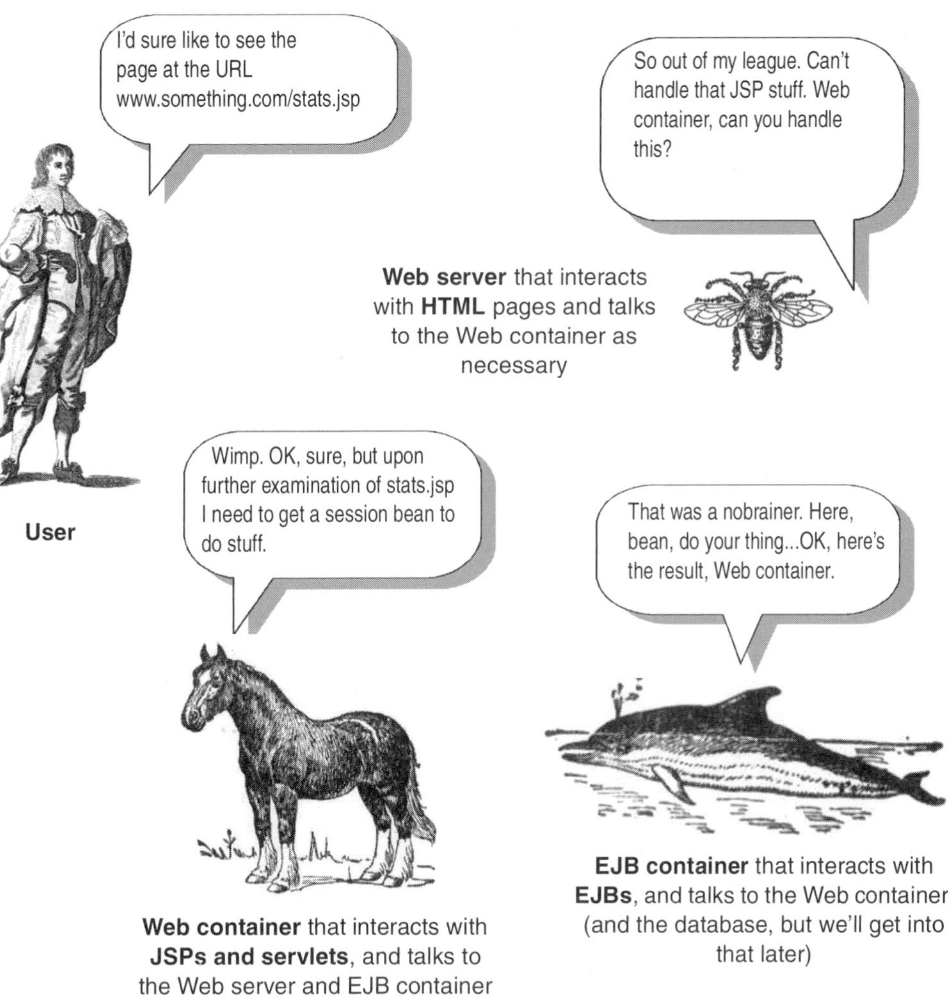

Figure 2-3 Client, Web server, Web container, and EJB container

So to sum up, here's what's in a J2EE application server when you go out shopping.

- An EJB container that provides resource management, security, and data integrity services to the part of your application that's written using EJBs
- A Web container that provides resource management and security services to the part of your application that's written using JSPs and servlets
- A Web server that does simple stuff in the language of the Internet, HTTP (the Web server might be included, or you might need to get your own)

The Web Server Isn't Always In the Picture

The Web container has the ability to read HTTP, deal with plain HTML pages, and otherwise do the Web server's job for it (much to the Web server's dismay). So sometimes the Web server isn't involved at all. However, the Web server does show up a lot, especially when there's no Web container and the Web pages want to communicate with EJBs.

We explained it because we figured it was easier for people to discover later, "Oh, the Web container can do the Web server's job too?" then to go "What's this Web server thing and what is it doing in my J2EE application?"

More on Application Server Services

Now that we know more about what's actually in an application server that provides all those services, let's talk a bit about what those services are.

Note: Keep in mind that of these services, only security is provided by both the EJB container and the Web container. There's also a little resource management available to the Web container, but only the same old resource management, garbage collection, that's available to anything made out of Java.

Conveniently enough, the three types of services are analogous to the Big Three characters that Dorothy meets in *The Wizard of Oz*. After all, if you've got courage, a heart, and brains, there's not much you can't do.

- *Data integrity*, or Brains – Data integrity includes things like making sure that if you pay for your pizza from Antoine's pizza shop and you're interrupted before you give your address for delivery, that either you do get the pizza like you expect, or you're not charged for the pizza and it's like the whole thing never happened.
- *Security*, or Courage – Security involves techniques for preventing others from messing with your pizza order, from getting into your credit card, from accessing beans that they shouldn't, etc.
- *Resource management*, or Heart – One kind of resource management is making sure that *objects*, the code representation of customers and orders and so on, get created and then killed off so they don't keep consuming memory. (This is Heart because it makes sure that everyone's treated fairly and gets what they need.) You get some resource management from the JVM, garbage collection, that you get in any Java application. Another kind of resource management is creating connections to the database ahead of time, to improve performance.

We'll go into each one in a little more detail on the following pages. This is a medium-high level look at each. We get into more detail in a chapter for each: Chapter 15, "Resource Management," on page 185; Chapter 16, "Data Integrity, Transactions, and Concurrency," on page 197; and Chapter 17, "J2EE Security," on page 207.

Data Integrity (Brains)

Data integrity is the brains of the outfit. The container does a set of things, in conjunction with the transaction management services in your database management system. The database management system is just the brains of your database; kind of like a librarian who's the brains of a library.

The container does a few different things, covered in the next sections.

Getting Stuff In and Out of the Database

One of the big responsibilities that the server can take over is stuffing data from your application into the databases, and pulling the right data out when it's needed for other operations. The server knows what tables and rows and machines the database is on, and it knows how to deal with all sorts of databases.

The application server can take over the responsibility for getting data in and out of the database. This is called *container-managed persistence* or CMP. Without this feature, programmers have to write a lot of database-related code. That's a lot of work.

Container-managed persistence not only saves work when writing an application the first time around, but helps with maintenance. Switching from one database management system to another is easier if the container is the one who has to deal with the change, not the programmers.

Keeping Related Tasks Together, Through Transactions

Imagine you're using an ATM. Put in your card and PIN, tell the machine how much money you want and from which account. The ATM software takes the correct amount out of that account, then spits out the correct amount of money to you. These steps form the money-getting-out transaction. A transaction is a set of tasks that should be completed all together or not at all.

Imagine if there was a power outage right after the money was deducted from your account, but before you received your money in the ATM money slot. That would be really annoying. It would be nice if, instead, that whole transaction were rolled back so it's as if you had never even started the transaction. You still don't get the money, but you don't lose the money from your account either. That roll-back feature is part of transaction management.

Security (Courage)

Security gives your site Courage; the ability to resist things that will compromise it. You of course need and want security. If unauthorized users are hacking in and deleting all your transactions, that's really annoying.

Security features include *security realms*. This is a list of who's who and what kind of user they are (administrator, peon, etc.). The EJB container looks at this list and at a few other files, and determines and enforces what users in the realm are allowed to do. You can specify that certain users can run some methods (procedures) for a particular session EJB, but not others. The getInfo() method would be fine for everyone to use, for instance, but setPrices() wouldn't. You can also specify what directories users can get to so that the servlets in the /everyone directory are accessible to everyone, the servlets in the /management directory are available to anyone who's assigned the Manager role, and the /admin servlets are available only to the person with the ID guido.

You can do security *declaratively*, which means the container takes care of it, or *programmatically*, which means you decide you can write the code better and you don't mind doing the work yourself. Programmatic gives you more control and you can do things with it more precisely.

Security is a big topic, and we'll go over it in more detail in the security chapter.

Resource Management (Heart)

Here's the Heart element. We decided that it's Heart because resource management is a kindly service making sure everyone's got the memory they need to do their jobs. Part of resource management in J2EE is stuff that you get just because J2EE is Java, and part of it is J2EE specific.

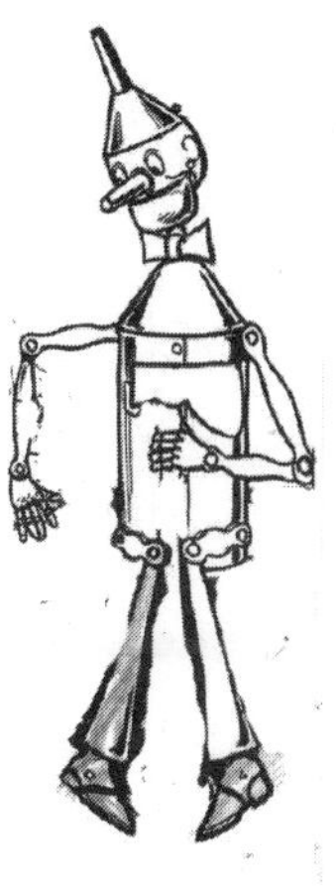

Memory Is the Big Resource

In regular human life, the big resource is, say, money or time. In J2EE application server land, memory is the thing there's never enough of.

Resource management is pretty much about memory management. Being smart with it, and taking it from things that are done with their share and giving it to things that need it.

It's not actually possible to have enough memory in your system to accommodate all the possible simultaneous processes that there could be, for a big enterprise application. That means resource management, management of memory and so on, is necessary.

Stuff the Garbage Collector Does for You Because J2EE Is Java

Java code doesn't automatically give its memory up when it's done using it. That would be nice, but it's just not proactive. So you have to have something that's always walking around, looking for memory no one's using anymore, and picking it up and throwing it in the recycling bin and bringing it around to the Memory Rental shop again. That's what the garbage collector does, which is what you get just for using Java, whether or not it's J2EE.

Connection Pooling

J2EE does its own specific resource management, as well. One of the things that needs to be done in a J2EE application is creating a connection to the database before the code can actually query the database for information. Doing that takes a lot of memory and can slow things down, so the container creates a bunch of connections ahead of time for use as needed. That's connection pooling.

There's a lot more resource management, which we cover in Chapter 15, "Resource Management," on page 185.

How Interfaces Make It All Work

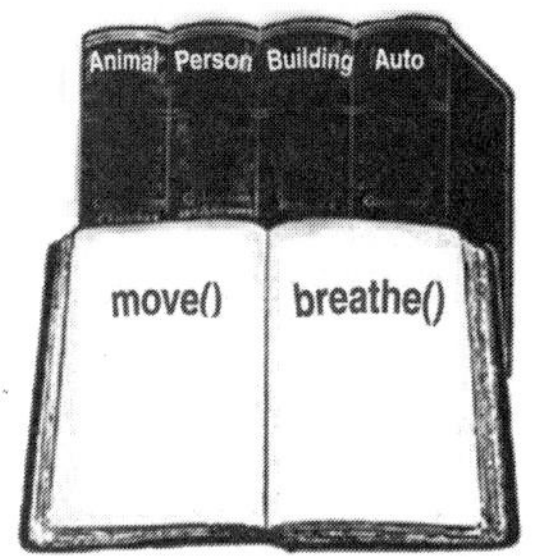

If you've worked on any software projects, you know that the project can go great and finish on schedule, or go sour and never end. You can have specifications up one side and down the other, and planning all over the place, and you can make everybody go on a ropes course retreat to learn to work together, but sometimes it just doesn't work.

So how in the world is it that these J2EE applications, thousands of them, actually work with the J2EE servers they're supposed to work with? Doesn't it seem odd that Sun just printed up this thing called a specification, the programmers read it, and boom, you've got great J2EE applications all over the place that work correctly and application servers that work right, too?

If that were the way things were set up, it wouldn't work all that well. The reason all these J2EE applications actually work is not just from following instructions.

It's all about *interfaces.*

A Java technology *interface* defines required general behavior without specifying the implementation. In plain English, an interface defines the "what" but not the "how."

For instance, when you apply for a job, you have to send in a cover letter and a resume (what) but you can send them in using PDF or text or HTML, you might have multiple pages for the resume (or cover letter, though we don't advise it), and so on. The rigid, protocol-oriented HR person receiving your information is going to be expecting those two things, and if you don't send'em in, she's going to freak, and start saying "Does not compute!" You have to send in a cover letter and a resume or the whole process just won't work.

Here's how interfaces can apply in programming. A programmer is told to create a method called `cookPizza` but exactly how he or she writes that code is up to the individual. The container needs this method because it's going to call a method called `cookPizza` at some point when it does its container business. However, the container really doesn't care about anything except that method existing. The container couldn't care less about how the actual pizza gets cooked. The programmer gets to do whatever coding is necessary to write the method. And there's a lot of different things to put in to make sure the method works and the pizza gets cooked correctly. A smaller pizza might need less time; a pizza with fresh basil spread on top might need a lower temperature. A pizza might even be deep-fried.

Looking at Interfaces Another Way

Let's say that Jennifer the Amazing Programmer we met earlier is working on some code for a zoo. She could create a blueprint (write code for) for an animal. Every animal has certain parts and behaviors. The parts of an animal include things like a circulatory system, respiratory system, digestive system, etc. The behaviors for an animal would include behaviors like breathing, eating, moving, sleeping, etc.

*These actions are **what** every animal must be able to do.*

She could also define the how.

For example, she could define how every animal must breathe. Maybe something like this—take air into the lungs and then release that air from the lungs. But what happens when she defines a fish. A fish is an animal and it can breathe. But does it breathe air using lungs?

Of course not. By defining animal as an interface you can achieve greater flexibility. You just define the what *(every animal can breathe) but not the* how *(air into lungs/air out of lungs). The fish which is an animal must be able to breathe but it is up the fish (dog, cat, or whatever) to decide* how *to breathe. You don't know or even care how a fish breathes (unless you're a fish). All you need to know is that it can breathe.*

Example 2-1 shows an *interface* on the left, and a partly coded *class* that implements (follows the rules in) that interface.

Example 2-1 Interface and class that implements it (approximation)

```
public interface Animal
{
   void breathe();
   void eat();
}
```

```
public class Dog implements Animal
{
   public void breathe()
   {
      inhale();
      smell s = computeBreathBasedOnRecentMeal();
      exhale(s);
   }

   public void eat()
   {
      while (foodInBowl())
      {
           swallow(Eating.DONT_CHEW);
      }
     if (Math.random() > 0.5)
     {
        vomitOn(locateCleanCarpet())
     }
   }
}
```

chapter 3

Introduction to JSPs, Servlets, and EJBs

"I do believe Marsellus Wallace, my husband, your boss, told you to take me out and do whatever I wanted. I wanna dance, I wanna win. I want that trophy, so dance good."

Mia Wallace, Pulp Fiction

So you've got containers and they provide services. You've got a Web server. Great. But what applications are they servicing? A container standing around all day flexing in front of the mirror, murmuring softly "Oh yeah...you've got transaction handling, baby..." doesn't do anyone any good. Containers exist because applications need them.

So there must be J2EE applications. And it's pretty likely that there are some special kinds of technology available to write the J2EE applications in, and some rules about how to write the applications to work correctly with the J2EE application server.

In short, who are the J2EE application server's dancing partners and what are they like?

Chapter in Brief

J2EE gives you more different kinds of technologies to use than Just Plain J2EE code. There are servlets and JSPs to deal with Web-enabled applications, session beans to do business processes, and entity beans to represent your data.

Here's what we talk about in this chapter.

- *Overview of J2EE Code*
- *Client Tier: Nothin' Here But Us Browsers*
- *Web Tier Technologies: JSPs and Servlets*
- *Business Tier Technology: Enterprise JavaBeans*

Overview of J2EE Code

Figure 3-1 illustrates the chunks, or tiers, a J2EE application is generally divided into. We'll be focusing on the servlets and JSPs on the Web tier, and the EJBs on the EJB tier.

The **client tier** just has, of course, customers, but in addition to them, just a **browser**.

This is the **Web tier**, sometimes (but not always) containing the **Web server** and **Web container**, plus all the HTML pages, JSPs, and servlets.

This is the **EJB tier, middle tier,** or **business tier**. It typically has the **EJB container** and all the Enterprise JavaBeans.

This tier is called the **database tier** or **persistence tier.** It's the tier where all the data is stored and where the **database management system** is located. It's in charge of dealing with requests to store and retrieve data, it's loyal, it's always there holding your slippers and/or your invoice records. (Hence the dog analogy).

Figure 3-1 J2EE tiers with different types of technology on each

The database-handling features aren't really the focus of this chapter, but the database does come into the picture since one kind of EJB is the in-memory representation of records in the database.

Client Tier: Nothin' Here But Us Browsers

There's nothing on any of your customers' machines that has anything to do with your application.

Well, that's not *quite* true. The pages from your application get sent over to them by the Web server. They're cached (stored) on the customers' machines for a while, then deleted. There's also the occasional cookie, which is a little text file that tells Amazon who you are when you go back an hour later, and allows Amazon to make, let's be frank, embarrassingly accurate recommendations. You might also, especially in a distributed but not online application, have some J2EE code on your customers' machines.

But for our purposes right now, just take the client tier where your customers hang out and forget it. The real goodies are on the other tiers.

Web Tier Technologies: JSPs and Servlets

JSPs are HTML with a little Java code inside, and servlets are Java code adapted for the Web, sometimes with a little HTML inside.

JavaServer Pages, or JSPs

JSPs are basically HTML on Java steroids; you can slip in various kinds of extra codes, plus actual Java code. They go on the Web tier and the Web container sends them to the client tier so users can see the pages.

Here's an example that uses regular HTML, then breaks stride for a moment to use a JSP tag to get a name. This line could appear in the middle of any page that otherwise just has HTML.

```
Thanks for requesting information about <I><%=
request.getParameter("topic") %></I>
```

Sometimes JSPs work on their own, and sometimes they call other parts of the J2EE family, like servlets.

Servlets

Servlets are just Java code for doing normal programming, *but* on the Web. They can handle being out there on the Web because servlets can speak HTTP, the Language of the World Wide Web. They understand all the commands that your browser sends across, including GET and POST commands. They also understand what the Web server says, since the Web server of course speaks HTTP as well.

What Servlets Replaced

If you really want to know

Servlets are J2EE's answer to CGI, common gateway interface scripts. CGI scripts are all over the place and great for smaller projects, but don't scale—grow as your business does—very well.

Servlets use and extend classes like HttpServlet which are specifically designed to deal with Web stuff and interact with JSPs. The following code appears in a lot of servlets. The doPost and the HttpServletRequest and HttpServletResponse are pretty much dead giveaways. Take a look at Example 3-1, not necessarily to read what the code is doing, but just to see the types of code used in a servlet so you'll recognize these elements in other code you look at on the job.

Example 3-1 Typical servlet code

```
public void doGet (HttpServletRequest myRequest, HttpServletResponse myResponse)
 throws ServletException, IOException
{
  some Java code that does stuff
}
public void doPost (HttpServletRequest myRequest, HttpServletResponse myResponse)
 throws ServletExeption, IOException
{
  doGet (myRequest, myResponse)
}
```

A Bit More About Servlets and JSPs

Servlets and JSPs both answer Web requests, whether the requests are something like "get me the description page for this item" or "find me all the books by Laura Jacobson."

JSPs are really good at providing great layout and some simple code/calculations and can contain all sorts of Java code in a variety of forms. Servlets are pretty powerful code and can generate HTML as well but it's not a great system. So we generally use both; JSPs are used for anything that's mostly layout but then needs a little extra Java punch, and servlets are used for anything that's primarily behind-the-scenes processing, business logic. They often work together; the JSP can ask a servlet to do something, then display the results.

Servlets and JSPs support the idea of *separation of concerns* (the object orientation thing about isolating unrelated chunks of code). JSPs most commonly do presentation logic, which means controlling how things look. Servlets most commonly do processing, the underbeneath stuff of *business logic*, which is just the guts of the program. Each is capable of doing both presentation and business logic, but JSPs are better suited to presentation logic, and servlets are better suited to business logic. We discuss separation of concerns more in *The Attributes of Object Orientation* on page 261.

The Web Deployment Descriptor Keeps Track of How to Run the Application

JSPs and servlets are pretty smart, and so is the Web container, but you can't just write the code and say "go!" You need to give a little bit more information about how to run the application in the form of the *deployment descriptor.* The deployment descriptor is just a big configuration file containing settings for how to run security, how to run the application, and much more. We talk about it more in *Web Deployment Descriptor* on page 107.

Business Tier Technology: Enterprise JavaBeans

EJBs, or Enterprise JavaBeans, are a whole different animal. While servlets and some EJBs can do similar things, the way a programmer writes EJBs is a whole lot different. And the way EJBs run and are managed by their EJB container is different, too.

Types of Enterprise JavaBeans

There are three kinds of EJBs: beans that represent things, beans that do things, and other types of beans that do things.

- Entity beans – Entity beans represent your database. An individual entity bean holds a record from a table in your database, like the record invoice 45991-A, or Baroness Hickenlooper's name and address record.
- Session beans – Session beans do stuff. They compute tax or they send information to another part of your application. They're your business processes. Session beans do what people would do if you were running your business in a world without computers. If you have a use case, you should probably have a session bean or five that correspond to it.
- Message-driven beans – Message-driven beans also do things. But they do things a little differently. Message-driven beans are like a butler who will answer the door when you're in the middle of a project but you're expecting someone to come by. The butler takes care of people who come by so that you can get a little work done.

All right, there might be a little more to it than that. We gave you the gist of each on the first go-around; here's a little more detail.

Entity Beans

Entity beans pretend to be the important things in your business like customers, invoices, orders, pizzas, etc. The things that you store information about in your database. Currently needed portions of the database are loaded into memory, assigned to entity beans, and boom, there's your database, floating around in memory.

A typical entity bean stands around holding a record from the database, and helps change the information. For instance, if an entity bean is holding a person's name and address and the address has changed, the bean might scratch out "910 Harrison Drive" and change it to "191 Mapleton." Or sometimes the bean might just take the record and squish it up and throw it away. Entity beans just do what would be done normally to the database, but in memory.

Nothing the entity bean does in its data-holding-capacity actually affects the database. This is up to the EJB container. The container is the one who pats the entity bean on the head, says "Good job!" and then does the actual corresponding changes in the database itself. The entity bean does the prep work, but the container is really in charge.

Now, you might well be thinking, "Why is this necessary in life? You've got a perfectly good database sitting there with very expensive database people taking care of it. Why duplicate all that in entity beans, especially when you've been telling us that there's not enough memory to go around?" And that's a very good question, especially given how complicated it can be to get data from the entity beans into the database and back again.

The point is the point which we have mentioned and will continue to harp on throughout the book: it's just good object-oriented application design. It's separation of concerns, encapsulation, all those good things.

Something still has to deal with communicating with the tables, of course. You don't bypass that. You just push the interaction with the database to the end of a particular process. That pushing is also one of the first principles of object orientation: put the things that have to do with databases in one place, off to the side by itself.

- J2EE applications are object oriented, and they understand objects. Objects are pieces of code that know information about themselves, and have things they can do. These same applications need to deal with the data from databases. Databases are organized in an entirely different way—a different paradigm, if you will. It's easier for the application to get at data if it's stored in an object-y way rather than in a database-y way.
- Now, granted, you haven't eliminated the need for objects to communicate with the database, by introducing a layer of entity beans on top of the database. But you have reduced the number of things that have to deal with the database, and given them special skills for doing so. These special skills came precoded from an application server, so you didn't have to write them yourself. That saves time and as much as you might hate to admit it, the application server folks might have done it better than you would have.
- Entity beans now are the only things that have to deal with the database and all the complexity therein. If it weren't for them, every session bean and servlet and possibly JSP that wanted to get anything out of or into or changed in the database would have to deal with SQL and database connections and allllll that stuff. Instead, entity beans take over the job, in tandem with the container, so all the other pieces of code, and all the people writing those

pieces of code, can be a little happier, a little more carefree, and get home from work before 10 o'clock.

Here's a condensed list of benefits.

- Entity beans sacrifice themselves so that they bear the brunt of dealing with the database, and no one else has to
- Entity beans separate the messy database connection stuff into one part of the application, so that it doesn't get mixed up with other things
- How entity beans communicate with databases is predetermined so that you don't have to write your own code to do it which might or might not be as well written or consistent

Not only have you encapsulated all this nastiness in one place, but with entity beans and CMP, it's all done for you. You don't have to do diddly. You tell it what the whole messy table thing looks like, and the container takes care of it.

Time Out for Jargon

If you
really want
to know

Entity beans reify the enduring business themes of your domain object model.

Yep, they sure do. Throw this sentence out at the next meeting with a straight face and see how many people nod as if they know what you're talking about.

It just means, entity beans are your data from your database, done up in little Java entity bean packages and running in memory for more convenient access rather than sitting sedately in your database, on the hard disk.

There's also a couple things called *bean-managed persistence* and *container-managed persistence* (BMP and CMP). They relate to entity beans and the database. Specifically. they relate to whether the programmer writes detailed code for how to get data out of the entity beans' big meaty hands and into the database, or whether the programmer leans back in her chair, sips her coffee, and says, "The container can take care of all that stuff." We'll get into that later.

Session Beans

Forget about computers for a few seconds. Imagine Antoine's pizza shop a hundred years ago. People did the work instead of computers. People created the pizza orders, added up the total order and asked for money, assigned delivery people to deliver the pizzas, figured out sales tax, put all the invoices for the day in the right filing cabinet folders, get sleepy in the middle of the afternoon and take naps, and so on.

That's what session beans do in a J2EE application. Session beans do what people used to do before computers. They send the invoice down to Receiving, or calculate sales tax, or schedule a delivery for tomorrow based on what delivery people are available, or say, "Hmm, this guy's ordering a lot of pizzas. Let's give him a coupon for our Gold Members Club." Session beans basically do the work.

Session beans are business logic.

More Business Logic? What About Servlets?

If you
really want
to know

Session beans and servlets do roughly similar kinds of things. However, they're designed to do it in different environments: the Web and a Web container; versus not the Web, and an EJB container. That's not to say you can't have session beans in an online application; it's just that the Web server doesn't talk to the session beans, and session beans don't speak HTTP. If you need to complete a business process and the result will be showing up in the browser interface, then you usually use servlets. But if the results of the business process are instead intended for the database or somewhere else that's not the browser interface, you generally go with session beans.

There are two types of session beans: *stateful session beans* and *stateless session beans.*

- Stateful session beans are faithful to one client for their lifetime. They sit there doing their session bean business logic, and they keep track of everything that has to do with that client and that process. The statefulness in their name has to do with the state, the data, gathered from the client they're working with. If Jeannie starts shopping, her bean stays with her until she orders that pizza and soda special or until she decides to work out and eat a salad instead, and logs off. Stateful session beans can remember everything their client tells them if that's what the application wants, keeps information around like their birthday or what items they've seen, and are ever so faithful.

  They carry around a lot of data with them which makes them useful in that respect, but slower.

  A stateful session bean is like a good waiter in a fancy restaurant who serves you and only you for the entire meal, bringing you menus, brushing the crumbs off the table, brandishing that enormous pepper grinder, and so on. (Except that the waiter isn't killed or its memory wiped after each meal.)

You could also think of session beans as the ideal boyfriend or girlfriend (though between us, they're a little dull).

- Stateless session beans will service any client's request, and won't remember anything about the last request. You could come to the same stateless session bean five times in a row, and she would greet you with the same vacuous, unrecognizing smile and do the one thing you asked her to do. Stateless doesn't mean they never remember any data; they can have their own private data like a variable that points to a database connection. They just don't remember state gathered from a client; that is, they'll do one thing with one piece of data collected from a client request, but then throw that state away.

  They don't carry around any state with them from one client request to another, so they're generally zippier than stateful session beans when it comes to performance.

  Stateless session beans are like that clerk at the coffee shop who never remembers you but always gives you the kind of coffee you ask for.

Figure 3-2 shows a stateless session bean at left and a stateful session bean at right. Look how closely the stateful session bean is paying attention to the guy she's having the conversation with. Yet the stateless session bean lost interest after the first question he asked her and is now just staring off into space.

Figure 3-2 Stateless and stateful session beans, respectively

Message-Driven Beans

The standard definition is that "Message-driven beans are stateless, server-side, transaction-aware components that process asynchronous messages delivered via the Java Message Service (JMS)."

This just means that you can have the message-driven beans do stuff for you when you're busy. The JMS (Java's post office) sends you the EJB container a message. You're busy processing 10,000 transactions a minute and don't want to have to drop everything and go check on whether there's enough database connections around. So the message-driven bean does it for you.

The message-driven bean is like a butler. You can tell him, "Oh, Jeeves, there'll be some people coming by sometime today to ask about the badgers we've got on sale this week. Could you keep a look out for them and handle it when they arrive? I'm going to be trying to get some work done."

The message-driven beans let the container concentrate on the main task at hand.

To do this in the application, you just specify in the deployment descriptor what messages you're expecting, from who, what message-driven beans will deal with said messages, and so on. You can have lots and lots of message-driven beans.

You might be thinking, after mulling this a bit, why the heck does something as powerful as the J2EE EJB container, which after all we chose to represent with a dolphin, need little butler beans to help it out?

Because J2EE isn't *multithreaded*. That means the container can't do more than one thing at a time. The container is fast, smart, and powerful but not so great with the multitasking. The container is like your geeky Uncle Alfred who can tell you when Easter will be in 2047 but if you ask him where the butter is at the same time, he'll totally lose track of the Easter thing. Or alternately he'll totally ignore you and keep figuring out Easter.

So message-driven beans let you simulate multithreadedness in your J2EE system.

The EJB Deployment Descriptor Keeps Track of How to Run the Application

Just as for the Web container, there's a big configuration file called the deployment descriptor that's kind of like a big Daytimer for the beans. The deployment descriptor keeps track of who's allowed to do what, what the names of all the beans are, and lots of other stuff. We talk about it more in *The EJB Deployment Descriptor* on page 154.

What's up With This "Bean" Name, Anyway?

The term *bean* is confusing since people go around talking about their beans doing this and that, and then about how their application does that and this, and the words get in the way of understanding that their beans *are* their application and vice versa. Beans go together to become an application.

Beans Are Just Java Code With a Twist

Beans are Java code. Beans are your application. A J2EE application, for instance, is often made up of a few JSPs on the front end to make the pages, a servlet or seventeen to do some complicated heavy duty processing for the front end, and a bunch of session beans to do the rest of the program's duties.

So why say *bean*?

The marketing folks and maybe Bill Joy and James Gosling dreamed a long time ago as they invented Java of an ideal world in which every piece of Java code could be reusable. That is, if it were written with the right extra bits of code that would let someone hook up to it, any piece of Java code could be reusable. The reusable code could flit happily from one application to another, doing good wherever it went.

Note: This doesn't happen quite as often as the founders would like but it's possible.

To be one of those reusable components, of course, a piece of Java code can't just be written willy-nilly. There are specific rules for coding them. Beans are written in a way so that, theoretically, you could send people your MarksUpPrices bean, they could pop it into their application, and boom, instant MarksUpPrices functionality.

What's a small unit of Java, in the coffee sense? Well, a bean, of course, so that's the name the big Java programming folks applied to a small unit of reusable Java code.

To make things just a wee bit complicated, there are of course two kinds of beans in Java, and they're entirely unrelated.

The Two Kinds of Entirely Unrelated Beans in Java

There's JavaBeans, and there's Enterprise JavaBeans or EJBs. They have nothing to do with each other, and work differently. How's that for a really silly naming job?

What JavaBeans Are

JavaBeans aren't really much in the news now, but a few years ago they were hot.

JavaBeans are really just very clearly, predictably written Java code and have nothing to do with J2EE.

If you read the object orientation appendix or if you know object orientation, you know that an object knows things about itself. These things are *attributes*. A Java bean, for every one of its attributes like `red` or `Nancy` or `19.99`, should have a way to set those attributes to particular values, and to just go get the value for a particular attribute. After all, if you create an object in Java like a particular red shirt, it would be silly if you couldn't go check to be sure it was red, or go "Whoops!" and change the shirt to blue.

The types of code that set and get the values of attributes are called, fairly logically, *getters* and *setters*. Any piece of Java code that has appropriately named getters and setters for all its attributes can be a JavaBean.

JavaBeans are generally entirely unrelated to EJBs. However, they're not entirely unrelated to J2EE. They've enjoyed a brief fashionable resurgence since JSPs; you can run a JavaBean from a JSP.

What Enterprise JavaBeans Are

Enterprise JavaBeans are written entirely differently from JavaBeans and have a whole nother set of requirements. They have to implement certain interfaces, and they don't interact with Just Any Other Piece of Code. They interact only with an EJB container, or with other EJBs. Nothing else.

EJBs can use all the services we've been talking about: security, data integrity, resource management. JavaBeans get squat.

So JavaBeans are nothing special, and EJBs are. We now want you to forget about JavaBeans for the rest of the book.

chapter

4

Multi-Tier Application Architecture

"It's hard to work in a group when you're omnipotent."

Q, Star Trek: The Next Generation

We've talked a lot about what J2EE is, why it's good, what it gives you, and so on. We've also talked about the different applications within it and how they're in different chunks, often on different computers.

Wouldn't it be simpler to not have all these pieces of code all over the place? Here, we'll talk about why people bother to tier up.

The Chapter in Brief

A tier is a chunk of code that performs roughly the same function. Applications are divided into tiers the same way that industries are divided up into chunks like raw materials, manufacturers, wholesalers, and retailers. Sometimes the tiers are on different machines, sometimes not. The standard tiers in a J2EE application are client (just the browser), Web (JSPs and servlets), business (EJBs), and persistence (database). Some applications use all four tiers. Some applications, like some that just use JSPs to go directly to the database and therefore don't have EJBs, have only two or three tiers.

Here's what we talk about in this chapter.

- *What Is a Tier?*
- *Why Bother With Tiers?*
- *Tier-Specific Reasons for Separating Applications Into Tiers*
- *Simple Architecture Sample*

What Is a Tier?

A *tier* is a chunk of code organized by function. Not a business function like all making chairs or making tables but a more basic type of function: getting information out of databases or displaying Web pages.

You can think of tiers as similar to the way raw materials, manufacturing, and retail are divided up in the world of clothing production.

If you want a pair of pants, for instance, you go to a clothing store. You don't go get the sheep and spin the wool and weave the fabric. Clothing stores specialize in selling clothing, which is a logical chunk of tasks in the clothing spectrum. Clothing stores talk to clothing manufacturers, not the wool wholesalers. Clothing manufacturers, in turn, specialize in the logical chunk of tasks in the clothing-making field. They talk to fabric manufacturers and to clothing retailers.

Tiers are about dividing things into logical groups that do their own particular thing, and provide the finished product to the things that need what they make. If clothing retail were divided into a multi-tier architecture, there would be a tier of businesses producing raw materials like sheep; a tier that creates things like thread from the wool on those sheep; a tier that takes the thread and weaves fabric; and a tier that creates the clothing for the end user.

Tiers are about specialization and efficiency, from raw to most distilled. Databases are raw data, whereas the JSP that displays Welcome, Baroness Hickenlooper! is very distilled.

Let's say Amazon is run on J2EE. It and other applications can be broken down into the following categories of program code, files, and other elements.

- Your browser – Amazon doesn't have to deal with this at all, just needs to make sure that their Web pages work with your browser.
- Presentation logic – Presentation logic is the decision-making processing involved in determining what the presentation will look like. It's not the layout itself.
- Business logic – Code that tells Amazon how the business is run, basically. Suggesting Elvis diet cookbooks to people who've ordered *The Bacon Cheeseburger Diet*, doing Valentine's Day gift specials in early February, getting all that information into and out of the database, and of course all the credit card processing, pricing, etc. Tax computation goes here too.
- The database – Stored stuff. Your orders and all the other gazillion people's orders, their huge inventory database, and everything else that just gets retrieved by the business logic. Sometimes referred to as persistence tier.

Why Bother With Tiers?

All the separation might seem like a pain at first. For one thing, when you've got code on different tiers, you usually need some special programming to let your code talk to the code off on the different tier. So why not put it all in one big lump on one computer? With J2EE applications as in life, the short-term quick way is not so good in the long term. There are lots of good reasons to separate applications into tiers; we cover a few in this section.

Note: If you're not familiar with object orientation and the benefits thereof, see "The Attributes of Object Orientation" on page 261 before you continue in this chapter.

Three Words: Maintenance, Maintenance, Maintenance

Anyone who used to work on '57 Chevrolets and now tries to even do an oil change on a '02 Toyota knows that the former is easy and the latter is a real pain. Because on the '57 Chevy, all the parts are right there in front of you, easy to find, and if you're working on the muffler belt you're not going to damage the seat-belt fluid dispenser. (If those parts in fact existed.) In later model cars, you practically have to take out the engine to get at the windshield washer fluid. And the more you fiddle with parts of the car, regardless of whether you need to fix them or not, the more likely you're going to break something next to it accidentally.

The same thing applies to maintaining code. Writing it right is hard, making it work is hard, and going in to fix it afterwards can be tough since you've gone onto another project by now and you've forgotten most of what you did. Worse, you might be the new guy going into code you've never seen before.

It'll be more manageable if when you go into fix each individual bug you only have to deal with the code where the bug is occurring. You don't have to learn how the database code works in order to change how sales taxes are calculated. Or to just update the login page.

Imagine a login page that also has SQL code in the page for sending the login info to the database, and has complicated security code in the page for encrypting the login. And of course there are rules for what acceptable values are for the login (name must be lowercase one word, password must be at least five characters), and so on. It's the most complicated page ever, and confusing even for the alpha programmers to fix. Any programer would most likely break it all immediately or spend three months figuring out how to fix it. It's be a whole lot better to have the SQL in one spot, the security in one spot, the business logic like acceptable login values in one spot, and the code for making the login page appear in another. Then you don't even have to worry about staying out of the way of stuff you don't want to break.

It's a Jungle Out There

The distributed environment itself is a whole lot more potentially wonky than a regular local application. Network issues, denial of service attacks, potentially billions of hits at the same time, database issues, etc. The environment is a whole lot more unpredictable than the safety of running on a nice little standalone desktop computer. Because of this, to eliminate the possibility of the whole application being taken down because one part of it succumbed to the dangers of distributed or online living, the pieces of the application are separated onto different machines.

A Distributed Application Is Pretty Complex, and Any Simplification Is Good

The structure of a J2EE application, when you look at everything that's going on, can seem pretty complicated. And to a certain extent it is, if only because you're not the one who designed it and it always takes a while to understand someone else's design.

So imagine if all your code is glommed together in one big pile. It's a lot more complicated that way than if the logical chunks are separated into tiers.

Tier-Specific Reasons for Separating Applications Into Tiers

We're past the general reasons, so let's look at it from a per-tier point of view.

The Importance of Separating the Database

The main reason to separate the database is that, like batteries, it's sold separately. It just is inherently separate. Everything else is just reasons why it's just as well it's sold separately.

The database is a pretty huge, important, lose-it-and-you're-dead, part of your application. You can't do business if you don't know how many orders in the ORDERS database you need to fulfill, and if other people get ahold of your customers' credit cards and use them inappropriately, you're not going to be getting repeat business for a while.

You definitely want this database to be secure as possible. In general, you want to keep the information secure, i.e. you want to not lose it, and you want to make sure no one else gets it. That pretty clearly points to keeping it separated from every other part of your application, not to mention your customers, with a really big firewall (protective software). If the database is part of the application, other people can get to it, and you have less control.

The Importance of Separating the Business Logic

Nothing's sure but death and taxes, and changes in tax laws. No matter how nicely you write your application, or how sure you are that certain things will always stay the same, they will always change. The marketing guy will show up one morning and say, "Hey, remember how I told you last week to sell a free Floozix with every Womplet? Well, Marcie was thinking how great it would be if we just offered them two Floozixes but at 30% off..." and after you've made him shut up and go away, your business logic will have to change. Again. And you'll have to buy yet another one of those mouthguards since you're gnashing your teeth even more at night.

All this just means that you should separate your business logic from your database. And you'll need it separate from the part of the application your customers are running, unless you want to ship out a whole new application, complete with migration procedures, every time you want to or have to change any aspect of the business logic.

Murphy's law still applies to any aspect of programming, of course: touch anything, and you will not only break it, but you will break everything around it, and the QA people will hunt you down and break your knees.

If you
really want
to know

The Deployment Descriptor Is a Nice Feature When it Comes to Maintenance

As we mentioned before, the nice thing about J2EE technology is that you can specify most of the configuration outside the program. This configuration is done in the deployment descriptor file, and can affect how the business logic behaves.

EJBs have *separation of concerns* built in. This is a good old-fashioned, remarkably logical principle from object orientation. EJBs are inherently separated from the code that deals with transactions and other services provided by the server.

EJBs are so componentized, i.e. divided into nice neat separate interacting bits, that you can switch your application from one database management system to another, say from Oracle to Sybase, without rewriting your application. The connection to the database is handled by the server, and by the configuration details you set up in the deployment descriptor. The deployment descriptor is just a big configuration file where you say. "do this when you start up, do that when this bean runs" etc.

The Importance of Separating the Presentation Logic

Who works on the application interface? User interface people. Some of whom are programmers, perhaps, but most aren't. The people doing the interface are different from the people doing the business logic. And they don't generally mix, and they don't like to share their source code files, kind of like cattle and sheep in the Old West.

They use different applications to do their jobs, as well.

All in all, it's a good idea to let the presentation people have their presentation files, and the business logic people have the business logic files.

Generally, JSPs do presentation well and servlets do the processing well. Each can also do the other function, but not as well. Let's take a look at a JSP (Java server page, for presentation) with some programming in it, and a servlet (programming) with some presentation in it. Each is a bad way to do what they're doing because the servlet is trying to do too much presentation and the JSP is trying to do too much business logic. Figure 4-1 shows a servlet trying to do what it's not as good at.

Bad example 4-1 Snippet of servlet code, which creates an HTML page (presentation in business logic)

```
...
out.println(docType +
"<HTML>\n" +
"<HEAD><TITLE>Hello, World Servlet</TITLE></HEAD>\n" +
"<BODY>\n" +
"<H1>Hello, World</H1>\n"+
"<P>Awful lot of work to just display text.</P>"\n +
"<P>And just think of the work to pass tags for </P>"\n +
"<P>formatting, links, forms, etc.</P>"\n +
"<P>Done by developers.</P>"\n +
"<P>Or Web designers who are used to Dreamweaver.</P>"\n +
"<BODY></HTML>");
...
```

Figure 4-2 shows a JSP.

Bad example 4-2 JSP, which has Java scriptlet code in it (business rules in presentation)

```
<HTML>
<TITLE>Happy JSP Spoiled By Too Much Java Code</TITLE>
<BODY>
<P>This page starts out fine, but then some scriptlet code, Java in the midst of HTML, comes along. Can your Web designer write Java? Ours can't. Shouldn't have to.</P>
<%
String linkTextFont = request.getParameter("linkTextFont");
boolean hasExplicitFont;
if (linkTextFont) !=null)
{
   hasExplicitFont = true;
}
else
{
   hasExplicitFont = false;
   linkTextFont = "WINGDINGS";
```

```
}
%>
<P>See what we mean? Plus how is a Java program compiler supposed to compile a JSP? It's easy to make mistakes in scriptlet code in JSPs and not so easy to find them.</P>
...
</BODY>
</HTML>
```

The Importance of Separating the Browser From Everything Else

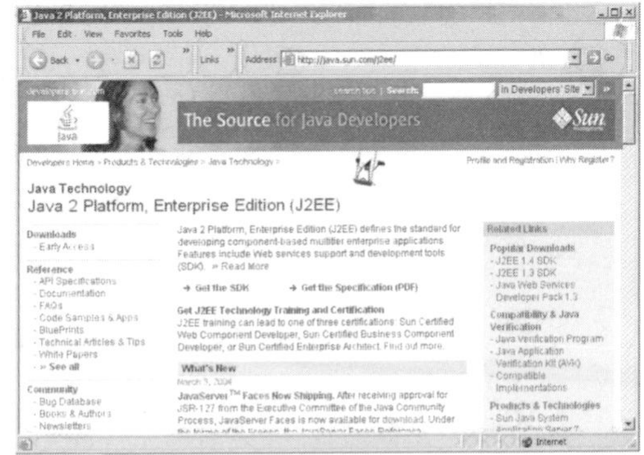

It's happened to everyone—you send out the fabulous new application, everyone's sitting around at the release party, when someone doing a demo notices that the main login page has a typo and says "Welcome to the Loggins Page." Suddenly you're getting calls from Kenny's lawyer.

Note: Kenny Loggins is an American singer best known for the theme to the movie "Footloose." In this example, he has an eternally vigilant Web-surfing lawyer.

As with business logic, it's a lot easier to update your application if you control it and have immediate access to it, and customers just access it with their browsers. If your presentation logic isn't on your customers' computers, it's a whole lot easier to spend five minutes with Dreamweaver fixing the user interface, than to cut and send out CDs every time you want to make a change. Having the browser be the only thing your customers have means you get to keep everything else, have total control, and save a whole lot of money on CD burning, support calls, and release notes.

Simple Architecture Sample

Let's put this together with a simple example.

Antoine's site www.antoinespizza.com, finally set up as a full J2EE solution, has just completed its final application development and he is pretty happy with it. They're using an Oracle database, BEA WebLogic as their application server, and decided to just run Apache Web server.

The Antoine's Pizza development team has grown and now has these main groups: the interface people, the Web developers, and the EJB developers.

Note: Remember what we said in *A Note About Antoine's Pizza Shop* on page 20—Antoine might not be using EJBs in real life, or if he were he might not be using entity beans. But we're using Antoine's as an example for everything since that's simpler.

- The interface people wrote a great set of JSPs for the Web site. The Web pages need a little bit of dynamically generated code, so they periodically ask the servlets for some help on those calculations.
- The Web development team wrote some servlets do calculations and requests.
- The EJB team wrote some heavy duty code that runs within the EJB container, to take care of the core business processes for Antoine's Pizzas. The development team did not write any security or transaction management or memory management code—the server took care of all of that. Which is why everyone on the team is still alive, sane, and has about as much hair as they used to.

So now when a customer visits www.antoinespizza.com she is treated to a beautifully designed online display (created using JSPs) of various pizzas. While navigating around the site, a customer can add the Hawaiian delight to her shopping cart and check out by clicking the checkout button on the Web site's checkout page (a JSP). This request is sent from the his computer to Antoine's Web server, which says "Agh! something for the Web container." The Web container hands off the request from the JSPs to the servlet that is waiting to process the order. The servlet gathers the customer's delivery, payment and item information. The servlet then calls on the EJBs, which are running on separate machines, to process, verify, and validate the information.

The EJBs validate her credit card and accesses the inventory and customer databases, which are running on yet another machine to update Antoine's inventory and add the customer information. The EJBs send an "A-OK" message back to the servlet. The servlet sends the confirmation JSP back to the browser. The customer will be enjoying the Hawaiian delight within the hour.

chapter 5

The Key Advantages of Using J2EE

"This is the burden we bear, brother. We have a gig that would inevitably cause any girl living to think we are cool upon cool. Yet, we must Clark Kent our way through the dating scene, never to use our unfair advantage. Thank god we're pretty."

Forrest, "Buffy the Vampire Slayer"

All right, you've decided that having an application server is a really good idea. You've got a system that's complex and big enough to warrant writing it so it interacts with an application server.

But some application servers are more J2EE than others. That is, some are J2EE and some aren't. Just being an application server doesn't mean you're a J2EE application server. You can use an application server without ever having heard of J2EE or being able to pronounce it.

So what's the point of specifically getting a *J2EE* application server? That's what we'll cover here.

Note that this is not a chapter on indoctrination; nobody in orange sheets and purple Nikes will be coming by for you in a van with *J2EE Junkies* painted on the side. We're just making a point here to differentiate J2EE application servers from those that ain't.

The Chapter in Brief

You have a choice from a variety of application server vendors; you're not stuck with one company. You can control a lot about how the application runs through configuration, without changing the code. It's Java, which has a whole set of advantages of its own. It's financially scalable, since there are free J2EE servers and there are some that are, well, not free.

Here's what we talk about in this chapter.

- *Get the Services From Lots of Sources*
- *Changing the Application Without Writing Code*
- *J2EE Is Java*
- *A J2EE System Is Financially Scalable*
- *You Get Automatic RMI*

Get the Services From Lots of Sources

Note: Just a terminology note here—we're going to get lazy and say *J2EE server* or just *server* a lot instead of *application server* all that time. Same thing.

Let's say that you've got a CD player. That's nice. You can buy any kind of CD with any kind of music to play in the CD player, which is right and normal. Think about how if you had a Floozix brand CD player that used the Floozix standard for CDs, and you could only buy CDs using that standard.

Now imagine that Floozix goes out of business and your Floozix CD player breaks. You have to go out and not only buy a Womplet standard CD player, but you have to buy all new CDs that run on the Womplet standard. That would really suck.

Wouldn't it be better if there were lots of companies that used the Floozix standard so that you could just get another CD player that uses the same standard, but from a different company?

Yes, it would. This is the logic that Sun followed by making the J2EE application server standard an *open standard*. Sun publishes all the rules anyone needs to know in order to build J2EE servers, and tells everyone how to build their applications to work with J2EE servers. That means lots of entrepreneurial-minded companies have gone into business building these servers. When you go around looking for a company to sell you a server, or when they come looking for you, you have a lot of choices. And once you pick one, if you don't like it, you can switch to another one.

Open standard means that J2EE is like other standards such as HTML or ASCII—there's a group in charge of the standard and they let everyone know what it is. This means that for instance, with the open HTML standard, you can look up how to make a heading bold, and type **<B>My Home Page</B>**, and every browser will interpret that correctly.

There are two types of features in application servers, the core standards and the optional standards.

- There's a core set of standards that all J2EE application servers have to comply with. They have to provide certain features for transactions, for concurrency, for security, and so on.
- There are also extra, optional, features that provide cool additional features. Application server vendors might or might not choose to make these features available.

Note: There's actually a third category. Some vendors take initiative and add their own features. If you write your application to use these features then of course you can't easily switch to a different application server.

If you're shopping for application servers, make sure you know what optional features the servers do or don't support, and think about whether you really need any of those optional features in your application. If you take advantage of optional features offered by one vendor, and then switch to another vendor who doesn't support those optional features, you'll definitely need to do a bit of rework on the application. Not nearly as much as if you had to rework it for a different application server standard, of course. And there's also the fact that the application server you switch to might support those optional features, too.

The other approach you can take is to just stick with the standard features when you write your application, and not rely on anything that might not be supported. That's definitely safer.

Changing the Application Without Writing Code

What if you want your application to run differently? Let's say you want your application hooked up to a different database. Or you want to change the number of connections open to the database at any given time, or some names in the code change.

Well, you probably have to change the code in the application, recompile it, etc. Right? Not necessarily. Some of how a J2EE application runs isn't even in the application itself.

The Deployment Descriptor

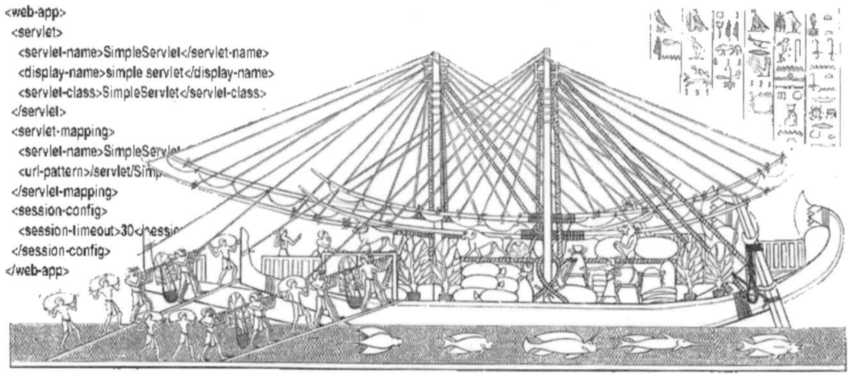
<web-app>
<servlet>
<servlet-name>SimpleServlet</servlet-name>
<display-name>simple servlet</display-name>
<servlet-class>SimpleServlet</servlet-class>
</servlet>
<servlet-mapping>
</servlet-mapping>
<session-config>
</session-config>
</web-app>

Some of how a J2EE application runs is controlled by a configuration file called a *deployment descriptor*. If you want to change any of the settings, you just change the information in the deployment descriptor. No touching the code and risking breaking something else in the code; just a nice neat little configuration file. (You still have to redeploy the application, which is not a trivial task, but at least you don't have to touch the code.)

What Deployment Descriptors Are Made Of

The file is created in XML. XML stands for eXtensible Markup Language. XML is a highly structured, user extensible, data-centric way to represent data. This just means that you can pretty much do whatever you want with it if you set it up right, and it can do a lot.

There's an XML deployment descriptor for your EJBs, and for your servlets and JSPs. Why use XML? Why not use a comma delimited text file? (That's just data in a text file with a comma after each piece of data like the first name, last name, and so on.) Heck, why not use that old chestnut, the database? One thing that makes XML so popular and an obvious choice for J2EE is that XML is platform independent; any computer can read XML. XML is relatively easy for a computer program to read and do stuff with, and surprisingly at the same time, humans can usually look at it and get the gist, as well.

A Little More on XML

We didn't want to do an XML hit and run, so here's just a little more info on XML even though it's not unique to J2EE. We'll get into it a little more later, especially when we cover Web services.

XML is a markup language. Big deal, you say? Well, kind of. Here's what a markup language is. *XML* and *HTML* are both markup languages, which just means that there's a piece of text in <> and then some more inside </>, which controls what the application reading the file does to the text in between.

`<center>My Heading</center>` would center the text `My Heading`. The browser knows how to center the text.

`<chapterheading>Welcome to the Big Picture</chapterheading>` means that the text `Welcome to the Big Picture` is a thing called a chapterheading. The application reading the XML file might then be able to look for all the headings and put them in a table of contents file, or might format the heading in a particular way, or might make sure that for every piece of text with that particular heading also has a piece of text following it labeled `introtext`.

You can also make up your own tags to define your data. That's the extensible part. HTML is not extensible; not unless you know someone influential at the HTML standards organization, which is called the World Wide Web Consortium or W3C. You can't go around just making up HTML tags that browsers will understand, whereas you can create whatever XML tags you need for your application.

J2EE Is Java

Java has a few advantages all its own. J2EE gets these advantages automatically, being based on Java and all. Those five key advantages of Java are:

- Write once, run anywhere
- Open standards (as with J2EE)
- Security
- Easier to write well
- Object orientation

For more information on each, see *The Gist of Java in General* on page 257.

A J2EE System Is Financially Scalable

Let's say you're one of those people trying to build a reusable vehicle for cruising around in space with. (First prize, $10 million!) You're doing a vast amount of calculating, it's a project involving a huge number of volunteers around the world, and you're in a big hurry since John from Arizona is way ahead of you on this. Therefore you've got a distributed project with some intense calculation needs. This might just be a good candidate for J2EE.

Do you have, say, $100,000 sitting round for a J2EE server? Given this stage of the business, probably not. On the other hand, you expect to get more money once you attract investors. Do you want to start out with a small non-J2EE application and then have to totally rewrite it when you've got enough money? Again, no.

Because of open standards, there are absolutely free J2EE servers out there. JBoss is one. (And there are free databases too, like mySQL.) You get an absolutely free *reference implementation* server with the free J2EE download from Sun. It's slower than commercial servers but it works.

Using J2EE means that when you've got a small budget and you don't absolutely need a high-speed, high-intensity server, you're fine. You can get the less fancy, less expensive, or free server.

Then as your business grows you can upgrade to a more expensive, faster, more robust (more fancy features) J2EE server. And since they're all J2EE, switching from one server to another isn't that big a deal.

That's what financially scalable is all about. You spend what you need to and as you grow, you can get a more expensive server to meet your growing needs.

You Get Automatic RMI

We've discussed the idea of talking to different pieces of code on different tiers. Or on different machines. Cool, huh? But *how* exactly do you make code A, on machine X, talk to code B, on machine Y? Or how does code A in Boulder talk to code B, in Dublin? Especially when code A never actually knows where code B is? Even if the machines are right next to each other, if code A is one machine and code B is on another, they might as well be across the world from each other. Code A can't just reach over and peak under the other machine's motherboard to see what's up. Code A doesn't even know what machines to look on.

Let's say that Jeannie, a faithful customer of Antoine's pizza, wants to know the pizza specials for that day. She goes to the specials.jsp page. Antoine has a big distributed system so that the JSP that does the formatting and lets customers submit a request for the specials information is on one machine, and the EJBs that figure it all out are on another machine. This is represented in Figure 5-1.

"What are today's specials in Boulder, Colorado?"
Code on machine X

"Tofu Sausage thin-crust."
Code on machine Y

Figure 5-1 Remote conversation between chunks of code

This communication is possible because of *Remote Method Invocation*, or *RMI*. RMI lets pieces of code that aren't local to each other communicate with each other.

The trouble is, regular old RMI is kind of like a bikini wax or running intervals—it's hard to do, it hurts a lot, even though you get spectacular results. It's basically the RMI House of Pain.

That's *plain* RMI, though. You get RMI built into J2EE, and you hardly have to do anything. Making remote code talk to each other in J2EE still uses RMI, but it's easier. Using RMI in J2EE is more like just shaving your legs, or going for a nice walk, instead of the RMI House of Pain.

The main point is that J2EE takes away RMI pain. We're not going to get into painful detail about RMI here, since the point is not that you need to understand how it works. The point is that you don't need to know how it works.

If you
really want
to know

If You Do Want to Know How RMI Works

We put in a very high-level explanation in the appendix, It's All About Communication: RMI on page 269.

chapter 6

A Walk Through a J2EE Process

"If it's to last, the getting of knowledge should be tangible...it should be smelly."

Giles, Buffy the Vampire Slayer

If you're anything like us, you do fine enough with theory but you want to see how it works. Let's think about a real world application that uses all this J2EE stuff: JSPs on the front end, through servlets and EJBs through to the database on the back end.

What happens, for instance, when you just want to create a login for the site? Say you've gone to Antoine's pizza site and you want to create a login so you can order those pizzas faster? Just what are those pieces of J2EE code up to during a process like that and is it really hideously complicated?

The Chapter in Brief

This chapter just shows step by step what the various aspects of a four-tier application do when confronted with a simple request from a client.

Here's what we talk about in this chapter.

- *A New Concept: Handles*
- *The Steps in a Simple Four-Tier J2EE Process*
- *That Was Simple???*

A New Concept: Handles

A new character you'll come across here is the *handle*. Some people use different terms for handles but it's good enough for now. When you've got beans and you want one bean to do something with another bean, you need to get a handle to it.

In regular Java, or in any regular object-oriented application, one object tells another object what to do; might call an invoice object's print method, for instance. To do that, the object needs a *reference* to the Invoice object. Just a special kind of code that lets you talk to that object.

J2EE is a little different since you don't get to have a reference to the object itself; you get a reference to a bean's remote interface which is kind of like the bean's personal manager. You can't get to the bean itself. And so since the mechanics are a little different, the EJB folks called the reference something different: a handle. A handle is just an EJB-style reference.

The Steps in a Simple Four-Tier J2EE Process

Here's the scenario.

Antoine's application at www.antoinespizza.com is a full-featured multi-tier application containing JSPs for the interface, servlets for Web-tier programming, EJBs for EJB-tier business processes, and the companies' financial and product information in a standard SQL database. They use an Apache Web server for the Web tier, a WebLogic Server EJB container and Web container, and an Oracle database management system for the database tier.

Jeannie the pizza customer is going to go to www.antoinespizza.com. She's going to register her name, email, and a password so she can order pizzas, design her own pizzas, talk on the pizza chat board, and so on.

So that's the scenario. Time for the process.

Are you sitting comfortably?

Then we'll begin.

1 **Fill in login information and click OK.**

The login page is a plain old HTML page. Jeannie fills in the information in a form on the page www.antoinespizza.com/loginspage.html and clicks the Register Me button. (She fills in her email as jeannie@yahoo.com and her password as thepurplepigeon.)

2 **Send the request to the Web server.**

The request to register Jeannie and the information about her are sent from the form, via HTTP (hypertext transfer protocol, just the language of the Web), to the Web server application on the Web tier computer. In this case, just to keep things simple, the plain HTML pages, JSPs, and servlets are all stored on the same computer, along with the Web server and the Web container.

3 **The Web server receives the request.**

The Web server is kind of the maitre d' of the application. It doesn't do much but knows where things should go. It receives the HTTP request from Jeannie's browser, says to itself, this login thing involves a servlet. That means the container needs to handle this.

The server didn't just decide that on its own, of course. The login form specified a servlet in the Login button, and that information was bundled into the request that the Web server received.

4 **Web server passes the request to the Web container.**

So it sends a message to the Web container that says, "Hey, got a request for you to do something, it's beyond me. There's some kind of URL associated with it, *you* figure out what to do."

5 **The Web container looks at the request and decides where to send it.**

The only thing the container has to work with is the URL that was sent over from the client in the request and passed to it by the Web server. It has to figure out from that URL what's going on and what it needs to do. So it follows the URL, says "Hmm. I've got notes here in my deployment descriptor saying that things that start with paths like this are servlets, and they're actually stored over here, so this loginservlet she wants should be right over there under the sink." (Or wherever the servlets are stored according to the Web mapping scheme written up in the deployment descriptor.) The container puts the jeannie@yahoo.com and thepurplepigeon information in a message, sends it over to the registration servlet under the sink, and says "Go, run, and here's the information you need."

Note: This is an example of how servlets and JSPs (and also EJBs) run *inside* their containers. The servlet didn't have to talk to the client or the Web server; it just takes its orders straight from the container, does its work, and then tells the container when it's done. In order to send these messages around, the container has been doing a lot of extra work checking security lists.

6 **The requested servlet connects to JNDI to get a session bean.**

The servlet says, "Finally, I have some work to do." It looks at the information that the container sent over in the message, and it realizes, simply because of how we've put together this example, that in order to do this, it needs a session bean to help it out. (A session bean is the kind of bean that does some actual work, rather than the kind of bean that stands around holding data, which is an entity bean.) The servlet is going to be under the impression, at least, that it'll be asking a session bean to do this work but what he's really going to get is a *handle*, a way to get power over, a session bean.

So the servlet does a *JNDI lookup*. Easy for it, you say. A JNDI lookup is basically just checking the big computer phonebook for how to get a session bean to do an errand for it on the EJB tier. JNDI stands for Java Naming and

Directory Interface. It's just how beans find other beans. (And more, but don't worry about that.)

The JNDI lookup is somewhere out there on your system, but you don't know and you don't care. It's probably on the EJB tier but nobody really cares. It just answers when you yell.

7 **Servlet retrieves a handle to a session bean.**

The JNDI lookup works just fine, and in the twinkle of an eye the servlet has a handle to a session bean.

Note: For those of you keeping track, this is one of those flaky but hardworking stateless session beans, who will service anyone at any time, not just sticking with one client through several requests and responses.

The EJB container says, "Hey, I'll bet a transaction is going on here. I'll put up a fence here and make sure all the rest of the steps don't get interrupted."

This is that transaction support we talked about. The container recognizes in the code the line "start transaction." It's nearly that simple in the actual code. That means that this is the Start of Something Big, or at least the Start of Something That Will Probably Have More Going On, and makes sure that from now on all the actions for this task stay together.

8 **Servlet calls a method on the session bean.**

Or rather, the servlet calls a method on the session bean's handle. This triggers the beginning of a transaction.

9 **The container creates a transaction.**

The container sees what the servlet did in the previous step and creates a transaction. This is assuming that the EJB deployment descriptor says that it should (which it usually will).

10 **EJB container pulls a stateless session bean out of the pool and conveys the servlet's request to that session bean.**

Depending on how the EJB container was set up, there are anywhere from a few to a whole sorority of stateless session beans already created and are hanging out in the session bean pool, eagerly waiting an assignment. The container pulls one out, stuffs the request from the servlet in the session bean's pocket, and says "Here. Take care of this."

11 **Session bean connects to JNDI to get an entity bean.**

The session bean looks at the request and goes "Whoa, I'm going to be messing with the database. I need an entity bean for this."

12 Session bean retrieves a handle to an entity bean.

It does the JNDI lookup and finds a handle to an entity bean. (To the Home interface for the entity bean, more accurately, but don't worry about that right now since we'll be covering the Home interface more later.)

13 Session bean asks the entity bean if there is already a record in the database with the email jeannie@yahoo.com.

That check is a business rule that's written in the session bean because the application doesn't want two people to have the same ID. That would cause a little too much referential unpleasantness.

14 Entity bean checks and says, Nope.

We'll say that there isn't another person already in the database with that email, so we will create a new record in the database for Jeannie.

15 The session bean asks the entity bean to create the user record.

So the entity bean and the container work together to create a new empty record in the right table or tables. This record creation is all done, however, in the entity bean. The container is pretending for now, and the session and entity beans actually believe it, that the entity bean is the database.

The bean might do additional verification or other stuff, as well.

As a result, what the session bean now has is a handle to the new entity bean which holds the new record.

Note: That's what happened in that step. But did you notice what didn't happen? The programmer wrote the session bean. That's all. The programmer did not write one line of code that dealt with actually creating the entity bean, getting the data in and out, creating a connection to the database, doing it efficiently, ditching the memory when it was gone, etc. This is because we're using container-managed persistence, or CMP, just letting the container do the work.

16 Session bean sends a request to the entity bean.

Next, the session bean sends a request to the entity bean, saying hey, here's some data, we need it put in the database.

17 Container receives request for an entity bean, tells the entity bean to complete the request.

The container receives the request and says, "Hey, you, entity bean, take care of this." The entity bean is still waiting around to do more work because we've got a transaction going on. Otherwise it would have dived back into the entity bean pool.

18 Entity bean completes the request.

The entity bean says in a very manly voice, "Yes, I'll take care of that," and stuffs the data into a file in its briefcase. (That is, the data from the request sits there in memory in the entity bean.)

19 Now the EJB container notices that the transaction should be complete and finishes things up.

The container copies the data that's in the entity bean into the database, sends the entity bean back into the pool to play, commits the transaction, and finally returns a "Done" message to the servlet.

20 The EJB container passes a "done" message back to the session bean.

21 Servlet says "Finally, I'm done."

The servlet has actually been completely unaware of all this processing by the container. It thought that it had just found an actual session bean, had directly spoken to the session bean and told it to register Jeannie, and that the session bean was now saying "Did it, thanks for the opportunity to work with you!"

22 Servlet builds and sends the response page.

The servlet creates but does not display an HTML page that says "Thank you for registering; a confirmation message will be sent to jeannie@yahoo.com."

23 Web container receives done message from the servlet.

The servlet says "Done!" to the Web container and passes the page to the container.

24 Container takes done message and passes it and the generated page to the browser.

25 Browser displays a "thank you for registering" page.

And that's all there is to registering a new user in a 4-tier J2EE system.

Simple, huh?

That Was Simple???

Yes, it was. Because what you care about is how much code has to be written. Let's take a look at what humans had to do in this scenario.

- A Web designer created a simple registration page.
- A programmer wrote a simple servlet to find a session bean and ask the session bean to create an account with a given username and password.
- The session bean asked an entity bean Home interface if the username already exists and if it doesn't, asks the Home to create an entity bean for that username and password.

That's all. All the complicated other stuff was done by the container. The entity bean didn't even have to store data; the container took care of that. And the container took care of making sure all those steps stayed together and didn't get interrupted, and took care of getting the database to lock and unlock rows, and do its database transaction business.

This might not actually be the simplest or best approach to this particular process; we used all the parts of EJB to show you how they work together, not to use this as a perfect example of implementing a login process. You could just cut EJBs out of the equation entirely if appropriate for a particular process.

Where J2EE really helps out is when the problem you're solving is more complex or overwhelming than the J2EE code you need to write and the rules you need to follow. So the benefits of J2EE are most evident in a really complicated process, on the other end of the scale from a simple login registration. However, the code and explanations for that example would run into about 1750 pages and that's just not what we're doing with this book.

chapter 7

Does a Cup of J2EE in the Morning Always Smell Like Victory?

"It's wondrous, with treasures to satiate desires both subtle and gross. But it's not for the timid."

Q, Star Trek: The Next Generation

"Life is pain, princess. Anyone who says differently is selling something."

Wesley, The Princess Bride.

Hey, it all sounds great! Beans, servlets, JSPs, big honkin' databases...sounds like a perfect way to implement your office scheduling system, eh?

If J2EE has all this power, why not just use it for whatever you can?

Well, the same reason you might not take the space shuttle to pick up a loaf of bread and a gallon of milk.

So when would you use J2EE?

The Chapter in Brief

The thing is, you don't have to do everything in J2EE. You can use some, none, or all of the technologies available. J2EE is not all or nothing: there are servlets, JSPs, two kinds of session beans, entity beans, and message-driven beans. If you go with J2EE you can use one or more of these. J2EE is an enormously complex system and the things you need to do with your application should be more complicated than the technology you use to build an application.

There are metaphorical dead bodies all over the place of applications done in J2EE that shouldn't have been, or which took on a full-fledged project with entity beans when a few servlets and some nice stateless session beans would have done the job just fine.

Here's what we cover in this chapter.

- *Should You Be Doing the J2EE Jig of Joy?*
- *When All You Have Is a Spoon, Everything Looks Like Ice Cream*
- *You Don't Need to Go All the Way*
- *J2EE Debates*
- *It Doesn't Hurt to Consult an Expert*

Should You Be Doing the J2EE Jig of Joy?

Gosh, if J2EE provides all these services, shouldn't everyone be using it?

Not necessarily.

Depends on how big or complex your system is.

Here's an example. The average person can usually take care of cleaning his house himself. This can take 1-10 hours a week, but it's manageable. Especially if he's just got himself to take care of, and he's got an entry-level marketing job that's paying $15 an hour and money isn't exactly flowing through his fingers.

However, let's say that this person has five extremely messy children, is a single parent, and a doctor. It would be kind of tough for him to tell his patients, "Sorry, can't operate on you Tuesday—the laundry's piling up and school lets out early that day." In this case it's probably a good idea for him to get childcare and cleaning professionals to help him out. He's spending money on it and he has to take the time up front to interview several candidates for each position, and of course has to do a little training once he's hired them. But overall, it's a good tradeoff.

Likewise, if you're going to go to the time and expense and complexity of J2EE, you don't want to be just doing some piddly little project that could be done more easily without it.

Here are some characteristics of projects that could likely benefit from J2EE:

- The project has a bunch of existing pieces of software that need to be integrated in order to work together.
- The project needs to be able to *scale* bigtime. Scale just means being able to handle increased load without rewriting the application. Scalability also means, ideally, handling increased load without throwing away the existing hardware and getting something enormous instead.
- The application will be distributed. (It's distributed either because it's online and therefore automatically distributed, or because of its need for performance and scalability and data storage space.)
- The project absolutely positively needs to be up and running all the time.

This is in no way the definitive list; there really isn't one since there are always exceptions (no pun intended).

It always comes down to research and using your judgment, whatever the project. This applies when you're choosing a technology like J2EE for a development project; or whether you're choosing a documentation tool and evaluating Word or Framemaker or (run, save yourself) an XML single-source application, be careful.

Read information by people who don't sell J2EE application servers or tools for a living, and talk to people and take a good long hard look at what your application's needs actually are.

When All You Have Is a Spoon, Everything Looks Like Ice Cream

This heading is a variant on a more common saying but we wanted to update it a little. It's one of the risks you'll run into when you're choosing how to approach a project.

One of the particular pitfalls in choosing technology is that people get excited and don't think clearly. If you're a geek, or if you know or love geeks, you might have observed that they can get a little obsessed with a technology because it's So Cool. Or alternately because it's the one they know, or perhaps because they want to learn it so they can put it on their resume. This is not a good enough reason to use J2EE. Or to do anything that takes more than a few hours. Nor is someone else using it successfully on an entirely different project a good enough reason.

You Don't Need to Go All the Way

The four-tier approach isn't the only way. Not everybody needs to have all four tiers, and using a different model that works better is a perfectly acceptable approach. And there's certainly no constitutional amendment that a J2EE architecture is a system composed of a client tier, Web tier, EJB tier, and persistence tier.

If you need massive scalability, for instance, you'll want to consider EJBs. That's one of their big advantages. If you don't need massive scalability, then you might not need EJBs.

Part of the Eight-Bit Path of Right Computing is the Right Tool for the Job. Some people go stampeding straight toward EJBs, but JSPs and servlets have a fair amount of power too. If you can do what you need with JSPs or servlets, you don't need to go farther than that.

So you don't need all parts of all four tiers. Here are some variations.

- Customers use a client container front end instead of a browser – A client container is a different approach to the part of the application the customers use. A client container is more of a classic approach to the user interface; it's more like a "normal" application front end.

  Most application server vendors give you tools to create a client container for your customers. The advantage of using it is that it incorporates the services of the container, so the customers get those services right there on their computers. You need to distribute the client container to the customers, of course, and they need to install it.

- Browser, Web tier, and database – Not everyone needs EJBs. If you've just got some Web pages that send data straight in and out of the database without a lot of fuss, this configuration is for you.
- Browser, Web tier, session beans, and database – Session beans and entity beans are both EJBs, but session beans and entity beans do entirely different things. You might not need entity beans to sit there representing your database; there's nothing wrong with having the session beans send stuff straight to the database. This of course means that you write the SQL code to get stuff in and out of the database yourself in the session beans, so you don't get container-managed persistence.

J2EE Debates

A lot of people have a lot of opinions about J2EE. Some of the opinions are more urban legend than reality; some are definitely valid in most situations. The main problem is that it's kind of hard to tell at first blush how valid a statement is. When people have an opinion in general in computer science, it's a *strong* opinion and it's not usually tempered by conditions like "well, in the projects I've seen..." or "I might be wrong about this but..."

We think that these opinions stem from a couple things.

- A bad experience or a good experience with a project, especially a death march project, can be overwhelming. Anyone involved in it wants to spread the gospel of their experiences.
- The other issue is that software architecture and development is just plain complicated, and it's very tempting to try to simplify it by saying "stateful session beans are evil" or "entity beans are evil" or "always use servlets instead of session beans". But you just can't simplify something complicated. As someone famous whose name we can't recall just now, "For any given problem, there is usually a very simple solution that is wrong." (Thank goodness no one ever runs the government that way, or there'd be trouble.)

If you read *Bitter EJBs*, you might come away with a strong feeling that JSPs and servlets are OK but everything else comes with its own personalized long-armed robot waving and crying "Danger, danger!"

Here are some, although by no means all, the debates you'll hear. What we want you to take out of this is not to go with any particular architecture but to conclude that the strength of an opinion does not necessarily correspond to its validity, and that above all you should take nothing on faith. Ask around, do some research, check out other people's experiences. "Look for the bodies." Some projects succeed. Some really, really fail. If you're looking around and you see a lot of projects that got completed, more or less, with servlets and JSPs and a database; and some projects that dies horrible deaths when they brought in EJBs or specifically entity beans; well, that's something to consider.

Debate #1: Entity Beans Are Evil

Entity beans get a bad rap because a lot of people use them when they don't need to. Another reason they get a bad rap is because they deal with persistence, a.k.a. getting data in and out of the database. Persistence is really complicated, period, so entity beans are going to be complicated too.

Another reason they get a bad rap is related to getting information in and out of the database. The container has the ability to take over the duties of taking data from entity beans and putting it into the database correctly, and of course bringing the data back out. This is called container-managed persistence, or CMP. However, prior to EJB 2.0, there were a lot of situations that CMP couldn't address. The main point of using entity beans is to take advantage of CMP, so that made entity beans less useful than they could have been. Getting a list out of the database of, say, all the houses for sale in a particular city, was problematic too for a couple reasons, which we talk about in *How to Stop Treating Entity Beans Like Objects: Home Business Methods* on page 133.

Another reason they get a bad rap is that there are add-on tools that promise to make entity beans as simple as waving a magic wand and saying "Abra cadabra persistence!" Sometimes they're great. Sometimes if your project is complex enough, those tools can actually keep you from ever finishing the project. If you use addon tools for making persistence easier, check out other people's experiences.

Here's the gist. People tend to forget the purpose of an EJB. Here's the deal. Computing power is a simple well-known equation of cost and power. You know how much it costs to get certain computing power. However, programmer ingenuity and results are not a simple equation. You don't know how much it costs in time and money to get certain results from a programmer. Development projects often don't go the way you expect, and the price is also usually higher than you expect.

The point of EJBs is to rely less on programmers and more on computing power. In an EJB project, you're throwing more hardware and fewer programmers at the problem. The result is more predictable.

Expect more reliability in terms of getting the project done right, and expect to throw more hardware at the project, and you will get what EJBs were designed to do.

Lots of programers don't like this or understand it since in effect it's threatening their jobs. It's like the protests against industrialization, ranging from those wacky saboteurs in their wooden clogs to Marx. Likewise some programmers today who don't like EJBs are throwing their Birkenstocks into the cogs of the development process when they have to do EJBs.

There is this tempting little possibility around the corner that the entity bean may yet get smarter than the programmer. Then, without any extra effort, you have all the benefits of fewer programmers without paying the price of more hardware.

This is not to say everyone should do entity beans all the time. The same "do it if it makes sense" rules apply. Just expect the right things from entity beans.

Debate #2: Stateful Session Beans Are Evil

A popular opinion is that stateful session beans should be avoided. Some architect groups dictate that stateful session beans are just not an option, period.

Now, sometimes stateful session beans, with their long memories and higher memory usage, are not a good choice. Sometimes you just need a stateless session bean to do one thing, then forget it all instantly once the task is done. Rinse and repeat.

However, sometimes they're fine, or at least the least of several evils.

One variable in stateful session bean performance is how they're used. If you ask a session bean to do only one thing, then the stateful session bean will drag things down. If you have multiple related requests, however, the stateful session bean can get better performance.

Another point is that performance is not the only thing to consider. This point is provided by Dan Johnsson from OmegaPoint consulting. The thing is, regardless of what kind of code you're writing, sometimes the business process you need to complete *requires* that you keep state around somehow. Keeping state around is not optional. You need to remember a set of search criteria or that *Buffy Season 6* has been put in the shopping cart. The customer will be pissed off if this information is forgotten.

Now, you don't *have* to keep that state around by using the stateful session bean's little backpack of information. You could store it in a number of other ways, including a cookie (that sneaky little file on your machine that lets Amazon recommend other books on That Topic to you). You could also shoot that information into the database and retrieve it when needed.

Now, of all these options and more—stateful session beans, cookies, the database—are stateful session beans going to be the slowest? Maybe. Maybe not. Performance is not the only thing to consider. Stateful session beans might be a little slower, but you need to consider extensibility (page 231), reliability (page 230), maintainability (page 232), and security (page 232).

A general guideline is that if the business process that the code is completing is stateful, then stateful session beans are a good solution. If the user interface is stateful, then HTTP sessions inside your servlets are a good solution. (HTTP session are just a way to make a servlet maintain state.)

That leads us conveniently to the next debate.

Debate #3: Session Beans or Servlets?

Anytime you want a meeting to go on forever or anytime you want to start a fight, just bring this up. It partly comes down to the technology, and partly to the skill of the team in question, the size of the project, and personal preference.

From a purely technical standpoint, a servlet and a stateless session bean are roughly comparable. They can both rush around and do business logic.

Session beans have all three services Session beans run inside the EJB container, which provides transactions and other data integrity features. The servlet container doesn't, though it does provide security.

Servlets do stuff for the user interface Servlets are generally for use in business logic that will be used in a browser interface, however. Servlets create data that the user will see, or that will affect what the user sees, in his or her browser. Session beans are generally for use when the results of the business process the bean is completing won't be showing up in the browser interface.

Entity beans lead to session beans over servlets Entity beans connect to databases and can be shared by multiple people. A Java object in a servlet, however, can't be shared simultaneously. So at that point, if you need that feature, you might want entity beans. And if you want entity beans, then you might want session beans instead of servlets.

This is because servlets are remote to entity beans since they're in different containers, but session beans can be local to entity beans (if you're using local interfaces, a new feature in EJB 2.0). Any remote communication is slower than local communication. Therefore you get better performance by using session beans to rush around and do things instead of servlets, if you've already got entity beans in the picture anyway.

If you're the analytical type, you might be thinking about that last paragraph and saying to yourself, "OK, the session beans are local to the entity beans so session bean-entity bean communication is local and therefore faster. But the browser is still remote from the session beans so browser-session bean communication is still remote. Any JSPs and servlets still in the picture are going to be remote from the session beans. Why is it good to have the session beans local to entity beans when there's still all that remote stuff happening?" That's a very good point—there's still that remote stuff even when you've got your business logic in session beans. But there's less. Here's why. The client just makes one, or at least very few, *remote* requests to the session bean. Then the session bean makes a whole lot of *local* requests to the entity beans. If you had servlets doing the calls to the entity beans, and of course doing them remotely, then there'd be a lot of remote calls from the servlet to the entity beans.

The right tool for the job You can focus on what to do by thinking, "OK, what are servlets *for*?" They're for running in a Web-based system. Servlets' primary purpose is to receive HTTP requests and generate HTML responses. Then think "What are EJBs for?" They're for representing your business processes (session beans) and your data (entity beans) but not really worrying much about the Web. If you aren't running in a Web-based system, then you don't really need servlets. If you don't need HTTP, then servlets can be quite inefficient. Basically, this line of thought is, a good piece of advice is to just use the tool that was built for the environment your application will run in.

General guideline If you have all the tiers in your application, for whatever reason, then business process should probably be handled by session beans. Processes related to the user interface should be handled by JSPs and servlets. Servlets are still about presentation more than business processes. Servlets are about computing things that go into the presentation.

However, if you don't have session beans then it's perfectly reasonable to do business computations in a servlet, as it is also appropriate if you have no web tier to do the presentation computations in a session bean.

Sometimes following the rules doesn't really get what you want. If you follow the rules and have servlets doing servlet things and EJBs doing EJB things, you might end up with a system twice the size you needed. If you can make your servlets do just a few other things that the EJBs were doing, you can cut the EJBs, decrease size of the application, increase performance, and feel very cool about what you made the servlets do.

And as always, keep in mind that applications grow. You might not need EJBs now, but will you? Remember what happened to Antoine—one review in *Cheese and Bread Monthly* and his business outgrew his application. If you want to scale, you'll need scalability, and EJBs are a good way to get that.

Any choice has got to be backed up by the right skills. If you're going to use servlets, make sure someone on your team can make servlets corner like they're on rails. If you've got an EJB expert team that views servlets with horror and deep suspicion, then you might be looking at an EJB approach. Not to recommend coding by resume but EJB alpha people are not going to be as good at servlets as alpha servlet people, and vice versa.

It Doesn't Hurt to Consult an Expert

We finished writing this section and thought, "All this sounds like the best thing to do is to hire someone to plan your application who's as smart and knowledgeable as a really good developer. But who doesn't have any of the programmer attitude or preconceived notions, and just wants to figure out the best way to solve the business problem."

Where do you find a mythological creature like that?

Then we realized that that's a decent definition of a software architect. That's what they do: take a look at what you need to accomplish and give you an overall plan that, when implemented, will do the right things.

Architects do a lot of valuable things, including evaluating how to make sure your application achieves the right qualities of service. For more information, see Chapter 19, "Good J2EE Architecture," on page 225.

part II

Deeper Into J2EE

"If Ford is to Chevrolet
What Dodge is to Chrysler
What Corn Flakes are to Post Toasties
What the clear blue sky is to the deep blue sea
What Hank Williams is to Neil Armstrong
Can you doubt we were made for each other?"

Lyle Lovett, Here I Am

The next step, now that you're solid on the point of J2EE and what's being accomplished, is to get to know the technologies better. There'll be some code, too. We won't throw tons at you, but enough so you'll see what the parts are and what code is involved.

We're going to cover what we've touched on already in more detail, plus introduce Web services, a new part of J2EE.

Here's what you get in Part II:

chapter 8

Web Servers and Web Containers

"Go web! Fly! Up, up, and away web! Shazam! Web it! Tally ho!"

Spiderman

We talked about Web containers, which are like EJB containers but for, well, Web code. And we talked about Web servers a little, too.

But these things become clearer in the retelling. So let's go over again Web containers and Web servers are, in more detail. We'll talk about what the difference is and why you need both. You'd think that a Web container, with all those services it does, could take care of all the Web stuff that needs to be done.

The Chapter in Brief

Let's say you use your browser to go to www.somebodyswebpage.com/about.html, the only thing that happens is that a Web server on that site takes your request, goes, "Hey, she wants the about.html page," and sends that page to you. If you went to www.somebodyswebpage.com/about.**jsp**, though, which is a Web page with extra Java steroids added, you need a Web *container* to be running on that site too. The container takes over when the Web server gets confused.

Here's what we cover in this chapter.

- *Web Server Overview*
- *More on HTTP*
- *More on What the Web Server Does*
- *What the Web Container Does*
- *The Web Container and Dynamic Content*
- *The Web Container Services*
- *How the Web Container and Web Server Work Together*

Web Server Overview

Note: The Web server doesn't inherently have anything to do with J2EE. Nothing at all. It was around a long time ago. But it's darned useful with J2EE nonetheless.

Anyone with a computer running a browser like Netscape can get to it. Why Netscape? Why a browser? Why can't you just use PhotoShop to get to the Web? Because you need two things in an application to get to the Web, and PhotoShop ain't got either:

- Ability to understand the protocol for transmitting information on the Web, HTTP (hypertext transfer protocol)
- Ability to understand the markup language for displaying information on the web, HTML

Anything, in fact, that runs on the Web needs to be able to handle those two things. So the Web server has those capabilities, too. And not much else. A Web server is just a simple application that can take requests from someone using a browser, and send back things like the Web page that that person requests. The requested pages are set up in a directory or directories that the Web server knows about and can locate. Once the Web server finds the requested page or file, it tucks the page into a series of commands called an *HTTP response*, and sends the page to your computer. An HTTP response is the way that the Web server has to package up the page to send it back to your browser. It's just the rules of the Web.

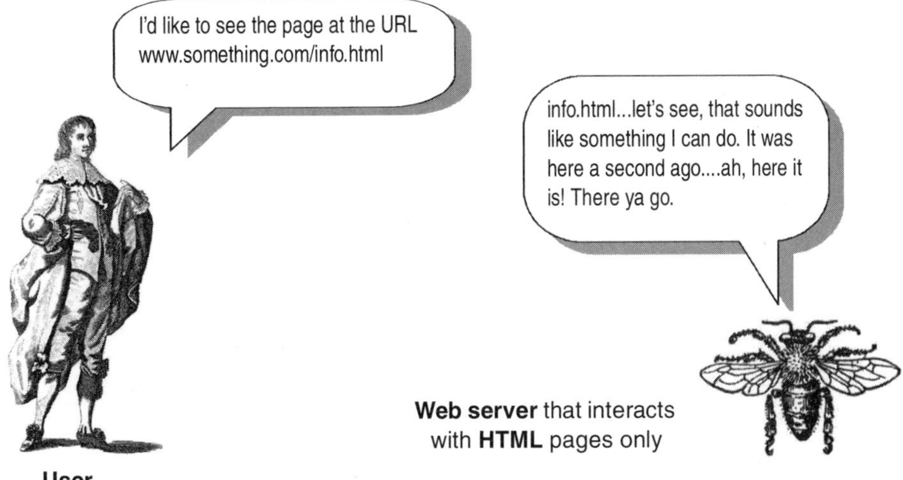

I'd like to see the page at the URL www.something.com/info.html
info.html...let's see, that sounds like something I can do. It was here a second ago....ah, here it is! There ya go.
Web server that interacts with HTML pages only
User

Figure 8-1 The user and Web server roles

More on HTTP

A Web server is simply an application that delivers files to people who ask for them, usually Web pages containing HTML, using HTTP as the communication protocol. It sits on some computer and just waits there patiently for an HTTP request. HTTP is the protocol (the language and conversation rules) that the request must be in.

Let's talk about the pizza shop again. Let's say Antoine's cousin Anita also runs a shop, and man, is she uptight about how you place your order. You can't just say "large, pepperoni, extra cheese." Store policy states that you have to say, "Hello Anita, my name is Bob. May I please have a pizza, pepperoni, extra cheese, large?" And if you deviate at all from that format, Anita will *so* ignore you.

HTTP is like that. Not complicated particularly, but you just have to follow the rules. Luckily, browsers and Web servers are all about how to do those rules.

The HTTP request itself is usually just to retrieve a specific file. If the Web server can service the request, i.e. if you just ask for a plain old preexisting file like a GIF or an HTML file, the Web server returns an HTTP response containing the file that was asked for. An HTTP response is just how the Web page you wanted is sent back to you by the Web server.

Anything you do is sent across in an HTTP *request*, and an answer is returned in an HTTP *response*.

- What is sent over in an HTTP request includes things like the type of browser you're using, what page you're on, and the data in the fields of the form you filled out a page (if indeed you did fill out a form).
- The response is the page or information you requested, with whatever else the Web server added.

Let's say you've gone to the site for this book, www.bigpicture-books.com. You open your browser and type www.bigpicture-books.com, which is basically the same as typing www.bigpicture-books.com/index.html. Then you press your Enter or Return key which is the Web equivalent of slapping a horse on its rear to make it take off.

Your browser creates an HTTP request that might look something like this:

Example 8-1 Sample HTTP request

```
GET index.html HTTP/1.0
User-Agent: Mozilla/4.76 [en] (X11; U; SunOS 5.8 sun4u)
Host: www.bigpicture-books.com
```

GET is the type of request. You want to get the file index.html from the Web server at www.bigpicture-books.com. Some other possibilities are HEAD which would just retrieve meta-data or information about the Web server and file. POST which is very similar to GET (we'll see the differences a little later) and a few others.

HTTP/1.0 is the protocol and version number.

User-Agent is the type of browser you are using.

Host is the Web server the request is being sent to.

There's a bunch of other data that can be sent in the HTTP request as well, but let's just keep it simple.

This request simply means that your browser would like to have the file index.html. The Web server on some computer at www.bigpicture-books.com receives this request, fetches the file index.html from where it's stored, "wraps" that file inside an HTTP response (don't worry about the details of wrapping), and delivers the response containing the page back to your browser running on your computer. Your browser interprets the response and displays that page to you.

More on What the Web Server Does

When you start up your Web server, it acts kind of like a phone operator. It sets up a network connection to listen with and waits for someone to call. That is, it waits for someone to make an HTTP request by entering a URL that it's responsible for into a client (usually a browser). When it receives a request it services that request, usually by fetching a file or asking the Web container to run a servlet. The server then wraps the information that it got from servicing the request into an HTTP response and sends the HTTP response back to the client.

If the request is for a servlet or JSP, the server forwards the request to the container. How does the server know that it's for a servlet or JSP? This depends on the server. For example, Apache uses modules that are plugged into the server. The modules are configured to look for certain URL patterns such as .jsp that are handled by that module.

The Web server is also responsible for managing resources to some extent. It will have to be able to service many simultaneous users. When, for instance, 200 requests for the Tuesday Night Special, Sausage'n'Ham Calzones, come in all at the same time, each user doesn't have to wait for the server to finish with the first person before it starts servicing the others' requests. That way hunger, riots, and of course madness lie.

The Web server will also act as a security guard preventing a browser from accessing other files that might be on the same computer as the Web server or accessible through that Web server.

When someone visits Antoine's Pizzas at www.antoinespizza.com, their Web browser is sending an HTTP request for a file called index.html from the Web server. At the same time the Web server is ready to service other requests. The Web server will send index.html back to your browser.

Antoine's index.html file is a welcome page that has a link to the menu. When you click on the menu link, your browser creates an HTTP request based on the way the link was written into the index.html file. The browser will create a request asking the Web server for the file specified by the link, for example, menu.html. The Web server will then deliver the file menu.html to your browser. If a file that you request doesn't exist or your browser doesn't have permission to access the file, the Web server will return a error.

What the Web Container Does

The Web container is a whole different thing. The Web container is very much part of J2EE and is far more powerful.

The Web container is responsible for helping the Web server service a request by invoking servlets or JSPs. It is usually a plug-in that you have to download for your Web server.

J2EE application servers typically come with a Web container for handling servlets and JSPs.

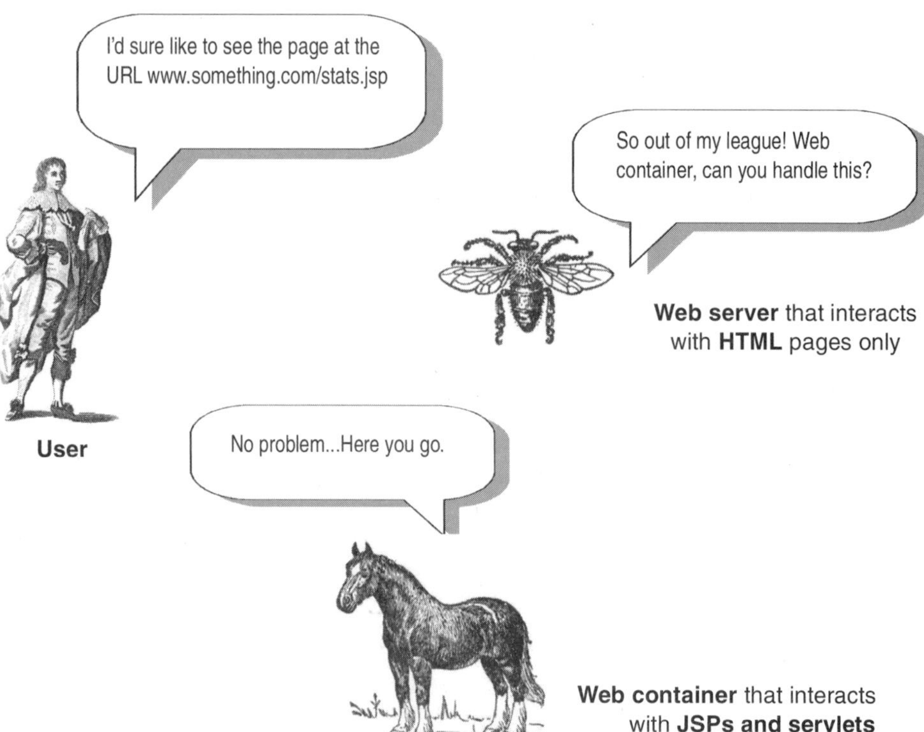

Figure 8-2 The user, Web server, and Web container roles

The Web Container and Dynamic Content

Basically, the Web container is different from the Web server because it manages *dynamic content*. Dynamic content is a file that doesn't exist already and is created on the fly by some programming logic.

What? Dynamic content doesn't exist? Let's back up for a second.

You could create *static content* by opening a text editor, typing in HTML, saving the file in a directory where the Web server can access it and voila, you can access the file through your browser.

Sometimes, however, you don't know what information the Web page should contain until it is requested. What if you wanted to create a Web page that contains inventory from a database? The contents of the database change constantly; you can't just type up a ThingsWeAreRunningOutOf.html page based on the INVENTORY table in the database, and have that be right for the next month, week, day, or even hour. If you did that, you'd be out of mozzarella pretty soon if it's not on the list, and if tomato sauce is on the list you might eventually stockpile so much of it you'd need to evolve sauce gills.

To keep that file up to date on your own and still have it be a plain old file, you personally or one of your minions would have to spend all day every day querying the database, then making the appropriate changes to the HTML file, then posting the new HTML file.

Wouldn't it be simpler if the checking, changing, and posting were all done by a program instead?

Some content needs to be very up to date, and to ensure this *content* is up to date, you create it *dynamically*.

Here's a way you might create up-to-date dynamic content for the ingredients needed for Antoine's pizza place. You can write a servlet (called InventoryDisplayer, perhaps) that would query the database and create the HTML page for you right there, on the fly. That created information would be dynamic content. And instead of saving it to a file like inventory.html you can have that same InventoryDisplayer servlet send its output directly to the Web server, which in turn displays it to the user. The Web container is responsible for starting the servlet and directing the servlet's output back to the Web server.

The Web Container Services

We talked a lot in the introductory chapters about how application servers provide security, resource management, and data integrity, and that also by the way in the J2EE application server there are two containers that really provide these services. What we didn't specify then, at least not in painful detail, is that the EJB container is really the big man on the services campus. The EJB container provides all three types of services, in spades.

The Web container, by way of contrast, just supplies security and a little bit of resource management. The resource management that it supplies isn't J2EE specific, but just what you get when you're Java, from the garbage collector. Not because it's a lazy, weakminded little container but because its servlets and JSPs don't really need as much. Different environment, different needs.

We'll get into security in Chapter 17, "J2EE Security," on page 207, and into data integrity supplied by the JVM in Chapter 15, "Resource Management," on page 185.

How the Web Container and Web Server Work Together

Let's say you've gotten way too hungry reading about pizza and you've finally gone to his site. You've looked through Antoine's menu of tantalizing pizza delights and have made your selection. When you click the Confirm Order button, the Web browser will send a request to the Web server requesting the URL www.antoinespizza.com/checkout.

Floyd, who Antoine has hired back as system administrator, has set up the site's Web server so that the URL will cause the CheckOut program to run instead of serving up a static Web page. The Web server forwards the request that's tied to the Confirm Order button along with anything that was entered into a form to the Web container.

The Web container starts up the program and monitors it. The CheckOut program calculates your total, modify Antoine's inventory and produces a confirmation page. The program creates HTML and sends it back to the Web container. The Web container holds onto the output until CheckOut is finished. When the program finishes, the Web container sends the HTML back to the Web server and the Web server sends the HTTP response containing the HTML back to the browser.

chapter 9

JSPs and Servlets

Charlie Kauffman: "I wrote myself into my own screenplay."
Donald Kauffman: "Isn't that a little weird?"

Adaptation

"Do you know what a metaphysical can of worms this portal is?"

Craig Schwartz, Being John Malkovich

We've taken a very high-level look so far at JSPs and servlets, the things J2EE programmers write to do stuff on the Web. But...what if you want to sit down and write a JSP? What does it look like? Do you create a file called mynewjsp.jsp and you're good to go, or is it a little more complicated? And what's this weird stuff about how JSPs are really servlets, when you run them? And while we're asking questions, why bother with EJBs when servlets, apparently, can do all sorts of fabulous powerful stuff?

It's time to take a deeper look at just what these things do, when you use them with other parts of the J2EE landscape, and take just a very small peek at the code.

The Chapter in Brief

Nice plain HTML pages are great but if you need to display the latest snow conditions or get Jeannie's latest order information out of the database, HTML just won't do it anymore. JSPs, HTML with Java code on the inside; and servlets, Java code with HTML on the inside; are sometimes the answer to this issue. You get a few techniques and frameworks to help you write JSPs and servlets, including the MVC design patterns and Struts for turning code into a deployed application.

Here's what we cover in this chapter.

- *Why Would Anyone Need Anything Besides Nice Plain HTML Pages?*
- *All About Servlets*
- *Overview of JSPs*
- *Tools and Techniques People Use Along With Servlets and JSPs*
- *Web Component Development Processes*
- *Introduction to Portals*

Why Would Anyone Need Anything Besides Nice Plain HTML Pages?

HTML is great for serving up static content; that is, Web pages that just sit there and look pretty. Mostly their content is the same, day after day, until some human changes it. As soon as you need to serve up content specific to a particular user like account information or a shopping cart, or content that changes by the minute or hour like stock quotes or snow reports, you need dynamic content. Using static HTML files for rapidly changing data gets very hairy very quickly. And not in a good way.

For example, if Al Timeter wants to log in and check his account information stored in your database, it would be very difficult, not to mention unsecure, to have this account information sitting in a static HTML file on your Web server. Even if it were easy and secure, you'd have to have one such HTML file for every user. All kept up to date, all the time. Unless you have an underground lair where you keep thousands of drones to do your bidding, this could be more work than you want.

Instead, it would be much nicer to be able to generate *dynamic content.* So when Mr. Timeter logs in, the Web server doesn't serve up a static HTML file. Instead, it calls on a servlet to create an HTML file on the fly. This program could easily access your database and provide Mr. Timeter with his most up-to-date account information.

You could create this dynamic content several ways. Which one you use depends somewhat on your circumstances and on the content itself. Two very common approaches for creating dynamic content are CGI and servlets. (We talked about CGI in Chapter 3, "Before J2EE: The First Online Tools," on page 41.)

All About Servlets

Servlets are really just some Java code that can run within a Web container, because servlets speak HTML and HTTP. Servlets were created so that you could create dynamic Web content.

How Servlets Work

Let's say Antoine's Web site has a form for logging in. When the user clicks the submit button, the information in the form is send along with the request to a URL; for example, www.antoinespizza.com/login

If the URL in this case were to refer to a static HTML file the Web server would simply send back a copy of that HTML file. However, in this case the URL refers to a piece of Java code (a servlet) on the server. So when the Web server receives the request, it doesn't serve up a file, but instead says "Hey, that's a servlet" and passes the request off to the Web container. The Web container says, "Hey, a servlet! I know where this servlet is," finds it, and passes the request off to the servlet itself.

The servlet can retrieve the information the user entered on the login form, and uses it to access a database or process the information any way it needs to.

Based on this information, the servlet can generate HTML and send it back to the Web container. The Web container then sends the HTML wrapped in an HTTP response back to the Web server, and the Web server then sends the HTTP response back to the Web browser. It's a lot like a baseball triple play.

If you
really want
to know

CGI

CGI, which people used for Web-enabled computing and processing before servlets came along and still use, works in a very similar way. The difference is that CGI uses C, Perl, or some other language.

The Web container will create a new process for each request to www.antoinespizza.com/login whereas a servlets will create new threads for each request. A process is more memory and performance expensive than a thread. In other words, servlets are generally faster and offer better scalability than CGI. Another huge advantage with servlets is that they are written in Java, so you get all of the benefits of Java including object-oriented design, platform independence, portability, the use of the Java class libraries, etc.

What Servlets Are Made Of

This example discussed a servlet that did some processing and then sent back a page: that is, the servlet dealt both with business logic and with presentation logic.

- *Business logic* is anything that manipulates data in order to accomplish something, such as storing data.
- *Presentation logic* is anything that controls how the application presents information to the user. Generating the HTML response within the servlet code is presentation logic.

Servlets often contain both business logic and presentation logic. This isn't that uncommon, despite our emphasis on how different types of logic Shouldn't Mix. Here's a short example in Figure 9-1. You can see that the Java code is the main part of it, and inside there are a few lines of HTML.

Example 9-1 Sample Servlet

```
// some import statements we're leaving out for simplicity
public class HelloServlet extends BigPictureServlet
{
  public void service(ServletRequest request, ServletResponse response)throws IOException
  {
    PrintWriter out = response.getWriter();
    // Generate the servlet response
  out.println("Hello, and Welcome to Antoine's Pizza!"); // the HTML
  out.close();
  }
}
```

Imagine if you had to write anything of significance within that servlet, like more text or some formatting text or a table. That would be really annoying to have to do in a servlet. And likely have more mistakes. The purists, the committed object orientation people, and people who just hate to write HTML code inside of Java code, like to leave the business logic to the servlets and designate as much presentation as possible to the JSPs.

Overview of JSPs

JSP is short for JavaServer Pages. A JSP typically contains HTML content and one or more kinds of Java steroids in the form of plain Java code or tags referring to external Java classes.

A servlet is Java code with (sometimes) HTML inside. A JSP is HTML with Java inside. So they're the same in that they do similar things in a similar context, and the opposite in terms of what's on the outside and what's on the inside.

The JSP tags allow you to embed dynamic content in a Web page. A JSP could contain, for example, Java code to define a variable or access a database, or a tag that reference Java code that can do just about anything. The JSP file sits on the Web tier along with servlets.

For example, you write a file called info.jsp, which contains JSP tags for accessing a database along with HTML for formatting and presenting the information from the database. In your browser you type www.antoinespizza.com/info.jsp and hit Enter. The Web server receives the request but doesn't simply serve up the file info.jsp. Instead, the server passes the request off to the Web container because it is a JSP. The Web container translates the JSP into a servlet and then compiles the servlet, as shown in Figure 9-1.

Wait—the JSP is now a servlet? Yep. That's how the Web container fiddles with the JSP so that it, the Web container, can deal with the JSP when the application is running. The original JSP with its nice simple HTML is still there and when Cilantro the Web Designer needs to make changes, he changes the JSP, not the compiled servlet that the container made.

The translation and compilation only occur on the first access to the JSP, and every access after that is faster because the JSP has already been translated and compiled. You can have the container just translate and compile everything all at once in a big batch once or twice a day or week, or you can let it happen when a user accesses a JSP.

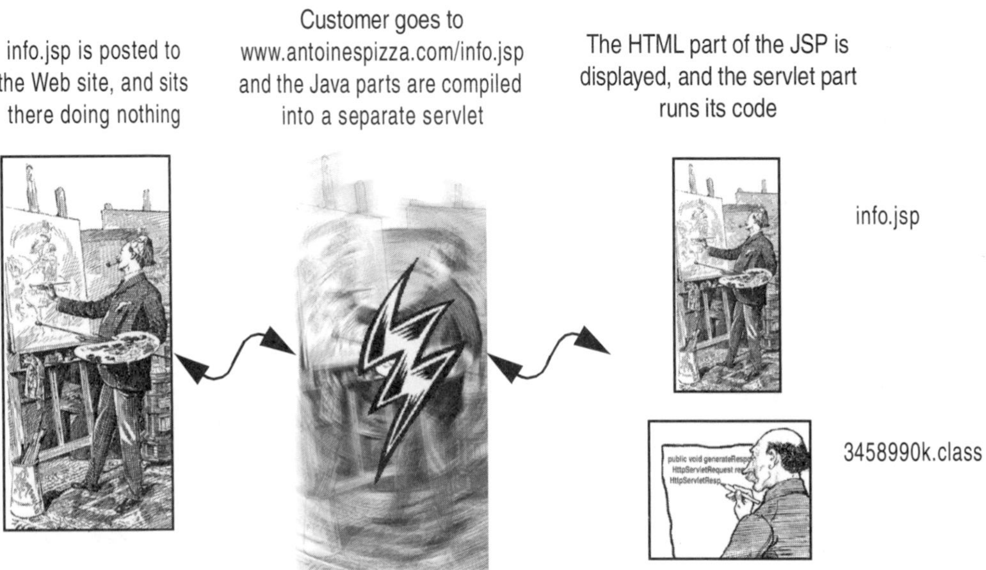
info.jsp is posted to the Web site, and sits there doing nothing
Customer goes to www.antoinespizza.com/info.jsp and the Java parts are compiled into a separate servlet
The HTML part of the JSP is displayed, and the servlet part runs its code
info.jsp
3458990k.class

Figure 9-1 A JSP becomes a servlet

Example 9-2 shows a simple JSP, with regular Java code in the middle.

Example 9-2 Simple JSP

```
<%! private static final String DEFAULT_NAME = "Customer"; %>
<HTML>
<HEAD>
<TITLE>Hello JavaServer Page</TITLE>
</HEAD>
<%-- Determine the specified customer name (or use default) --%>
<%
String name = request.getParameter("customer");
if ( (customer == null) II (customer.length() == 0) ) {
customer = DEFAULT_NAME;   // Java code
 %>
<BODY BGCOLOR='white'>
```

```
<B>Hello, <%= customer %>. Don't eat the brown pizza.</B>
</BODY>
</HTML>
```

The Kinds of Java You Can Put in JSPs

There are a couple different ways you can add that Special Something.

Scriptlets

As you saw in Example 9-2, you can type actual Java code in a JSP, right there in the middle of the HTML, and the Java code will run. Assuming it's written perfectly. Using scriptlets can cause JSPs to get very ugly very quickly (hard to read and maintain). Including scriptlets also puts more responsibility on the Web page designer because now either he has to learn new tags and also be a skilled Java programmer, or you have two people (a Java developer and a Web designer) working in the same file. The code used in the scriptlet is usually there to handle presentation logic. The other tags and HTML handle the presentation.

So scriptlets are allowed, but they are not necessarily the best way to incorporate Java code into a JSP. Not on a grand scale, that is. They're harder than plain HTML, and they're way harder to maintain and debug. Scriptlets are like using an old tshirt to make coffee because you've run out of filters. OK, it'll work, but really not something you want to do on an ongoing basis.

In Figure 9-3's scriptlet, a conditional statement is used to determine how to greet customers on a login page. If the variable **p** (pizzas ordered that month) is greater than 10, then the customer is greeted as a pizza club customer. If that condition isn't true, then a plain greeting is displayed in the JSP. Java code is in bold.

Example 9-3 Short scriptlet example with a JSP

```
<%
if ( p > 10 )
{
// the next three lines display the indicated words in the JSP if the condition is true
  %>
  Welcome, Pizza Club customer!
  <%
}
else
{
// the next three lines display the indicated words in the JSP if the condition is false
  %>
```

```
    Welcome!
    <%
}
%>
```

It works, but imagine pages and pages of all that Java code, some of it a whole lot messier and more complex.

Custom Tag Libraries

A better solution for incorporating Java code into a JSP is to use custom tag libraries. They do involve more work upfront but are easier to maintain and offer a better separation of concerns. Custom tag libraries give you the power of scriptlets without the mess.

How does it work? A Java developer writes some Java code called a tag library by following the tag library rules. This code defines and documents a new JSP tag. The Web designer simply learn a little about the new tag and can use it within the JSPs he creates. This separation makes the application not only easier on Cilantro and all his brethren but easier to maintain. It would be much more difficult to find every place a scriptlet has been used than to simply change the tag library code.

Using custom tag libraries is also pretty nice because the tags are reusable. Just refer to then and boom, they're in the JSP. With scriptlets, you're in cut-and-paste city.

Why is cut-and-paste city a bad place to live? Cutting and pasting once or twice is fine but once you've done it 113 times, you get sick of it. Cutting and pasting means that maintenance takes a long time. Cutting and pasting also means that you're almost guaranteed to make mistakes during maintenance because everyone makes mistakes selecting the right thing to copy, and selecting the right thing to paste over. It's all just a very manual, human-error-ridden process.

Example 9-4 and Example 9-5 show doing something with a scriptlet looks next to doing it with a JSP. This code just fills in a form with an address.

Example 9-4 Using scriptlets

```
<TD ALIGN='right'>Address:</TD>
<TD>
<% String addressValue = request.getParameter("address");
if ( addressValue == null ) addressValue = ""; %>
<INPUT TYPE='text' NAME='address'
VALUE='<%= addressValue %>' SIZE='50'>
</TD>
```

Example 9-5 Using custom tags

```
<TD ALIGN='right'>Address:</TD>
<TD>
<INPUT TYPE='text' NAME='address'
VALUE='<pizzaorderform:getReqParam name="address"/>' SIZE='50'>
</TD>
```

There's no actual Java code in there; the Web person just needs to know the name of the custom tag library and what input values it needs. This means your Web designer Cilantro just needs to know that the form submission tag library is called Address and that it needs a text value called address. Just the name and the data is needs to receive, and the order of the data.

Web Deployment Descriptor

The deployment descriptor is the Web container's checklist of where it wants to go today and what to do with all the parts of the application. It's basically the answer to the question, "OK, you've given me all these servlets and JSPs, now what do I do with them?" It tells the container about what kind of security to use and where to look for the lists of who can and can't do stuff; where the servlets are; and all sorts of other stuff so the container knows how to do its job.

The file itself is XML. (See *A Little More on XML* on page 67 for some background.) XML, or eXtensible Markup Language, is a standard way of writing up information by indicating what type of information is enclosed in it with tags.

You can edit the deployment descriptor directly, but nobody except a hard core vi user would actually do so. You update the settings in the deployment descriptor with graphical interface tools you get along with the application server.

Example 9-6 shows a small example of what you might find in a Web deployment descriptor.

Example 9-6 Web deployment descriptor

<web-app>

This tag is the start of a Web application.

<servlet>

Within a Web application there are several parts. Servlets can be one part of a Web application. This line says that there is a servlet in this Web application.

<servlet-name>**SimpleServlet**</servlet-name>

This line tells the name of the servlet.

<display-name>**simple servlet**</display-name>

This line provides a display name for the servlet. This name is the one you'd see in development tools. (What's a display name for? You might have a particular rule for creating the regular names of the servlets that's great for coding but not human friendly. Display names help you see more easily what you're dealing with.)

<servlet-class>**SimpleServlet**</servlet-class>

This line provides that name of the actual servlet class for this servlet.

</servlet>

This tag is the end of the servlet section, which could then be followed by several more servlet tags.

<servlet-mapping>

This tag begins the servlet mapping information. This information describes how a browser can access a servlet.

<servlet-name>**SimpleServlet**</servlet-name>

This line lists which servlet we are creating the mapping for.

<url-pattern>**/servlet/SimpleServlet**</url-pattern>

This line is the relative URL for accessing this servlet. To access this servlet you would have to enter something like www.myserver.com/servlet/SimpleServlet in your browser to get this servlet to execute.

</servlet-mapping>

This tag identifies the end of the servlet mapping section.

<session-config>

This tag begins the session configuration for this Web application.

<session-timeout>**30**</session-timeout>

This line states how long a session can be inactive before it expires.

</session-config>

The end of the session config section.

</web-app>

The end of the Web application section.

If you
really want
to know

Why Use EJBs When Servlets Can Do So Much?

On their own, a servlet and a stateless session bean are roughly comparable. They can both rush around and do business logic. However, the Web container and the EJB container have very different capabilities. We discussed when to use each in Chapter 7, "Does a Cup of J2EE in the Morning Always Smell Like Victory?," on page 79.

Tools and Techniques People Use Along With Servlets and JSPs

It's not just plain old hand-coded servlets and JSPs all day long, seven days a week. There are frameworks, methodologies, and sometimes small stuffed toys that people use to make servlets and JSPs do their bidding.

The Ever-Popular MVC Pattern

MVC is an acronym that stands for Model-View-Controller. Basically, MVC is a way to represent the parts of an application. It's a techy way of dividing up how the Web part of the application looks, how it acts, and where it stores the information. Which is just the same old separation of presentation, business, and persistence logic we've been blabbing on about pretty much since the beginning of the book.

- *Model* is the data itself. Like your customer mailing list. Entity beans are a common way to make the model.
- *View* is the particular view of the data. For instance, you might have a view that shows the customer mailing list with all the snailmail addresses that are in the model but none of the email addresses that are in the model. JSPs are a common way to make the view.
- *Controller* determines what data shows up in the view, and updates the view when the model changes. Servlets are a common way to make the controller.

The view shows the model and accepts input. It is what the user sees and interacts with to get stuff done. The controller validates the input, translates user input into model actions, and selects the view. It is what processes the users' requests, coordinates the activities of the model, and decides what the next view should be. The model represents application data and business rules. It is what enforces the business rules and interacts with the data.

The point of MVC is just good old-fashioned separation of presentation and business logic.

Struts

They have nothing to do with your car's suspension system, though the name works if you think of it as an MVC suspension system. Struts is an open-source framework for building Web applications based on the MVC pattern.

Struts does for MVC what J2EE does for enterprise applications.

For example, the C in MVC stands for controller. Struts provides various built-in extensible controller classes that you can use for your application. It also provides classes for retrieving data from the user. All of this functionality is provided with Java classes, JSPs, and XML descriptors.

Struts came around for the same reason as any new technology comes around—to make something easier, better, and/or faster. It was developed to make creating, developing and maintaining complex Web sites faster and easier. (That is to say, it's not meant to help you develop a family Web site with the pictures of your new house and the holiday newsletter, but it could help you if you were putting together a big ol' database for your entire extended family with a big genealogy database, a few forms for entering and correcting data, and a Yahoo! Maps type functionality for plotting where your family has lived.) It also makes it easier to convert a non-MVC application into an MVC application by providing the glue that holds together the existing code with the new MVC model.

Struts was originally created by Craig McClanahan, and the Apache organization maintains it through a project called Jakarta. Struts is an open source framework, so just about anyone can contribute. Apache maintains Struts but it's actually produced and written by many volunteers.

Some people love Struts. Some think it's evil. Some think it's a really good solution for 10% of the projects out there. So with Struts as with everything else, check it out, do your research, see whether it would solve the problems you need to solve.

Surf to http://jakarta.apache.org/struts to learn more about it.

Web Component Development Processes

All right. Let's say you find yourself on an actual Web component development project. A serious JSP party situation. Here are a few things you're probably going to be doing.

Web Development Roles

For a large Web application project, the development team is often organized into small groups. Each group provides a different skill set and therefore takes on a different role in the project. Alternately, sometimes there are very few people on a project and you'll have one person doing one or more roles. The point here is that these are roles, and can be fullfilled by a bunch of people or just one. There are four different roles:

- Content creator – The content creator is responsible for creating the view elements; that is, the stuff the user will see. The creator often wears a black turtleneck and has lots of hip pop culture posters and action figures in her cube.
- Web component developer – The Web component developer is responsible for creating the controller elements; that is, the stuff that validates user input and determines what the user should see.
- Business component developer – The business component developer is responsible for creating the model elements; that is, the stuff that represents and enforces the business rules for the application.

- Data access developer – The data access developer is responsible for creating the elements that represent and manipulate the data,; that is, the stuff that accesses and manipulates the database.

Deployment

Let's say you're a technical writer and you've got a little Web site to help you get contract jobs. You've put together a few plain HTML pages, listing your resume and a few projects from your portfolio. You create the site on your computer hard disk, and then when you're ready to go live you copy the files to your file server. Everything's the same on your hard disk as on the file server. Same files, same directory structure. After all, why would they be different? No reason at all. Not with that project, at least.

Development and deployment would definitely be different, however, if your little getting-hired Web site were a big ol' Web application with JSPs and all that. The situation changes entirely. Your directory structure when developing is completely different from when you're deploying the application. So how do you get from one state to another, when you've got hundreds of files that all need to be in a very specific structure?

You go through a rigorous *deployment process* to compile, rearrange, copy, and much more.

What the Development Structure Is Like

Here's what the development situation is like. You typically have your source files in a source directory structure and compile the classes into a separate but similar directory structure that contains just the class files from the servlets. To make things even more interesting, in order for the Web application to run on the J2EE Web server, the class files must be in yet another completely different directory structure within one of the Web server directories.

And you don't simply copy the directory structure to the Web server, instead you need to create an enterprise archive (.ear) file that will contain a Web archive (.war) file. The WAR file is simply a file in zip format that contains the correct directory structure for the Web server and a deployment descriptor. The EAR file is also in zip format and contains the WAR file and JAR files containing EJBs and or helper classes if the application uses EJBs or helper classes. When you deploy the ear file the Web server just unzips the file and copies the .class files into the appropriate server directories.

The Web deployment descriptor contains configuration settings for the Web application. It contains stuff like the name of the servlet class, the URL that maps to the servlet, the session timeout, etc. The name of the servlet class might be pizza.CheckOutServlet and it might be *mapped* to a /checkout URL after the domain name. Like www.antoinespizza.com/checkout. To access this servlet you'd have to visit the URL www.antoinespizza.com/checkout The Web server will know to invoke the pizza.CheckOutServlet to receive a request for that URL because of the mapping in the deployment descriptor. The deployment descriptor could also contain security information.

Build Tools for the Deployment Process

As you read earlier, to build a Web application you have to write source code, compile the source code, create a deployment descriptor, package the compiled code and deployment descriptor into a war file and deploy the war file to the Web server.

Each step could contain a lot of typing at the command line or lots of clicking in an IDE. (An IDE is an integrated development environment, and has tools like color display of parts of the code that make writing code easier than just typing in a plain text editor. IDEs also often include build functionality.) A popular way to automate and make these tedious steps easier is to use a build tool. A build tool allows you to write instructions or steps and execute those instructions with a single command. Using a build tool you'd simply create a file that contains the commands that you want to issue (compile, create the WAR file, and deploy), then each time you make a change to your code you'd simple issue the build command and it would perform all the steps from your build file.

The make command has been a very popular build tool. Apache makes a build tool called *ant* which is probably the most widely used today. Ant is a newer build tool that uses XML for creating the build file. Because ant uses XML, it is more portable than make. Ant also alleviates some of the other headaches that developers encounter with make.

Ant is more portable than make is because ant is written in Java, and so far no one has decided to make fourteen different variants of it like they did with make.

Introduction to Portals

This is a fairly large can of worms but we wanted to just peek into it without really opening it too wide, and mention *portals*. You're bound to come across them sooner or later if you haven't already.

A portal is a set of features grouped together conveniently, and customized for its users. If we were marketing people, we'd say that the features are grouped seamlessly. The effect is of going to a single Web page even though multiple pages, services, features, etc, are displayed.

The benefit is roughly comparable to buying a Home Medical Kit instead of hunting all over for the separate pieces: the Ace bandage, the ointment, the iodine, and so on. Except that you get to design the Home Medical Kit, and then poof, instantly send it out to everyone in your family. And it's dynamically updated whenever necessary with the latest in ointment technology.

Figure 9-2 is a portal. It looks like a Web page, but it's Much More.

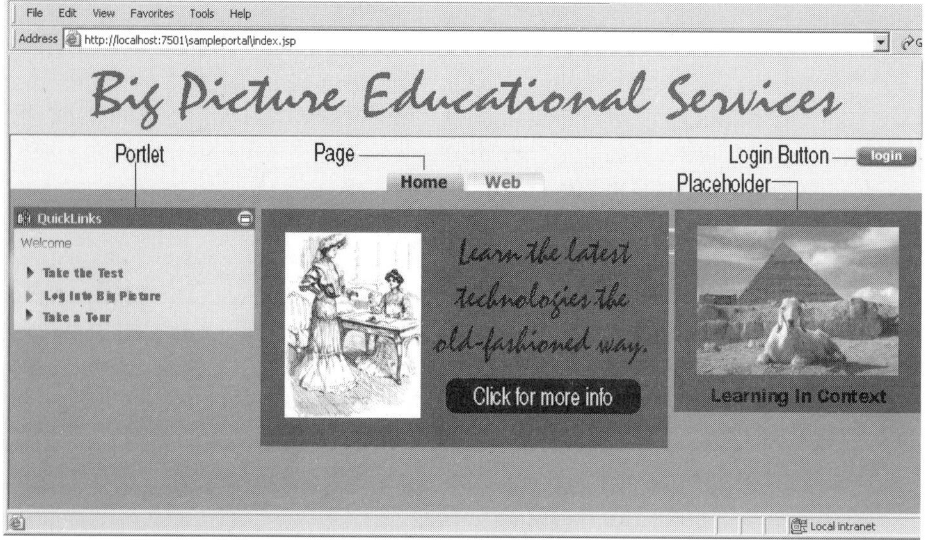

Figure 9-2 Portal

A portal is part technology and part marketing buzz, as outlined in Table 9-1.

Table 9-1 What the heck is a portal?

What It Is to the User	***Technology***	***Marketing buzz***
It looks like a plain old Web page at first. But it's made up of subparts that might show you the weather in Oregon, and give info from HR.	You can make a portal with anything as long as it fits inside a Web page and/or JSP and/or servlet.	Marketing people like portals because they get to use phrases like *seamlessly* and *feature-rich*.

Table 9-1 What the heck is a portal? (Continued)

What It Is to the User	***Technology***	***Marketing buzz (Continued)***
The point is to combine lots of functions into one page. And also that these functions are the ones that you need. Companies often make their own portals specifically designed for the information their users need. And users, too, can customize their portals to add or modify the look and content.	It's made up of portlets, other Web pages...pretty much anything. Portlets are cute little reusable bits of Web content that fit into portals. Kind of the portal's EJB. But, you know, not an EJB. Theoretically, you the programmer could just grab someone else's portlets, stuff them in your portal, and zammo, it works.	They also like it because portals are theoretically easy to customize to a company's Unique Needs, and most portal development kits include cool stuff like different *skins* (color schemes).
Portals usually have multiple versions of themselves, using the ever-popular tab navigation method.	There's a variety of portal development kits out there, including BEA's WebLogic Portal. Development kits include premade JSPs, servlets, portlets, portlet creation and portal creation windows that theoretically even the most technically challenged business analyst could use. And a lot more that we won't get into right here.	Here's what the folks from BEA's WebLogic Portal say about portals. "A portal is a feature-rich Web site. It provides a single point of access to enterprise data and applications, presenting a unified and personalized view of that information to employees, customers, and business partners."

Most of the big portal development kits out there are based on JSPs and servlets, and therefore of course fit into the Web tier of the typical J2EE application architecture. But they're optional, not required. You can swim the J2EE sea all day long and come out without having seen even the smallest portal.

chapter 10

Introduction to Enterprise JavaBeans

"I'm an old-fashioned kind of gal. I was raised to believe that the men dig up the corpses and the women have the babies."

Buffy, Buffy the Vampire Slayer

Time for beans. Some say they're the heart and soul of a J2EE application and everything else is just trotting back and forth across the Internet with pretty Web pages. (Not while the Web component developers are in the room, of course.)

But we'll let you make up your own mind. First question to think about: are Enterprise JavaBeans just JavaBeans used in a big distributed enterprise system? And secondly, if not, why in the world did the marketing people call them that?

You might also be wondering what the point is of EJBs when servlets and JSPs seem to have covered a fair amount of territory.

The Chapter in Brief

EJBs are just your business objects and processes, written according to the EJB coding rules. There are three kinds of EJBs: entity beans, representing your objects (user records, inventory); session beans, representing your processes (calculating sales tax), and message-driven beans which are like little messenger boys you can send off on errands while you go on to another task. You get guidelines from Sun to help write EJBs, not the least of which are roles for who works on beans, blueprints, sample code, design patterns, and of course interfaces.

Here's what we cover in this chapter.

- *Three Kinds of Beans*
- *Guidelines From Sun to Help With Development*
- *The EJB Structure Is Enforced By Interfaces*

Three Kinds of Beans

Here's a quick restatement of what the types of EJBs there are.

- *Entity beans* are used to represent data in the database. The entity bean brings your data up out of the dark, dank database into the sunshine of RAM. Entity beans also ensure that when multiple people try to access them at the same time, the data doesn't get screwed up. The container or a programmer can take the data from the entity bean when all the processing is done and stuff it back into the database.
- *Session beans* do business processes. Session beans provide the business logic and workflow associated with the J2EE application. There are two kinds, *stateful* and *stateless*. A *stateful* session bean is used to manage the state of a user's session on the server. An example of a stateful session bean would be a shopping cart, which remembers data, or state, gathered from a series of requests and responses with the client it's assigned to. A *stateless* session bean just participates in one single action with a client, then forgets everything about that action and can start all over again fresh (and not weighed down with the data from the previous action) with someone else. Or with the same client.
- *Message-driven* beans are like butlers who deal with everyone who wants to talk to the container while it's trying to get some work done. You can create a

bunch of message-driven beans to deal with messages you're expecting from other parts of the application, from your suppliers trying to sell you more pizza toppings, messages from the container about needing additional resources, etc.

We'll talk more about each type of bean in Chapter 11, "More About EJBs," on page 123. This chapter is more about the Whole EJB Thing.

Guidelines From Sun to Help With Development

It's always nice to get some guidelines. Here's what you can get from Sun to help build J2EE products.

The Development Process Is Supported by Blueprints and J2EE Patterns

There are software design patterns you can use to help you write applications. We'll cover this more later but a pattern is a broad blueprint that outlines a reproducible way to solve a particular problem or address an issue. For example, the arch is a pattern that architects use to build certain buildings and structures. The architecture for J2EE was designed using many popular object-oriented patterns. The popularity of J2EE itself gave rise to many newer patterns for use when building a J2EE application.

Sun's Java Blueprints are a different set of guidelines, including sample code, that will help you not only to design a J2EE application but also to design it well. For J2EE, the Java PetStore Sample Application is the example that demonstrates J2EE using Sun's Java Blueprints.

More on patterns in general is coming in Chapter 20, "Design Patterns and UML," on page 235.

The EJB Process Is Supported by Application Development Roles

The EJB architecture was developed to support different roles to make it easier to divide up the work, just like a factory with an assembly line has different roles for workers. Some are responsible for making the parts like the engine, chassis, transmission, etc. Some are responsible for putting those parts together to make a whole car. Some are responsible for making sure the factory is up and running.

You've already seen Web development roles, in *Web Development Roles* on page 111. The development roles for an EJB application have some similarities but are different to support the specific needs of EJBs. The roles are as follows.

- The *application component developers* are the people who write the EJB that make up the application.
- The *application assembler* is responsible for taking all the different components and packing them up into a single file called an enterprise archive file (EAR file).
- The *deployer* takes enterprise archives and sets them up, or deploys them, to work on the server.
- The *system administrator* is responsible for installing everything and making sure the server is up and running.
- The *tool providers* are the people who make the Integrated Development Environments (IDEs) and tools to make it easier to assemble and deploy an application. Examples are WebSphere Application developer (WSAD), Sun ONE studio, JBuilder, and WebLogic Workshop.
- The *server providers* are those who develop the J2EE application servers. You can see a list of these in *J2EE Products* on page 279.

Although these roles seem very black and white, they are really more in the gray area because most of the time people fall into more than one role. It would be more difficult to assemble a car if you didn't have at least some idea of what each of the parts were. The same is true for the development roles. It would be very difficult for an assembler to assemble an application if she didn't know anything about being a component provider.

Also, projects tend to understaffed. (Shocking, we know, but true.) People need to take on multiple roles to get the job done. Likewise you could have multiple people in the same role. On an automobile assembly line you have component developers; one that makes engines and ones that make transmissions. Likewise some application component developers might be working on a Customer EJB but other would be working on the Item EJB.

The EJB Structure Is Enforced By Interfaces

Note: If you didn't read *How Interfaces Make It All Work* on page 36, or if you don't already know what interfaces are, take a look at that section first before you keep going.

The EJB architecture takes full advantage of interfaces and requires certain interfaces to be present for each bean. The interfaces are what allow the developer to specify *what* has to happen; primarily what methods the container can use.

Interfaces Mean Structure and Consistency in the Development Process

Interfaces force the developer to adhere to the coding structure that EJBs rely on. These interfaces contain certain methods. By having interfaces the container can know exactly what is supposed to be done. It is up to the container and the EJB class itself to determine how things get done. If you do not provide these interfaces or don't follow the rules for EJB, the EJB container will not deploy the application and will complain at you—error, danger Wil Wheaton, or hopefully something more meaningful about what you did wrong.

Let's go back to the car assembly line example. One way CarsRUs can make sure that their employees follow the rules is by giving the Employee only one way to do something. If they wanted to make sure that blinker lights aren't put into the head light plug and vice versa then they can design the headlights so that they will only fit one way into the headlight socket. And do a similar thing for the blinker lights. Another way that they can enforce the rules is to check and inspect that things are being done correctly. So managers would walk around checking the work of each employee.

Note: Just as Henry Ford brought efficiency while taking turning workers into disenfranchised robots, programmers sometimes feel a little like they're on an assembly line when they switch to EJB.s. The more maverick-like of developers generally don't like EJBs because they're not as fun. See also Chapter 7, "Does a Cup of J2EE in the Morning Always Smell Like Victory?," on page 79.

Interfaces Mean the Container Can Do Its Job

The container can't just keep calling the bean like you call your cat in at night, saying "OK, bean402, you have got to get over here right away. Somebody needs that data you're holding" and standing around tapping its toe. The container needs to know that when it says `jump(4);` the beans won't even ask how high but will in fact jump the specified height. Otherwise everything would take a really long time to do and the container would go Stark Raving Mad. (You really don't want to see a container go postal.) In order to take advantage of the container, EJB developers need to make sure that when the container tries to run certain methods—and it will—that those methods are there.

If you
really want
to know

Looking at Interfaces and the Container Another Way

It's kind of like when your mom offered to pay for and organize your wedding. All the headaches of ecru versus cream, all the endless meetings with the rental people, all that hassle is over. However, now anything you really want to do, like having baby corn in the salad or changing the time, has to go through your mom. You get great services from your mom, but now you have to go through her and follow her rules.

To take a look at the interfaces as the plain old code you need to write for EJBs, see Chapter 12, "Looking Inside Enterprise JavaBeans," on page 145.

chapter 11

More About EJBs

"What makes them differments in beans, Owl?"

"I don't rightly know, Porky, being busy as I is with atoms an' the world an' all.

"Well...but I be dogged if I can figger you all kin 'splain about atoms and how to blow up ever'thin' an' you don't even know beans."

Walt Kelly, The Incompleat Pogo

There was a lot of what in that last chapter, but not a lot of *how* and *why*. Here are some deeper questions to ponder as we move on.

So here's a question for you. Let's say there's an entity bean for an Invoice. There's also a separate entity bean for a Line Item. So for every Invoice object, say invoice #3221, there are also a few Item objects corresponding to it. How does the Invoice object know that it has Line Item objects and how to get ahold of them? If the Invoice object is deleted, do its Line Items linger on?

And another question. What if you switch from one database management system to another. Do you have to go into your EJBs and update all the database code?

The Chapter in Brief

We get into more about entity beans and session beans in this chapter: how they work, including container-managed relationships which are very likely better than sliced bread, in the EJB world, at least. They make connecting related beans much easier. And we go into session beans, stateless versus stateful and how each is useful.

Here's what we cover in this chapter.

- *Entity Beans Overview*
- *How Entity Beans Function in a Simple Process*
- *Entity Beans and the Database*
- *How to Stop Treating Entity Beans Like Objects: Home Business Methods*
- *Entity Bean Pooling*
- *Session Beans Overview*
- *Stateful and Stateless Session Beans*
- *Session Bean Pooling*
- *How Session Beans Are Used*
- *Talking to Session Beans and Entity Beans With Local Interfaces*
- *Message-Driven Beans*

Entity Beans Overview

So the entity bean holds data. Fine. How does it get the data, how does it hold it, how do other beans do stuff with the data afterwards, and how does all that work?

An entity bean thinks it's the database. It thinks it's the be-all and end-all of data storage. But it's not—it's an in-memory version of the database, more or less.

How Entity Beans Function in a Simple Process

So the entity bean holds data, and it has a bean class and a Home interface (we go over this more in Chapter 12, "Looking Inside Enterprise JavaBeans," on page 145.) OK, fine. How does an entity bean work?

Let's join our example we used before, already in progress. Antoine is signing up on his own Web site, registering to make sure things work right with the signup process. He's submitted his email to a JSP, which sent off the request to register to a session bean.

A Session Bean Working With an Entity Bean

The session bean needs to find out if Antoine has already signed up, since creating two identical records would be silly and confusing. This is just good standard business logic. It also knows that if Antoine doesn't already have a record, the bean needs to make sure one a new record gets created for Antoine in the database. Since that's the whole point of his registering.

The session bean has gotten the *handle* to the *Home interface* of the type of entity bean it needs. Not to the bean itself but to the bean's Home interface. Let's say it's the User entity bean. The session bean thinks, "I'll use the find method to see if there's already a record in the USERS database for antoine@yahoo.com."

In this scenario, just for convenience purposes we're going to assume that there isn't already a record for Antoine.

Geek Note: Finding Records

If you really want to know

When a session bean uses a find *method to see if something's already there, and if there isn't one already (**failure** to find), then that means that the process of adding a user will be a **success**. And if the session bean does find a record there already (**success**) then the process of adding Antoine's user record will **fail**. Fun, huh? So be careful about assuming what people mean when they talk about success and failure in development meetings.*

Having concluded by using the find method that it's OK to go ahead and add Antoine's record, the session bean creates a new record in the database using the create method of the User entity bean's Home interface.

Once the session bean has done that, the create method returns a new handle, this time to the bean itself. So the User entity bean reluctantly drags itself out of bed and stands there yawning while the session bean calls the entity bean's set methods on it. (The bean has set methods in addition to those find and create methods.)

The exploratory part of the process was done with a handle to the Home interface, but when the session bean needed something to be actually done to the database, it used a handle to the entity bean itself.

Getting the Data Stored

This entity bean thinks it's the database. So when the process from our previous section is complete, registering Antoine, the entity bean tucks Antoine's new user records into the right folder in its duffel bag, and says "All taken care of, the data is stored."

The session bean hears that the entity bean has completed the storage task. What it gets back from the create method is a handle to an actual entity bean instance. This instance is roughly comparable to an in-memory copy of a row in a database.

Then, assuming that nothing went wrong, and confident in the knowledge of a job well done, the session bean flushes a little in pride and says, "Well, I finished that job!" to anyone within earshot but most particularly the container.

The container of course is listening, says "Good job!" but also thinks, "Hey, must be the end of the transaction." The container knows that the entity bean is not, in fact, the database. So the container pats the entity bean on the head to congratulate it and whisks Antoine's user record file out of the bean's duffel bag and sends it to be actually stored, this time, in the database. This is *commitment*. The container is all about commitment, but only under the right circumstances. Everything went right, nothing went wrong, and nothing was interrupted, so it's OK for the registration transaction to be completed and stored in the database.

No one on the development team had to write code for anything that connected to the database. This is because the application is using *container-managed persistence*, or CMP. Which is what you've just seen; the container takes care of everything and makes sure all of the data is tucked into the database in the right places, at the right time, or rolled back (not committed to the database) if something went wrong.

Of course, some programmers think they can do it faster and better, and sometimes they're right. In which case they use bean-managed persistence and have to write the code to connect to the database themselves. Which might be faster, but means you lose the ability to just pull up stakes one day and say, "Hey, kids, pack your bags—we're moving from Oracle to Sybase!" or some other database switch.

Entity Beans and the Database

Let's look at a broader example of what the entity beans do with the database.

Antoine's Entity Beans

Antoine has lots of data to keep track of. His data is in several tables within a database. He has tables for customer information like names and addresses. He has inventory information so he'll never run out of pepperoni. He has order information so that he can keep track of who ordered what and send coupons to his good customers. All of the data within these table are represented by entity beans. His application has entity beans coming out its ears.

This means whenever a customer orders a pizza from the Web site, the entity beans that represent the inventory, orders and customer tables are quite busy. A servlet will gather the information like the customer's name, address, phone number, the type and size of pizza, etc. The servlet passes the request off to a session bean that will coordinate the activities of the entity beans. So the order information will go to the order entity bean which will result in a new row in the orders table. The inventory information will go to the inventory bean so that the inventory is reduced by the proper amount and the customer information will go to the customer bean so that a new row will be inserted if this is a new customer.

How Entity Beans and What They Hold Correspond to the Actual Database

Before leaping off the bean topic, we'll finish up with a closer look at that data the entity beans are holding. We've talked about how entity beans hold data, and they correspond to a row in a database. That's about right: they correspond to, or they represent data from the database, but they aren't a copy of a row in the database. This is because good object-oriented design, and good database design, aren't the same. Yet they both need to handle the same data. Annoying, huh? Luckily, the container is clever enough to deal with this disparity, given some good design and instructions on your part.

Each table in the database doesn't have to map directly to its own bean. In other words, you don't have to have an entity bean for every table in your database. You might have a customer table and an order table in your database. This doesn't mean that you have to have a customer bean and order bean. (Assuming you're using EJB 2.0.)

Also, one entity bean can actually map to several tables or parts of several tables. An order bean could map to fields in the customer table, orders table, and the items table. So when an order bean is used in the J2EE world, it could actually update several tables in the database world. If this weren't possible then you'd either have to redesign your database tables to match a good object-oriented design or use an object-oriented design that matched the data but didn't follow good object-oriented design principles. Neither of these scenarios is desirable. Fortunately J2EE allows your bean to map across multiple tables so you don't need to worry.

Bean-Managed Persistence

In BMP, the programmer does all the work. He or she writes all the code for inserting, reading, updating, and so on. Which just means basically, more work for the programmers with all that SQL code, but they get to do it their way and often though not always it's faster.

Container-Managed Persistence

In CMP, the container handles the implementation of the code necessary to insert, read, and update an object in a data source. The programmer doesn't need to write code for that.

Figure 11-1 Container-managed persistence: the EJB container and the DBMS take care of pretty much everything

The container communicates with the DBMS and the programmer doesn't have to do much at all. You just need to map which data in the bean goes with which field in the database. The mapping between entity beans and your database is done when you're getting your application all ready to run, after it's coded. Most database tools allow you to see the database schema and match your bean data to the data in the table with a drag and drop style tool.

CMP is the ideal way to develop an application because it requires less code changes by the application developer when the data model changes. However, to provide this flexibility, CMP doesn't generate the most efficient SQL queries. So performance is a little slower.

CMP is one of the nice additions to EJB 2.0. You need an EJB 2.0 compliant application server to use this feature.

Container-Managed Relationships

Container-managed relationships sound kind of like a blind date with a Tupperware saleswoman. On the contrary, it helps out with CMP.

When you have a database, you have relationships between the data. There are invoice IDs, and there are line items on the invoice. And those relationships are built into your relational database by those intensely devoted database admins and the relational database management system.

Likewise since entity beans represent your data, there are relationships among the entity beans. A purchase order needs a buyer and a seller. A credit card needs a customer. Your invoice entity bean is related to your line items entity beans.

How do you make sure the entity beans know about each other? Is it even important for them to know about each other? The answers are, in 2.0, they know about each other with *container-managed relationships*, and *Yes*, it's important.

CMP and CMR Fields

You know *CMP* is container-managed *persistence*. *CMR*, or container-managed *relationships*, is the concept of mapping objects to each other. CMR fields are the way to define these relationships in the deployment descriptor. A bunch of big words in order to say "Objects that are related are written up in that big XML deployment descriptor file that the container checks when it runs the application. Then when the application runs, lots of stuff about those object relationships happens automatically, which is good."

Figure 11-2 shows examples of objects that have relationships: a customer has multiple orders, and each order could have multiple items on it.

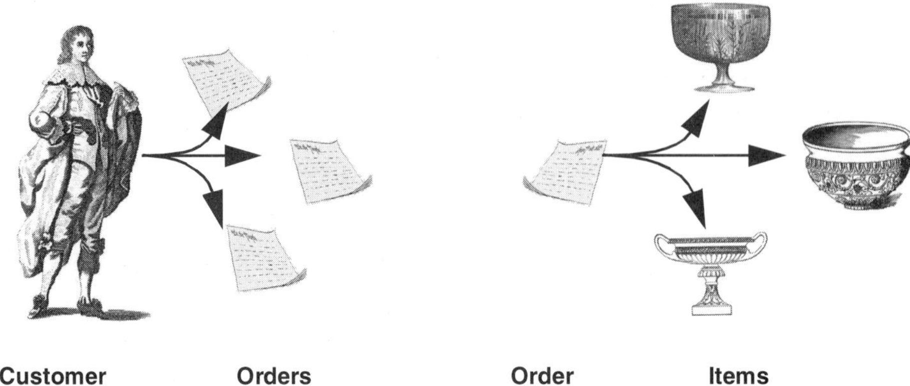

Figure 11-2 Things in an application that could have container-managed relationships

The EJB container maintains the *referential integrity* of the entity bean relationships. That just means that if one of the objects changes, the related ones change accordingly. For example, let's say you've specified a container-managed relationship between Orders and Items. It's a one-to-many relationship because an invoice for a customer's order can have a lot of different items on it. If the customer calls back five minutes after placing the order and says, "You know, I was shopping because I was depressed and now I feel better, so cancel that order," you delete the Order object. But you don't want a lot of random Item objects floating around, so those need to be deleted to. Without CMR, you have to write the code to make sure all those objects get deleted too. With CMR, the deletion just happens. It's a wonderful thing.

Likewise the changes can happen in the deployment descriptor and show up in the code. Let's say we're in Antoine's application. He's set up a relationship between Employee objects and Location objects. One *employee* can only work at only one location, such as the Fargo 13th street *location*, as in Figure 11-3.

Figure 11-3 Employees are associated with a location, in the database and in CMR fields

Antoine's fiddling with the application design, however, and now he wants to set up a relationship between *Employee* objects and *Manager* objects. This is because he's got freelance employees who make pizzas in their own homes or deliver all over the place; it's not logical from a business standpoint to associate employees with locations anymore. He goes into the deployment descriptor and changes *Employee-Location* to *Employee-Manager* as in Figure 11-4.

Figure 11-4 Employees are now associated with a manager, in the database and in CMR fields

When he deploys the application, the container automatically drops the old relationship and replaces it with the newly formed relationship.

Free to Be EJB

CMR isn't just about relationships between beans. It's also about relationships between entity beans and tables. And what that means for how you get data in and out of tables. Because CMR makes it easier, CMR lets EJB be EJB.

What does that mean? Let's take a look at entity beans and tables for a second.

An object is made up of a bunch of attributes. A Pizza object might have size and baking time and toppings and price and specials list IDs and customer and things it's sold with and much much more. An object is just defined by whatever's in it. Now, a brief segue to databases. An entity bean corresponds to your data in the database. And a database is made up of tables that are much more uptight, very nearly square in fact, about what are in them. Tables are made up of things that are all alike, based on what they are rather than how they're used.

So let's say you've got a $12.99 large pepperoni-bacon pizza that's cooked for 12 minutes, showing up on the MeatLovers list, and was just sold to Jeannie along with some Pepsi. What table does this Pizza object correspond to? As shown in Figure 11-5, it corresponds to a lot of tables.

Figure 11-5 Object trying to correspond to tables

How do you the programmer specify that the Pizza object is made up of partial rows in multiple tables? Prior to EJB 2.0, in the dreary land of no CMR, you had to do it very painfully by hand. Lots of code. And because you were writing all this stuff by hand about how the entity beans related to the database, you couldn't use container-managed persistence, CMP. You had to use BMP instead. And CMP is one of the major advantages of having J2EE in the first place. So if you had even slightly complex entity beans that didn't map nicely to tables, you lost a major portion of your J2EE capabilities.

Luckily, now with EJB 2.0 and container-managed relationships, you can do all that automatically. You set up the relationships in the deployment descriptor; you say that the Pizza object is made up of these three fields from the Item table, two fields from the Toppings field, four fields from yet another table, and so on. The container keeps track of all that, you don't have to write complicated code, and when the underlying tables and fields change as they will, you just have to change the deployment descriptor (we'll get to that in a bit), not the entity bean code.

Note: It's the *local interface* that the beans have relationships to, not the bean itself. See *Talking to Session Beans and Entity Beans With Local Interfaces* on page 141.

An EJB Query Language

The EJB 2.0 specification also introduces a query language called EJB Query Language, or EJB QL. It's a substitute for SQL, and has Special Powers specifically for EJB.

EJB QL defines query methods—finder and select methods—for entity beans with container-managed persistence. It's supposed to be portable across EJB containers.

EJB QL is based on SQL92. However, it's been enhanced to allow querying or navigation over entity bean relationships. That is, a query can begin with one entity bean and, from there, navigate to related beans (defined using the lovely and talented container-managed relationships). For example, the query can start with an Order bean and then navigate to the Order's line items. It can also navigate to the products referenced by the individual line items, and so forth.

So that's the point of using EJB QL instead of SQL? Why learn all this new stuff? What EBJ QL gives you is the ability to manage the container-managed relationships we were just talking about. EJB QL builds on the container-managed relationships specified in the deployment descriptor, so when you write up a query statement, you specify it in the deployment descriptor. The container then generates the QL implementation for the query. So you need to set up your queries ahead of time in the deployment descriptor; they're not for the impulsive, flighty set on your J2EE development team.

How to Stop Treating Entity Beans Like Objects: Home Business Methods

Home business methods are another feature in EJB 2.0 that can make entity beans a much better experience. All in all, entity beans in EJB 1.1 were kind of like those free ski passes that you can use anytime except for blackout days...which were all the time. EJB 2.0 is more aware of what kind of things you need to accomplish and provides better ways to actually do that.

To fully understand what the point of home business methods is and why they're such a benefit, we need to take a brief trip down Object Orientation Lane.

Note: If you aren't familiar with object orientation, read *The Attributes of Object Orientation* on page 261.

Sometimes a House Is That House

Let's say you're using a plain old Java real estate application. You were out walking in your neighborhood and you saw a great house, 910 Harrison Drive, that you want to find out more about. You go into your application, you ask for information about 910 Harrison Drive in Kalispell, Montana, and you get information about that house. Under the covers, the application created an instance of that particular house, and gave you information about that individual house, possibly using methods like getColor(), getPrice(), and so on.

Those methods, methods you use on a particular house, are instance methods. You use them once you've created an object for one unique thing. And that makes sense, since if you want to find out the color or price of a particular house, you want a method that will give you that information for one house.

Sometimes a House Is Houses in General

However, let's say you never saw that gorgeous house for sale. Let's say you're currently living in Boston, planning on retiring to Montana, and you want to know what houses are for sale there. You log onto your real estate application and you just ask for all the houses for sale in Kalispell. The application can't use those same instance methods since you haven't specified a house instance, which also means it hasn't create a house object yet. Those instance objects only make sense, and only work when, the application has created a house object. And there's no way you can tell it how to create a house object because you know squat about houses in Montana. (For all you know, they just live in old dinosaur caves.)

Sometimes a house is that house. Sometimes a house is just Houses In General. You need the code tools to express both conditions.

Trying to get information about things you don't know about and you haven't created an instance for, using instance methods, is like a cat chasing its tail. And not nearly as adorable.

However, clearly it is possible to get a list of things when you don't know specific information about one of them, such as all the houses in Kalispell or all the kinds of pizza Antoine has. You've done it hundreds of times. We all have. So what does your Java real estate application do instead of using instance methods, to provide you with a list of houses?

Instance Methods or Static Methods for That House or Some Houses

To get information in general, plain Java programmers use *static methods*. Static methods apply to things in general rather than particular instances of things. (Apparently the word *static* makes sense if you used C.)

- Instance methods need a thing to be created already in order to work.
- Static methods let you find out about things without creating an instance first.

> For instance, if you had a getHouses() static method in the real estate, it wouldn't require an instance, and would return a two-dimensional array (just a detailed list) of the houses you requested. (The method might be something like getHouses(String city, String state, float price) so that you could specify location and price, and get back a set of houses that met those criteria.)

The point is that there are two kinds of methods in Java, *instance methods* for particular instances and *static methods* when you don't have a particular instance in mind. One useful application of static methods, though certainly not the only one, is to get a list of occurrences of the object. You could use a getMenu() method, for instance, in the Pizza object, to get a list of all the kinds of pizzas Antoine sells. You can't use static methods when you need instance methods, and vice versa. Or if you do, extreme wackiness ensues, of the bad variety.

Why Do You Care About Instance Methods and Static Methods?

You care because until EJB 2.0, entity beans didn't have static method functionality. Not in a good way, at least. They had something that was similar to static methods but you didn't get a lot of flexibility in writing them.

These structured slightly static methods are *finder methods*. Finder methods are perfectly respectable ways to get a list of things without creating an instance. You can use a House entity bean's finder method to get a list of all the houses for sale in Kalispell.

You can try to get a list. What you actually get back in code terms is a remote reference. Not just one but two for every house. One for requesting it and one for responding. So you've got this list of information, and every time you look at one item in that list, you remotely request it, and a remote response gives you the info. Remote is *slow*.

Let's say no one in Kalispell ever leaves because it's a big retirement community, so the result from using the finder method is a whopping list of five houses. OK, big deal. You get the address for each house, so that's ten remote operations.

If you want to get the address, the price, and the square footage, though, each stored in a separate field in the database, that's 30 remote operations.

And let's make this more realistic, since Kalispell is actually a boomtown, the new Aspen of northwest Montana, and there are 2,457 houses for sale there. If you get three pieces of information for each of those houses, that's 14,742 remote operations.

This is the issue with finder methods. They don't exactly scale. Which sucks if one of the qualities of service you need is scalability.

This can be somewhat annoying. There sit the entity beans, representing your objects, representing your data in the database, and they're missing some pretty significant functionality.

What Did EJB Programmers Do to Simulate Static Method Functionality in EJB 1.1?

What would the programmers have done to create the functionality we mentioned, of being able to find all the houses for sale in Kalispell?

They often skipped the finder method thing and used session beans, writing all the regular code and database access code themselves. Which means they didn't get any of the services from the container like container-managed persistence or anything related to entity beans.

They couldn't put the methods in the bean class along with all the normal methods, because it didn't make sense and it wouldn't work. It would be like going out and buying a house in Kalispell, just in order to find out what houses are for sale in Kalispell. Which is not only difficult but if you don't know of any houses for sale in Kalispell, it's darned difficult, too.

And they complained a lot and went around saying no one should ever use entity beans. Which at the time had a fair amount of validity.

Business Methods in the Home Interface Solve the Problem

Finally the EJB 2.0 folks said to themselves and their managers, "Hey, it's kind of stupid to have entity beans that most people can't use." So they came up with a number of things including business methods.

Business methods are, more or less, static methods. They provide the same sort of capability of doing things in the general context of a class rather than to a particular created instance of it.

You put business methods in the Home interface. The Home interface is where the finder methods currently go, and are also where the standard create methods and other methods go that the container itself uses. The Home interface is a very lovely, logical place for something to go that's going to simulate static methods.

Business methods return a two-dimensional array of Strings (a detailed list of text, more or less), instead of a remote reference for each item found.

Entity Bean Pooling

The server reserves the right to *pool bean instances*. That's all very well, you say. What's it for and how does it work?

It's for saving time and resources and being ready when a sudden customer onslaught happens. Creating beans takes work, so you might as well have a bunch of them ahead of time so you're not caught unprepared. If you have an Item entity bean, for instance, the server can create a bunch of instances of the Item bean so that if there is a mad rush on the items they sell, then the server doesn't have to waste time creating bean instances to service the requests.

All these instances, created usually when the server starts up but at other times too, are then just sitting around in the pool, available as needed but not consuming as much memory as if they weren't pooled.

Then when the need arises, the server can just pull a bean from the pool. There can be a pool for each type of bean: customer, pizza topping, etc.

How big does a pool get? Well, that depends on how you configure the container since most containers allow you to change a configuration file to create more or fewer beans.

Session Beans Overview

Session beans do things. They might compute, request, make a note of various pieces of information and carry that info back and forth.

The key thing about session beans becomes whether they're stateful or stateless. An important part of understanding that of course is, what is state?

What's State?

Stateful session bean
keeping state its
client is telling it

State is a slightly fuzzy concept, not because it's difficult but because the term is used for different but related concepts in different contexts. The state we're talking about, more properly called conversational state, is what a stateful session bean remembers from previous messages and can use when processing more recent messages.

State is the means to the end, and the end is the completion of the business process. The business process might be a customer buying a pair of red suede pumps, or the results to a personality quiz that reveals you are most like the dark-haired Power Puff girl. The point of the whole process is receiving red suede pumps in exchange for money, or discovering your true nature. All the state collected along the way, like your credit card and shoe size and favorite scent, are just incidental to the main goal.

State is information gathered in a conversation, a series of requests and responses, between objects. Why not just give all the information at once, though—why have the conversation? Why ask all those questions back and forth? Because neither party knows ahead of time what information to provide or request.

Let's say you're filling in a tax program, like Quicken. It asks you if you have any dependents. If you do, then the next window tells you to give information about them; if you don't have any, there's no point in providing information about them. Conversational state is a good way of asking for the right information. And state, just plain state, is the information that is accumulated during that conversation.

State is not any data that an object carries around. State is data specific to a conversation, several requests and responses.

You might or might not, depending on the process, need a bean to remember the state of something through multiple steps of a process. Through multiple requests and responses, back and forth. Being stateful, or having state, or remembering state, means that you can use information you received from request/response pair A as you continue forward into request/response pairs B, C, and so on.

Example 11-1 A conversation with a session bean, with state

You: Hi, I'd like to register as antoine@yahoo.com

Thing with the ability to keep state: OK! .... Done!

Client: And yes, I'd like to sign up for the pizza of the month club.

Thing with the ability to keep state: OK, and I still know your login so I'll just use that as the email to sign you up with....Done!

Example 11-2 A conversation with a session bean, without state

You: Hi, I'd like to register as antoine@yahoo.com

Thing without the ability to keep state: OK! .... Done!

Client: And yes, I'd like to sign up for the pizza of the month club.

Thing without the ability to keep state: Who *are* you?

Let's talk more specifically about statefulness and statelessness as it relates to session beans.

Stateful and Stateless Session Beans

There are 10 types of people: those who understand binary, and those who don't. (If you're one of the latter, ask one of the former why this is funny.)

And there are two types of session beans: stateful and stateless.

A *stateful session bean* is faithful. A stateful session bean is like a good waiter in a fancy restaurant who serves you and only you for the entire meal, bringing you menus, brushing the crumbs off the table, brandishing that enormous pepper grinder, and so on. (Except that the waiter isn't killed or its memory wiped after each meal.)

A *stateless session bean*, on the other hand, is like that clerk at the coffee shop who never remembers you but always gives you the kind of coffee you ask for.

Figure 11-6 shows a stateless session bean at left and a stateful session bean at right. Look how closely the stateful session bean is paying attention to the guy she's having the conversation with. Yet the stateless session bean lost interest after the first question he asked her and is now just staring off into space.

Figure 11-6 Stateless session bean and stateful session bean, respectively

Stateful session beans give you the capability to hold a conversational state for a client, like the kind of state you need for a shopping cart. There are any number of ways to handle a conversational state in an enterprise application, but if the state needs to be close to the business logic, then it should probably be in a stateful session bean. A shopping cart is an example of a stateful session bean. A stateless shopping cart would be a shopping cart with a big hole in the bottom.

Servlets (with HttpSession objects) are a decent way to do shopping carts, too. Session beans aren't the only way.

We talk more about state and various ways to hold it in *Debate #2: Stateful Session Beans Are Evil* on page 85.

Session Bean Pooling

We talked about entity bean pooling. Now for a little equal time with session beans. We talk about bean pooling more in Chapter 15, "Resource Management," on page 185.

- Stateless session beans aren't expected to have state, so your container can have a big pile of blank ones already created in the bean pool, ready to use whenever your application needs one.
- Stateful session beans are not pooled. They're activated and passivated, which achieves the goal of effective memory management but in a different way.

How Session Beans Are Used

Here's how session beans might work in Antoine's Web site.

When you are ordering your pizza online from Antoine's, you are greeted by a pretty welcome page, a JSP. After you've browsed around and placed your order, a form, another JSP, appears where you enter your customer information. The form also displays a summary of your order.

All of this information is sent to a servlet, which verifies that you've supplied all of the information requested and that you've entered valid data—for example, you've entered a phone number containing 10 digits (area code plus number). The servlet sends this request to a stateless session bean that will use entity beans to execute the business logic. It will make sure that you are not ordering something that was out of stock and check to see that your credit card verifies, etc.

Talking to Session Beans and Entity Beans With Local Interfaces

Every bean needs a *component interface*. A component interface is just the bean's interface. Component is a nice general (or alternately vague) term for a chunk of code, including beans. So component interface just means the standard interface for the bean that every bean needs. Because EJB is just that way.

Session beans and entity beans in 2.0 can have two types of component interfaces: a remote interface and a local interface. Both are component interfaces, but one's for local communication and one's for remote communication. A bean can have either a local or a remote interface, or both.

- The *local interface* is a standard Java interface that does not inherit from RMI. (For info on RMI, see *It's All About Communication: RMI* on page 269.) Using local interfaces means that you don't need to go through all that serialization and deserialization business.
- A bean that needs to have remote capabilities at least some of the time uses a *remote interface*. In so doing the bean inherits from RMI and interacts with distributed clients. In the EJB 2.0 specification, a bean typically uses its remote interface to expose its methods across the network tier. What does that mean? It means it winks and says coyly "I'll be over here if any of you remote objects need me or these seventeen methods of mine. Come up and invoke me sometime." Or technical actions to that effect.

Message-Driven Beans

The regular definition is that "Message-driven beans are stateless, server-side, transaction-aware components that process asynchronous messages delivered via the Java Message Service (JMS)."

In the next sections, we'll explain what that actually means.

Message-Driven Beans: The Butlers of the Application

The message-driven bean is just like a butler. You can tell him, "Jeeves, there'll be some people coming by sometime today to ask about the badgers we're selling. Could you keep a look out for them and handle it when they arrive? I'm going to be trying to get some work done."

To do this in the J2EE application, you just specify in the deployment descriptor what messages you're expecting, from who, what message-driven beans will deal with said messages, and so on. You can have lots and lots of message-driven beans.

The messages themselves could be anything. It might be a customer saying Hey, I want to buy a pizza. It might be a disk drive failing. It might be a supplier telling you there's a special on dried lutefisk pizza toppings. *Message* means that it's information sent around by the Java Messaging Service, or JMS.

Why Do You Even Need Message-Driven Beans?

Now, why is it that an application that's as powerful as a J2EE application even needs help? Why does the application need these little bean butlers? With all the resource management and all that stuff, why bother with message-driven beans?

It's because the J2EE application is kind of like an ultra-smart geek. Powerful and very capable and all that, but not real good with the multi-tasking and time management. Picture a full-on geek working in the lab on some cool new invention. You knock on the door. Again and again. He is so not answering, since he can either work or he can sit around waiting for people to knock on the door, but he can't do both.

Multithreading is what other applications can do that allows them to deal with incoming requests while they're still working on their current project.

Multithreading is however not available in J2EE. But obviously there's always more than one thing going on at a time. If you're J2EE and you don't have message-driven beans, how do you deal with the need to address incoming messages.

- You could have a plain Java process going on that does allow multithreading but then you'd be half J2EE and half not, and while it works, it can be messy.
- Or you could sit around waiting for the messages. But in that case you get no work done at all, which isn't acceptable.

Message-driven beans let the application get some freakin' work done without ignoring incoming messages.

It's Message-Driven, Not Message Driving

A lot of very smart people gap out when they think about message-driven beans and think of them as little beans that go around delivering messages. As if it's the urge to deliver messages that drives the beans. That's not correct. Message-driven beans are message *driven*, not message *driving*. They're not the post office. They're what sits there next to the mailbox and opens the mail and shrieks "I might already be a winner!" (Or whatever the appropriate response is to the message.)

After all, you don't need message-driven beans to send a message. Sending means just popping the envelope in the mail, or the code equivalent. Pop, there it goes. Where you need the asynchronicity of message-driven beans is when you're sitting there getting some work done, and yet here come the girl scouts and the friendly religious folks and your neighbor who wants to borrow your forklift.

One convenient use for message-driven beans is when you need to integrate your dandy new J2EE system with an old less new-and-shiny system. Your old system doesn't know J2EE but it often does know messages. The Java Messaging Service that message-driven beans work with can talk to anyone. The old system has to have a message-driven architecture. There's a lot of them out there; a lot of old IBM systems have message driven architectures. How do you know if your old system is message driven? Ask someone who built it, or check to see if it has *MQ software*, which is typically an indicator.

chapter 12

Looking Inside Enterprise JavaBeans

“‘Oh, Auntie Em, there’s no place like Home.”

Dorothy, The Wizard of Oz

We’ve talked an awful lot about the theory of beans, local interfaces, Home interfaces, etc. But we haven’t actually shown you any real code yet.

Needless to say, from what we’ve said already this is not going to be Hello World. However, you’ll see that beyond the fairly strict structure and the not quite clear terminology, there’s simplicity hiding in the background and peering out at you.

The Chapter in Brief

You don't really know EJBs until you've seen how they're written. EJBs are really a departure from "normal" code. So you're going to see the Home interface, the component interface, and the actual bean class, for each type of bean. And you'll get to take a look at an EJB deployment descriptor which allows you to do an immense amount of tuning and other configuration but without ever touching the code and risking breaking it.

Here's what we cover in this chapter.

- *The Code That Goes in an Enterprise JavaBean*
- *What It Takes to Be a Bean*
- *The Home Interface*
- *The Component Interface*
- *The Bean Class*

The Code That Goes in an Enterprise JavaBean

Note: You're not supposed to know how to code EJBs after this section, and you're not supposed to understand EJBs fully after this. There's more coming later on how EJBs work, how they interact, what they're for, etc. Looking through the code here should just make you think, "Dang, these are some highly structured rules for coding" and your eyes should glaze over a bit.

We don't usually show as many code examples as this chapter has. But the thing with Enterprise JavaBeans is that they're a little wacky and highly structured when it comes to how you code them. With a normal piece of Java code, you have a fair amount of freedom. You just write some code using any of several possible options. There are preexisting Java classes, there are some interfaces around, you could write your own interfaces, you could even hardcode your Strings if you're that kind of sicko, and so on. With EJBs, the rules are far more defined. So since the system of interfaces and class files is part of what makes EJBs different from other code, we're going to show you a bit.

What It Takes to Be a Bean

When you write a session bean or entity bean, you really only need four things. Simple. Or rather, when you write a session bean or entity bean, you absolutely must have four things. How you view it depends on if you're one of those grue-half-full or grue-half-empty sort of people.

These things are:

- **A programming code file called a Home interface**

  The Home interface contains methods for getting ahold of a bean so the container can grab onto it and do stuff to it like creating an instance.

  In a bean, you also have the **implementation of the Home interface** that the container creates. But nobody on the development team needs to write that code. More on this later.

- **Another programming code file called a component interface**

  A component interface contains the business methods.

  If you thought this was going to say remote interface, that's so five minutes ago. Component interface is the new term.

- **Yet another programming code file called the bean class**

  This is the part of the bean that does the real work; that does the main business logic. The bean class contains *callback methods*, which the container will call on the bean when it gets a request.

- **An XML file called the deployment descriptor**

  There's just the one for the whole application but you have to make your mark in it for your bean.

The Home Interface

The Home interface contains methods for getting ahold of a bean so the container can grab onto it and do stuff to it. One of the things that the container needs to be able to do is to create a new instance of the bean.

What's an Instance?

If you
really want
to know

An instance is a particular unique specific bean that does a specific job, as distinct from the plain old bean class. The instance is like a cookie; the bean class and associated interfaces are like the cookie recipe. Cookie recipes don't taste very good, and J2EE applications don't do squat if you don't have instances of your beans. If you'd like more information, see Objects and Classes on page 265. An object is the same kind of thing as an instance.

Programmers don't create instances of beans; the container does. And it's going to be awfully hard for the container to create the instance without a `create` method somewhere around. Thus one of the methods in the Home interface is `create`.

The Home interface is kind of like a hostess at a restaurant. In fancier restaurants you don't find your own table and order your food directly from the chef; you ask the hostess to find you a seat and the hostess assigns you a waiter who talks to the chef. You ask the waiter for your food.

The Home interface is usually developed by the bean developer. If you really want to know, the Home interface should extend `javax.ejb.EJBHome`. (Sometimes people talk about EJBHome instead of the Home interface. This is another example of confusing terminology.) The Home interface allows the container to create instances of the EJB (more on that a little later) and also allows the client to create, remove, or find an EJB.

You can also put business methods in the Home interface, as of EJB 2.0. See *How to Stop Treating Entity Beans Like Objects: Home Business Methods* on page 133 for a little more information on those.

Now, an interface that just sits there lookin' pretty and laying down the law about what but not how is pretty much useless without an implementation. Without the how. So the container, helpful as always, is the one that creates a class that *implements* this Home interface. Again, the container works hard so you don't have to. So in a bean, you also have the **implementation of the Home interface** that the container creates. But nobody on the development team needs to write that code.

Example 12-1 shows a simple Home interface for a session bean.

Example 12-1 Simple Home interface for a stateless session bean

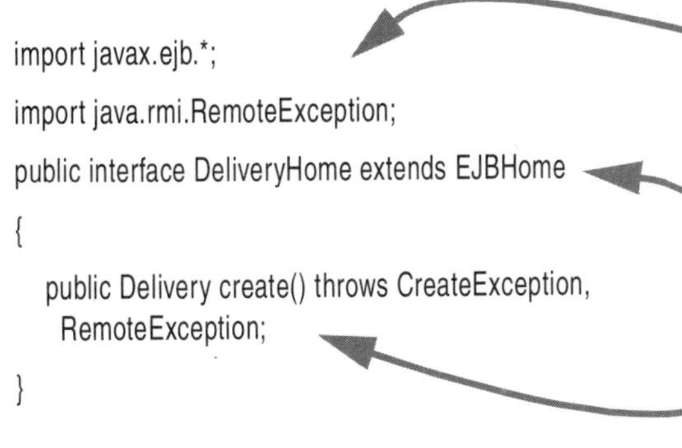

```
import javax.ejb.*;
import java.rmi.RemoteException;
public interface DeliveryHome extends EJBHome
{
   public Delivery create() throws CreateException,
     RemoteException;
}
```

Administrative hoohah, just taking advantage of the pre-made Java classes for EJBs and for error handling, a.k.a. exceptions.

The Home interface has to have this line to follow the EJB rules.

The container needs to be able to create the session bean, so there's the method for creation.

Example 12-2 shows an example of the Home interface for an entity bean. (A remote one.)

Example 12-2 Simple Home interface for an entity bean

```
import javax.ejb.*;
import java.rmi.RemoteException;
import java.util.Collection
public interface PizzaHome extends EJBHome
{
   public Pizza create (String pizzaName) throws CreateEx-
ception, RemoteException)
   public Pizza findByPrimaryKey (String key) throws Finder-
Exception, RemoteException)
   public Collection findByType (String type) throws FinderEx-
ception, RemoteException;
}
```

Administrative hoohah, just taking advantage of the pre-made Java classes for EJBs and for error handling, a.k.a. exceptions.

The Home interface has to have this line to follow the EJB rules.

The container needs to be able to create the bean and find it, so it needs some methods that do that.

The Component Interface

The Home interface contains administrative details like creation that could be the same for any old application.

By way of contrast, the *component interface* contains the business methods, the guts of your application. This is because you cannot simply tell the bean "give me a Pizza." You have to ask the container by using the component interface. The container can then start a transaction or check security, or do whatever before it goes and tells the bean to service your request.

The container is like a waiter. You don't tell the chef your order, you tell the waiter and the waiter makes preparations like taking you menu or removing your wine glass before he goes and tells the chef.

The component interface is developed by the bean developer and the application server provides an implementation (makes a class based on the interface). It should extend javax.ejb.EJBObject. The component interface contains the business methods that can be called by the client. The component interface acts as a proxy.

If you
really want
to know

Isn't the Component Interface Supposed to be Called the Remote Interface?

In previous versions of the EJB specification, this was called the remote interface. Because it had to be a remote interface. You had to assume that the bean might be right next door or in Poughkeepsie or St Petersburg so you had to give it a remote interface. (We talk about this in the appendix, It's All About Communication: RMI on page 269.)

However, now with local interfaces, it ain't necessarily so. That is, the interface formerly known as remote might be local or *remote. So the EJB folks came up with another term for it, a component interface. Got it? Good. Heck, if it were easy to understand, everyone would be doing EJBs.*

We discuss local interfaces more in Talking to Session Beans and Entity Beans With Local Interfaces on page 141.

Example 12-3 shows an example of a component interface for a session bean.

Example 12-3 Simple sample component interface for a stateless session bean

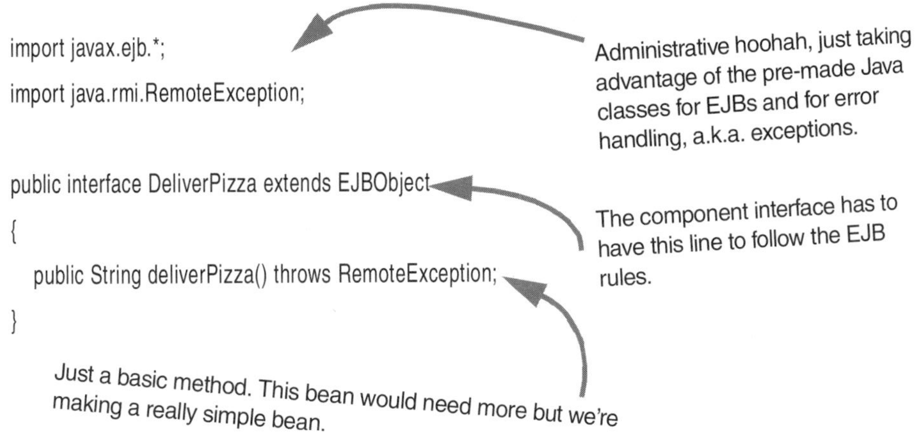

import javax.ejb.*;
import java.rmi.RemoteException;
public interface DeliverPizza extends EJBObject
{
public String deliverPizza() throws RemoteException;
}
Administrative hoohah, just taking advantage of the pre-made Java classes for EJBs and for error handling, a.k.a. exceptions.
The component interface has to have this line to follow the EJB rules.
Just a basic method. This bean would need more but we're making a really simple bean.

Example 12-4 shows an example of a component interface for an entity bean.

Example 12-4 Simple sample component interface for an entity bean (remote, not local)

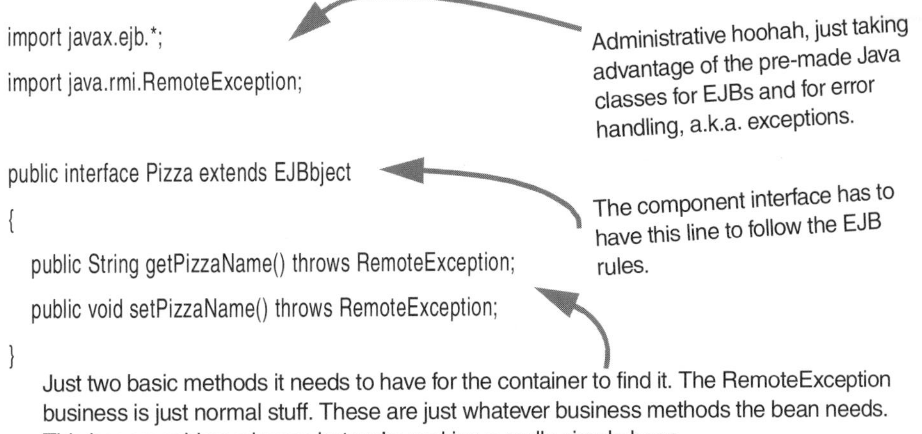

import javax.ejb.*;
import java.rmi.RemoteException;
public interface Pizza extends EJBbject
{
public String getPizzaName() throws RemoteException;
public void setPizzaName() throws RemoteException;
}
Administrative hoohah, just taking advantage of the pre-made Java classes for EJBs and for error handling, a.k.a. exceptions.
The component interface has to have this line to follow the EJB rules.
Just two basic methods it needs to have for the container to find it. The RemoteException business is just normal stuff. These are just whatever business methods the bean needs. This bean would need more but we're making a really simple bean.

The Bean Class

The *bean class* contains *callback methods*. These are the methods that the container will call on the bean when it gets a request. When you ask the container to create a bean, the container can do some stuff and then it will tell the bean to create itself or get ready for action. If you tell the container "give me a Pizza", the container can do some stuff and then it can tell the bean "give me a Pizza."

When the container gets the order "give me a Pizza," it can do things like start a transaction, check security, etc. When the container gives the bean the order "give me a Pizza," the bean will actually make the pizza. The bean is like the chef. The chef is responsible for making the food and reporting to the waiter and management.

The bean class is developed by the bean developer and contains the implementation of the method defined in the component interface. It should use javax.ejb.SessionBean or javax.ejb. EntityBean.

That just means, it should be a session bean or entity bean, and to designate the type, you put the line implements javax.ejb.SessionBean or implements javax.ejb.EntityBean in your code. This sucks in preexisting definitions of these interfaces, and saves your having to type out all the definitions that are required in every bean.

We'll throw in just a bit more code here. The first one's a simple session bean that doesn't do much but shows you the structure. The second is a very simple Pizza entity bean. You'll see lots of the same methods between them.

The first example in Example 12-5 is just a tiny bit of business logic that prints out the words Welcome to Antoine's Pizza.

Example 12-5 Simple session bean that just displays a welcome message

```
import javax.ejb.*;
public class HelloCustomerEJB implements SessionBean
{
   private SessionContext context;
   public String hellocustomer()
   {
      String ret = "Welcome to Antoine's Pizza";
      return ret;
   }
   public HelloCustomerEJB()
   {
   }
   public void ejbCreate() throws CreateException
   {
   }
   public void setSessionContext(SessionContext theContext)
   {
      this.context = theContext;
```

```
    }
    public void ejbActivate()
    {
    }
    public void ejbPassivate()
    {
    }
    public void ejbRemove()
    {
    }
}
```

Example 12-6 shows a simple example of a simple Pizza entity bean. The point of this example is to show you that there are some methods with very specific names and functionality like ejbCreate, and ejbActivate and ejbPassivate, that you just have to write. And then you write normal code like methods to get and set the type of the pizza: pepperoni, Lutefisk Lover's, and so on.

Example 12-6 Simple entity bean class for a Pizza bean

```
import javax.ejb.*;
public class PizzaEJB implements EntityBean
{
    private String pizzaType;
    private String primaryKey;
    private EntityContext context;
    public String ejbCreate(String type)
    {
        pizzaType = type;
        primaryKey = this.getPK();
        // database hoohah
        return primaryKey;
    }

    public String getPizzaType()
    {
        return pizzaType;
    }
    public void setPizzaType(String thePizzaType)
    {
        pizzaType = thePizzaType;
    }
    public void ejbActivate()
```

```
    {
    }
    public void ejbPassivate()
    {
    }
    public void ejbRemove()
    {
      // and some other code that's not important to this example
    }

    // some other code that has to do with contexts
    public void ejbLoad()
    {
      // and some other code that's not important to this example
    }
    public void ejbStore()
    {
      // and some other code that's not important to this example
    }
    // some more methods that have to do with the primary key
}
```

The EJB Deployment Descriptor

You've seen the Web deployment descriptor; the EJB container has one as well. The deployment descriptor is the container's checklist of where it wants to go today and what to do with all the parts of the application. It's basically the answer to the question, "OK, you've given me all these beans, now what do I do with them?" It tells the server how many spare database connections to have sitting around, what database it should connect to, who can do what to the beans in the application, and a whole lot more along those lines.

The deployment descriptor also contains information about the bean like the kind of bean, entity, message-driven, or session, transaction and security information and other configurable information about the bean.

You set up the deployment descriptor for your application, telling the server exactly what to do, and the server goes off and does it. The deployment descriptor contains stuff like usernames and what groups they belong to, information on how to find each bean using JNDI (like a phone directory operator), the database that the application is using, and so on.

The file itself is XML so you can theoretically edit it directly, but nobody except a hard core vi user would actually do so. You update the settings in the deployment descriptor with GUI tools you get along with the application server. Then a whole big redeployment process needs to be done to make the change effective.

Here's a small example of what you might find in an EJB deployment descriptor, with commentary on each line.

Example 12-7 Sample EJB deployment descriptor contents and comments

---

```
<ejb-jar>
```

The beginning of the deployment descriptor.

```
<enterprise-beans>
```

This is the section where each EJB will be configured.

```
<session>
```

The first (and only) bean in this case is a session bean.

```
<display-name>PizzaShop</display-name>
```

The display name is what you will see in the server tools and IDE.

```
<ejb-name>PizzaShop</ejb-name>
```

The ejb-name tag is used to identify this ejb in other parts of the deployment descriptor.

```
<home>pizza.PizzaShopHome</home>
```

The fully qualified name (i.e. including package) of the Home interface.

```
<remote>pizza.PizzaShop</remote>
```

The fully qualified name of the remote component interface.

```
<ejb-class>pizza.PizzaShopBean</ejb-class>
```

The fully qualified name of the ejb class.

```
<session-type>Stateless</session-type>
```

The session bean type can be stateful or stateless.

```
<transaction-type>Container</transaction-type>
```

Who will manage the transactions: the container or the bean? (That is, will the programmer will write all that code, or will the programmer just say, "Container, just take care of all this.")

</session>

Plain old tag for ending the session bean.

</enterprise-beans>

Plain old tag for ending the EJB section of the ejb-jar

</ejb-jar>

Ends the ejb-jar.

---

chapter **13**

The Database

Walter Neff: "You'll be here too?"
Phyllis: "I guess so, I usually am."
Walter Neff: "Same chair, same perfume, same anklet?"
Phyllis: "I wonder if I know what you mean."
Walter Neff: "I wonder if you wonder."

Double Indemnity

The Moving Finger writes; and, having writ,
Moves on: nor all thy Piety nor Wit
Shall lure it back to cancel half a Line,
Nor all thy Tears wash out a Word of it.

Edward Fitzgerald's translation of "The Rubaiyat"

The database. Lots of related data, called records, in lots of big lists, called tables. Not as glamorous as the other parts of J2EE, but very necessary. Just because it's not glamorous, though, doesn't mean it's not complex. Think about multiple users accessing it. How do you make sure that two users don't edit the same data at the same time—or is that even a bad thing? And think about all your entity beans. How do they know where to send the data to: what row, what table? What if multiple records are involved? There's a whole lot to deal with when you've got data storage that goes beyond just listing your income in a spreadsheet.

The Chapter in Brief

The database just keeps track of whatever you tell it to. It's big and complicated because not only is it important to make sure you keep track of the data, but finding and getting the data out fast is tough. Changing the data without goofing things up is even tougher. The *DBMS*, or database management system, is like the intense but very smart librarian who gets books in and out of the stacks for you. Entity beans are hand in glove with databases since entity beans represent data from the database.

Whenever you code an application, you have to keep in mind what will happen to the data in the end: how to get it in there, and how to get it out. You also need to make design decisions about the database based on what the goals are for how the application will perform.

Here's what we cover in this chapter.

- *Things You Already Know That Are Related to Databases*
- *So, Just to Be Absolutely Clear, What's a Database?*
- *There's the Database, and the DBMS*
- *Why We Need Databases and DBMSes*
- *Communication With the Database*
- *How Database Data Corresponds to J2EE Application Data*
- *The Data Access Object Pattern*

Things You Already Know That Are Related to Databases

CMR is the container's way of making sure that the same relationships between items in tables stay related in the application. See *Container-Managed Relationships* on page 129.

You also know that entity beans stand around pretending to be the database. You can review this in Chapter 10, "Introduction to Enterprise JavaBeans," on page 117.

So, Just to Be Absolutely Clear, What's a Database?

The information is stored in tables, like CUSTOMERS or INVENTORY, which conceptually are really just spreadsheets but stored in a database. Tables have a bunch of rows or records, each of which is a single record of information, like Jane Jones name and address. Each cell is a piece of information, like Jane or Boulder, and each column is information like FIRSTNAME.

Figure 13-1 shows a couple records in a table and the parts in each.

CUSTOMERS Table

FIRSTNAME column

CUSTOMERS

	FIRSTNAME	LASTNAME	ADDRESS	CITY	STATE	POSTCODE
Jane's record	Maude	Jones	404 Found Avenue	Boulder	CO	80303
	Steve	Santos	1688 Ashley Lake Road	Kalispell	MT	59901

Kalispell cell

Figure 13-1 Simple example database table

It's more complex with a normal working database containing hundreds or thousands of tables. However, there's not much you need to worry about. There's the tables, and then there's all the other stuff that your database administrator gets to chuckle and rub her hands about.

Your J2EE application might have a bunch of different databases. This is no more complicated than having one database; you just specify which one or ones you're using in the deployment descriptor.

There's the *Database*, and the *DBMS*

The database just sits around holding data. Sometimes it hums snatches from Broadway musicals softly to itself but mostly it doesn't do much. And that doesn't do anyone any good. Like a library without a librarian.

Therefore you need a DBMS. A database management system. The DBMS is really what you're buying when you buy a database, since you fill up the database yourself with your own data. The DBMS is the librarian for your database. A librarian does things like sending some books out for interlibrary loan, brings requested data up to the front to customers, tells some customers "sorry, that's checked out" and other duties. The DBMS does the same kinds of things for the database.

When people say "What database are you using?" they usually mean the DBMS such as Oracle or Sybase.

What's an RDBMS?

If you
really want
to know

You might hear "RDBMS" too, which means pretty much the same thing except it's Relational Database Management System. All the database brands you'd use with J2EE are relational, anyway. Relational just means that the data is grouped logically in tables, with customers here and inventory over there and orders up there, behind the sink. Sometimes the tables contain the relationships between the tables, so that you can tell which orders contain which inventory items, and which customers placed which orders.

Why We Need Databases and DBMSes

Think about your family's birthdays. Theoretically a manageable list of information. You remember that.

Now imagine you're a manager with 37 very emotionally sensitive direct reports. You probably need to write down a list of their birthdays. But a piece of paper will do since it's not that long a list and birthdays don't really change that often. And you're the only one who needs to get at the list.

Now imagine you're in charge of the Department of Keeping Track of People in your country and everyone and their intern needs to retrieve or record births, deaths, divorces, names, addresses, pets, favorite colors, income, jobs, and whatever other personal information is tracked. Paper is no longer an option.

You need a database. You need to record enormous lists of people's names and addresses, hooked somehow to the corresponding list of the same people and their job and income information, hooked to the information about their favorite colors.

But it's not just that you need to record the information. You need some major software intelligence to make sure that people can get the information out again. Write-Only Memory is a funny idea but not that useful. You need to make sure that multiple people can access the database at once. And you need to make sure that when multiple people access the database at the same time they don't screw things up. The system needs to make sure that when Bob from the tax department is updating Baroness Hickenlooper's information, that it doesn't goof up Sheila who's reading Baroness Hickenlooper's income.

So a database serves two purposes: data is recorded fairly permanently, and can be used without being screwed up.

This means you need a database, and a DBMS.

Communication With the Database

You read about container-managed relationships, which are the container's way of making sure that the relationships between records in tables stay related in the beans in application. See *Container-Managed Relationships* on page 129 for a brief review.

Database Drivers

Every database has its own special way of dealing with SQL commands, of course (because otherwise it would be too simple and no fun). So there's a *driver*, just a little software interpreter sort of program, for each type of database. A driver is kind of like an interpreter for the database, taking incoming commands and translating them appropriately for the database. There's one for each brand of database, and you get them from that company, usually just downloadable from their Web site.

SQL: Esperanto for Databases

All these database management systems speak SQL, a beautifully human-like, English-like, language. Anything who wants the database management system to do anything to the database speaks SQL to it. If a container, or an OpenOffice.org document, or anything wants anything from the database, they ask the DBMS for it, in SQL. It's like Esperanto, but successful.

Standard SQL operations, just stuff you can do to databases, are read, write, delete, and update (change the data). Or CRUD: create, retrieve, update, delete. These are all things that the EJB container can ask the DBMS to do to the data in the database.

How Your Application Talks to the Database

Depending on your application structure, you might have an EJB tier that talks to the database, or you might have your servlets or JSPs talk straight to the database.

How Web Components Talk to the Database

If you want your servlets or JSPs to talk to the database, you can do it pretty simply. You can just create an HTTP connection, using Java's standard HTTP connection class, and then throw your SQL request at it, like "Select FIRSTNAME, LASTNAME from CUSTOMERS where POSTCODE = 80303."

How EJBs Talk to the Database

There are two ways to do this. Let the container get data in and out of the database, or do it yourself. CMP, container-managed persistence; or BMP; bean-managed persistence.

Here's how it works if you just let the container do it. The container takes care of *everything*, all the communication and messing around with the database. For all your application knows, databases and SQL and drivers and all that business don't exist. Your J2EE application lives a pretty carefree existence.

If you
really want
to know

Pooling Database Connections

The container also takes care of pooling database connections, which we'll get into later in resource management. Pooling database connections is done because it takes a fair amount of time and energy for the container, or anyone, to get the database's attention so it will do what you ask. Therefore the container creates a whole bunch of premade database connections so they're ready when needed. This helps performance. Database connection pooling is also a good idea from a purely economical standpoint. Some databases are priced based on how many connections can be used at once, so pooling is a good idea.

The container knows how to talk to the DBMS, knows all about how to send data off to it, ask the DBMS to seal off a record while the container is messing with it, etc. The container also knows how to use entity beans to hold data while it's being manipulated (tax calculated, order being totaled), and then when it's done, taking it from the entity bean and asking the DBMS to send it to the right place in the database.

This means that since your application runs just fine without knowing that it's with a SQL Server database, you can switch it over to an Oracle database without even telling it. You just tell the container.

Each database vendor handles the DBMS work very differently. Even with the assistance of drivers and SQL to standardize somewhat how one writes code to connect to databases, the additional level of separation, the container, brings a huge additional benefit, a big leap, toward making application development and maintenance and portability (switching databases) easier.

So the people developing the application don't have to know much more besides how to write code for their own business: selling beanbags, selling handyman services, or whatever. And this is really the point of J2EE.

But what if you like to do it yourself? Then you can write the persistence handling code yourself. This is called BMP, bean-managed persistence. It just means you've got some good programmer on staff who wants to write the database handling code himself. It's called *Bean-managed* because the SQL code goes inside bean code. Your programmer wants to do this because he thinks he can write code better than the container and make everything work faster. Whether BMP is a good idea varies a lot. Depends on the project and of course who you talk to.

How Database Data Corresponds to J2EE Application Data

Your database has one way of organizing data, in tables. You have INVENTORY and CUSTOMERS and ORDERS and so on. You also have an INVCUST table that stores customer IDs with their order IDs, and a TAXCALC database for all that nasty but required sales tax info.

Object-oriented Java applications also hold data. Create a Pizza object from the Pizza class, which inherits from the FoodWithCrust class. (Pizzas and Calzones are both in the FoodWithCrust class. Spaghetti and other noodley foods would be in a Pasta class.) Call it newPizza and assign it the values of large and pepperoni and redsauce, and there's the data. You also have a Customer class so you can do stuff to customer records, an Orders class so you can, of course, receive and process orders, and so on.

So what tables do you store those objects' data in?

They don't correlate real well. Objects are one thing and tables another, and the best structure for one is not the best structure for others.

Luckily, in EJB 2.0 and later there are container-managed relationships. You just specify in the deployment descriptor how your objects correlate not only to the database, but to each other. Fun for all. See *Container-Managed Relationships* on page 129 for more information.

The Data Access Object Pattern

The Data Access Object pattern, or DAO, isn't something that *enables* an application to get at data. The application can already do that. DAO makes the whole application *easier to maintain.* The DAO is a data retrieval specialist. It takes over data-getting-and-retrieval duties and being able to do it in many different ways.

You use the DAO if you're using BMP, since DAO is a way to separate the data retrieval code from the rest of the application. If you have BMP you have data retrieval code; if you're using CMP, you don't.

The DAO pattern is, like so many other things, just good object orientation. It supports the idea of separation of concerns. It takes the database code and puts it in one chunk so that when you need to change it, you don't have to go hunting high and low throughout your application: you just go to the DAO pattern.

The DAO allows entity beans to not care how the data is stored, which is similar to using CMP. Your application just says, "Hey, DAO, get me the info about customer ID 78655 and don't bother me about the details." And the DAO goes around sniffing out the data you want, talking to your DBMS. Between the two of them, they figure it out and get the task done.

Now when you need to change databases you don't have to go into the application and mess with it, potentially breaking all sorts of things. You just change the data access object.

A business logic component, maybe an EJB, will have a reference to the data access object interface. Anytime the application needs to do database-related stuff, the application just tells that hardworking EJB to go get the data.

The code for the data access goes in a separate regular Java class that implements an interface. The interface contains the data access methods (like getCustomerAddress). This class is the data access object.

Figure 13-2 shows the basics of what the DAO does.

Your application just connects to the DAO when it needs to get into and out of the database.
All SQL code for getting data in and out of application is separated and put here.
Your database, which you can switch without messing with the main part of the application.

Figure 13-2 Data Access Object pattern

chapter 14

Web Services and SOAP

"Room service? Send up a larger room."

Groucho Marx

"For your convenience, we recommend courteous efficient self-service."

Sign in a Hong Kong supermarket

The buzzword du jour (well, along with XML) is Web services. Sounds awfully good, doesn't it? Just...go to the Web and get a service. Whoohoo!

There's that vague marketing word again, though. *Services*. So we need to know more. What does the Web services technology offer? What does it do; what do you have to do if you want to write one?

The Chapter in Brief

There are two things: the idea of Web services, just having a service out there that someone can hook up to, and the technology of Web services, which means specifically using WSDL and SOAP and lots of other standards. Web services are part of the latest (at the time of writing) release of J2EE, and you get a lot of J2EE tools for creating Web services.

Here's what we talk about in this chapter.

- *Intro to Web Services*
- *What Are Web Services Really For?*
- *How Web Services Are Defined and Structured: XML and SOAP*
- *What About Performance?*
- *Distinguishing the Web Services Technology From the Web Services Implementation*
- *Tools for Creating Web Services*
- *Web Services Walkthrough for Antoine's Pizza Business*

Intro to Web Services

This section tells you a bit about what Web services are, how they're put together, and why everyone's making such a big deal about them. We'll also talk about XML and SOAP, a technology and a protocol that are used to write and structure how the Web services are run.

Just a Definition

A Web service is a specific technology that is one way of making a function available over the Internet. Like the Internet equivalent of being able to say, "Marge, beer me," and suddenly getting a beer. Only you need to go to www.margebeerme.com to run the Web service using SOAP and WSDL and all that the other stuff that's used when you do Web services. The possible application of Web service technology on this site would be a service for finding the best wholesale prices on sweet nutty brown ales, or getting a list of distributors who could bring you some nice weiss beers all the way up in Yukon Territory, by Tuesday.

The folks from Sun tell us that Web services are software systems designed to support interoperable machine-to-machine interaction over a network in a heterogeneous environment.

You might also hear people saying that Web services are "compute functionality over the Internet" which is true but does not provide any additional meaning. So do RMI, RPC, Jini, CGI, etc. We're just throwing that phrase in because you'll hear it a lot.

Who the Players Are

There are three main players in Web services:

- The client who uses the service,
- The provider who, well, provides the service
- The directory where the client finds services and the provider lists services.

Web Services Basics

A Web service can be considered a service-oriented architecture, which consists of a collection of services that communicate with each other (and end-user clients) through well-defined interfaces.

Here's the translation. That just means that computers that might not otherwise be able to talk to each other can use Web services to communicate. XML is the core of Web services, and XML is extra readable so everyone can handle it. And it means that when you write code for Web services you need to use interfaces, which you've read about in this book a fair bit in relationship to EJBs, RMI, and J2EE in general. (Interfaces are just plain Good, kind of like using your seatbelt or eating a balanced diet.)

The XML in question is a set of open standards, such as the Web Services Description Language (WSDL), the Simple Object Access Protocol (SOAP), and Universal Description, Discovery, and Integration (UDDI).

- WSDL describes how to use the Web service

- SOAP is what you use to use the service, and what you get back from the service
- UDDI is about how you tell people that your service exists, and how they find out

JAXR and JAX-RPC APIs are used too. We'll get into the acronym soup as we go through the chapter.

The Typical Web Services Example

The typical example that's thrown around is a Web service that lets you ask for a stock quote, and sends right back the amount that stock is worth right now.

This type of service is requested either regularly or whenever the client wants it, and the answer is returned immediately. You might also set it up to return a response later, if the processing is going to take a long time. If you're asking what the best route is to follow from Manhattan to DC, while passing two or more Krispy Kreme stores, and you want to avoid construction, the processing could take a while.

Generally, Web services are used in a B-to-B way. B-to-B refers to commerce or other business-related tasks performed over the Internet between businesses, rather than between a customer and a business. Business to business or B-to-B actions might be a salesperson for retailer X going to the Web site for wholesaler Y to order more parts for the items that retailer X sells.

That means Antoine would use a Web service from ToppingsRUs to find the cheapest topping for his pizzas, and caterers or people throwing Super Bowl parties would use a Web service to find pizza purveyors like Antoine.

What Are Web Services Really For?

The point of Web services is not primarily to use them to write applications from the ground up. The most useful implementation of Web services is to use them to stitch together existing systems that otherwise might not be able to talk to each other. (That's where XML comes in—it's Esperanto for the Internet.)

This goes along with the point that Web services are often used for B-to-B communication. With B-to-B automation Antoine doesn't have to phone Tracy in CheeseRUs customer service to ask for twelve more boxes of cheddar.

However, Antoine's Pizza and CheeseRUs didn't consult each other when they created their businesses' applications. CheeseRUs might be using J2EE, or some simple CGI system, or .NET, or some obscure homegrown sort of system.

It's also unlikely that the CheeseRUs folks could just extend their own application to communicate easily with Antoine's Pizza's software.

That's a clear indication of the need for Web services. Web services let lots of different types of applications communicate with each other.

How Web Services Are Defined and Structured: XML and SOAP

Web services use configuration information in XML to specify the structure of the stuff that's sent over the Internet, using the SOAP protocol over HTTP. (We'll get through all those acronyms in this chapter.)

What's XML?

Briefly, XML is just a way of identifying what type of information something is and what structure the information should be presented is, as well as the information itself. If you didn't see it, there's a brief description in *A Little More on XML* on page 67.

You can specify any type of information in XML, whether it's something that's required for a particular technology like `<messageheader>04rtt012x</messageheader>` or just something for your own pet project like `<typeoffood>Pizza</typeoffood>`. Then other programs can take a look at that XML, saying (in code) "Hmm, I need the value for a `typeoffood`...oh, here it is. `Pizza`, got it."

That's an example of sending around *data* inside an XML document. XML can also be easily used to define the *structure* for a message. For instance, in a document it could be used to specify that a chapter heading must be followed by an introtext, which must be followed by a heading level 1, and so on. If you submitted a document that stampeded straight from the chapter heading to heading level 1, the XML validation process would gack on you and prevent you from submitting that document.

Even if the validation process didn't happen and you submitted a document without that structure, it wouldn't be that big a deal. We'd all manage to carry on and find meaning in life.

However, what if you were dealing with a medical company and it was really, really important that certain information be included correctly in medical documents? If a patient has a medical allergy, then you must also include degree of reaction and other information. If the patient is taking other medications, you must include them. The XML validation can verify that the correct pieces of information in this document are included. The validation could also just make sure you're filling in the form the right way, which would be great, since filling in medical forms correctly is right up there with root canals and meeting your in-laws for the first time.

If you were putting together a cat object using XML, you'd want to make sure that the body was between the head and the tail and that each leg ended in one paw. Otherwise, you get some pretty wacky cats. XML can make sure the cat is built right.

The point here is that XML is very powerful when it comes to verifying that something has all the right parts, in the right order.

What's SOAP?

SOAP, simple object access protocol, is a different way to communicate remotely. (It's kind of like RMI; see *It's All About Communication: RMI* on page 269.) It's a system for exchanging objects, data, ectoplasm, information about red suede pumps, whatever, over a network.

It too is XML based, so you set up how you want to do it with the programming language of your choice for the actual processing. It uses XML to do things like say how big and how structured its requests are that it's sending over the network.

It specifies how to say what the data types are. Data types are things like an integer such as 34, a String such as "Hi There", and so on.

We're talking about it here because SOAP defines a system, or framework, for exchanging XML documents across the Internet. Why exchange XML documents? Because you have to for Web services.

- The XML document is what tells you how to decode this glob of data you just got over the Internet. And likewise it tells the gob-sending-party how to package up the data the right way.
- SOAP specifies, among other things, what is required and optional in a SOAP message and how data can be encoded and transmitted.

The Web Services Registry: UDDI

Universal Description, Discovery, and Integration (UDDI) is the standard for registering Web services in a central location. The UDDI registry receives queries about what Web services are available and sends back information about the Web services available.

Analogy for How Web Services and SOAP Relate to Each Other

Let's say you're ten years old, and you have a treehouse. Every other kid in the neighborhood has a treehouse, too, and you send messages back and forth to each other over a surprisingly sophisticated system of bottles and strings. Some of these strings stretch all the way over into the next county and you never see some of these kids. (It's a weird little system, but you like it.)

You don't even know who's out there or what they're like, but you want to communicate with them. For one thing, you get kind of hungry up there in your treehouse and you're wondering if anyone out there delivers sandwiches. You're also a prank specialist so are eager to share your services for covering houses in toilet paper.

So you climb down out of your treehouse, get a piece of bark and a crayon, write up what you do in your house-toilet-papering service. You also write up what you need to know to do it (the address, square footage, degree of coverage desired), and just where your treehouse is. You write it up in a very specific structure that all the kids have agreed upon, and you nail it to the Central Tree o' Information.

Note: In reality outside the analogy, this tree is part of the Web services specification, UDDI, and everyone knows how to find it. When you wrote up your services, the structure you wrote it in followed the WSDL structure and the document you wrote is a WSDL document. This is the WSDL document that describes a Web service and what it can do. WSDL is the grammar, the structure for how to write it. In the WSDL document, you've described for all the neighborhood kids how to do the SOAP things that will get the house-TPing service out of you.

When you're down there at the Central Tree o'Information, you see a few other pieces of bark hanging up there with information scrawled on them. One of them expresses the ability on behalf of the bark-scrawler to provide sandwiches for anyone who asks, and another expresses the ability to find the best time for anyone to sneak out of the house at night.

Note: These are the WSDL documents from other Web services.

You're pretty interested in this sneaking-out thing this kid is talking about, so you take a good look at the piece of bark he put up, then go back to your tree house and put together your request. He needs to know your address, your name, any siblings, whether you have a security system, and whether your house faces east. You write it all up according to the **S**pecific **O**rders **a**nd **P**articulars code that the neighborhood kids use to write their messages when they want services done. And, since this is a strikingly diverse neighborhood and you kids speak at least a dozen different languages among you, you write the message in Esperanto.

Note: In non-analogy world, this means you use the SOAP standard that tells you what structure your message should take, what type of information, etc. And you write it in XML (as opposed to Esperanto). Note that the standard for the structure is different from the language. Just as you could fill in an employment application form in English, Spanish, and so on, the *structure* and the *language* are different.

You put the message in the Coke bottle that you use to communicate, you pick up the right string that'll send the Coke bottle to the location of the boy who does this best-time-for-sneaking-out service, and send it off. (You know where to send it off to since one of the things in the WSDL document for that service is the URL where the Web service hangs out.)

Maybe a half hour later, you get back a message. You open it up, you look at the message, and you use the special message decoder ring that's part of the **S**pecific **O**rders **a**nd **P**articulars code to figure out what he said. It says "You are never going to be able to sneak out of your house because your mother is Chief of Police, you idiot." You sigh gently and think, well, it was worth a try.

Have I Been Reading Too Long or Are All These Technologies Starting to Sound Alike?

If you got all excited about that brief reference to RMI and read through the appendix, *It's All About Communication: RMI* on page 269, you might be thinking there are Common Features between RMI and Web services. They both have a central registry of objects (which can do things) and services (which can do things). CORBA (underpinnings of RMI) and plain RPC can handle it too, though CGI couldn't.

So what's the point of SOAP when RMI was around already? Well, one thing is that RMI is for Java and doesn't branch out much beyond that. Whereas SOAP can communicate with anything. Some people think that's SOAP's best feature, that it can talk to anything. If you want to hook up a Java application to a VB application, for instance, SOAP'll do it for you.

There's also politics, of course. (There's always politics.) Some people didn't want to use Java, or open standards, so they invented another approach.

What About Performance?

We don't usually talk about binary right off the top like this, so brazen and all, but we'll try to make it as painless as possible.

You might be wondering about performance. After all, with SOAP you have to send across so much information about the message, all that XML. The overhead of sending the message might take up a whole lot more system resources than just sending it over the normal way which is a little more computery and compact.

Well, OK, you might not have been wondering that. But we're bringing it up anyway. Here's the deal with Web services and performance.

Web service protocols are very fat. What makes them nice and human readable, and readable by any application, also makes them fat. And that means that running Web services over the Internet are going to be hogging the bandwidth buffet.

Here's why. Every single data field is identified this way, coming and going:

```
<pizzatype>sausage</pizzatype>

<bakingtime>40</bakingtime>

<deliveryorpickup>pickup</deliveryorpickup>
```

Look at all that. There's way more text to lug around in the identifier fields than in the data itself.

Here's what the problem is. Text, XML. is different than the usual way data is sent around.

How Data Is Usually Sent Around

A *byte* is a computer number between 0 and 255. When you're doing normal computer science, sending information around, you take advantage of the fact that every number from 0 to 255 has been assigned a predefined meaning. 32 means space, 65 is a capital A, and so on.

Computers also have a predefined way of representing numbers in the range

-32768 to 32767

That's 65,536 numbers in that range, and any number in that range can be represented by just two bytes.

If you
really want
to know

How Big is a Byte?

A byte is really small. In most email systems, one character is one byte.That email you just got from your buddy asking you to his barbecue this weekend probably was maybe 5k. 5 kilobytes. 5120 bytes. So a byte is 1/5120 of that dinky text-only email you just got this morning.

So if you want to send a piece of information, say just a number 17,788, you can use the appropriate two-byte code. Your message weighs two bytes.

How XML Is Sent Around

Or you could ignore the predefined code and write it out longhand in text. You've used five bytes instead of two. Expand this to an entire system and you've got a huge amount of extra space being taken up because you're ignoring the predefined code.

That's what you're dealing with in XML, and with SOAP and Web services, There is no set of predefined assignments to make things more efficient. Not only that, not only is the actual data you're sending a lot bigger than in a system that has a predefined code, but you have to send all this data around saying "this is what I'm going to send," then say what it is you're sending, and then say "this is what I sent."

Let's say you just wanted to send the number of bananas that you have on hand in inventory, which is 14,090.

Using the regular computery binary approach:

```
14090
```

Using the format required for Web services:

```
<value name=number_of_bananas type=int>14090</value>
```

Here's the score:

Binary: 2 bytes Web services: 52 bytes

Sure, the example is mildly exaggerated, given that most XML setups won't be as verbose as `number_of_bananas`. But many are.

That's the deal with Web services and performance. It doesn't have the same predefined codes that most applications use to decrease the size of the information sent around the Internet. You get huge packages of data sent around networks as a result. And that's bad for performance.

Distinguishing Web Services Technology From Web Services Implementation

Web services actually have nothing inherently to do with Web services.

Let's try that again. Technically, Web services are just some standards, some APIs, some ways of writing code. But in a generic sense, you can get services from the Web easily, without any kind of Web services technology.

Due to their name it's easy to see them as The Way to get services from the Web, like getting the fastest route to Poughkeepsie or the best price on flights to Paris.

Have you ever compared flights to Paris?

Probably. You probably went on Expedia.com, asked for flights Denver-Paris, and then got a list of flights from various airlines.

That's a common implementation of the Web services technology.

Done without a shred of Web services code.

Probably though not necessarily done with servlets and JSPs. Maybe even CGI.

So that's the point. The capability of doing Web services the Implementation is not new. It's pretty old. Web services the Technology is a new way of providing Web services the Implementation.

Whether you use Web services the Technology depends on whether you even need to do WSTI (Web services the Implementation) and whether WSTT (Web services the Technology) is the best way to do it. Which takes us back to *What Are Web Services Really For?* on page 170.

Tools for Creating Web Services

For Web services to work, and of course this applies to lots of technologies, the system sending the request and the system receiving the request have to have at least some clue how to talk to each other. So Web services has chosen XML as its Esperanto.

You also need something to write the programming logic that does things with the XML and SOAP and all that. Java is one tool for writing the programing logic. We'll tell you here about the Java tools for doing Web services.

JAXM and JAXR

JAXM is the Java messaging service API that you can use with Web services. JAXR, the Java API for XML Registries, lets you get at standard business registries over the Internet. Business registries are basically just online yellow pages. You can get at the information in them, as well as register a business, using JAXR. It gives developers a uniform way to use business registries that are based on open standards like ebXML or semi-open industry-led specifications like UDDI.

SAX and DOM

SAX and DOM are two different ways to evaluate XML documents. And put together, the names sound vaguely salacious, which is fun.

- SAX, or the Simple API for XML, looks at things in order, one at a time. It goes through the document saying "Here's a thing", then forgets about that, then says "Here's another thing", and so on. It does also know about the structure of the document; if it's going through a document defining a cat and it just went past whiskers, it knows that nose and eyes are coming up and that hitting paws instead would be wrong. However, you can't rewind it, you can't look ahead of the current position, and you can't compare items in the document.

- DOM, or the Document Object Model, is a lot more powerful. It builds a representation of the whole document in memory at once, which is great if you need to be able to jump throughout the document, compare items, and so on. However, think about taking a whole XML document and putting it into memory. That takes a lot of memory. Theoretically, DOM can take an infinite amount of memory, if the document is big enough.

The Java Web Services Tools

This will sound just a bit confusing because JAX and RPC both do a few different things.

- JAX is the name for any one of a number of Java APIs for doing XML.
- RPC stands for remote procedure call. It's an industry standard way to call remote when you don't have objects. It's been around for ages.

Together, they let you write a group of procedures that make up a Web service. JAX-RPC is the Java API for doing remote procedures calls. Remote procedure calls just means calling stuff across a network, as you might expect.

JAX-RPC implements the protocols required for Web services, but also some similar ones that do the same thing in a different way.

Setting up Web Services

You put the Web service on the tier where your Web container is, and the service runs inside that container.The Web service sets up kind of a sandwich board of itself, a descriptor of what it is, using a Web Services Description Language (WSDL) document. A WSDL description is (of course) an XML document that gives all the important information about a Web service, like its name, the operations that can be called on it (like `getWholesalers` or `computeAveragePrice`), the parameters for those operations (do you have to send it the name of the company whose stock you want to check, the four-letter abbreviation like BEAS, or both?), and the location of where to send requests (the URL where the Web service hangs out). Think of it as the Web service's online personal ad. Anyone who wants to can then read it, see what it's like, and see how to access it.

The WSDL document is just an interface.

Writing anything involving RPC usually involves dealing with a lot of complicated programming plumbing to make the data fly around across the Internet, but JAX-RPC takes care of a lot of it automatically so programmers don't have to deal with it. This is similar to the way that the container takes care of all the serialization and stubs and skeletons in RMI, and all the programmer has to do is check the JNDI lookup and then let'er fly.

Creating a Web Service Using JAX-RPC

Developing and deploying a Web service using JAX-RPC isn't *all* that painful.

Writing the Code for the Server Side

The service itself is basically two files, an interface that declares the service's remote procedures and a class that implements those procedures. The interface definition, for instance, could contain all the methods a wholesale cheese distributor might want to make available to its prospective customers such as checkCheesePrice, placeOrder, placeOrder, etc.

Once all the code is written, the developer packages it all up, along with its XML deployment descriptor, in a WAR file. (WAR is Web archive, and is just like a JAR file except that it's spelled differently. JAR files are basically ZIP files.) There's usually a tool to help you do all this deployment, and to make the WSDL description, too. (The Web service's online personal ad.) Then everything goes where all the servlets and JSPs and other Web components go, so the Web service can run inside the Web container.

Writing the Code You Need on the Client Side to Run a Web Service

Now you just write the code that calls the methods you want, like getCheesePrice. This code is compiled and packaged up, and hooked up to the GUI for the Web service, which you typically have. The user clicks the button for Get Cheese Prices or Find Cheese Distributors, the button is hooked up to the right method call in the Java code, and the Web service is off to the races.

As with other things you can do in J2EE, there's a whole bunch of logistical networking stuff being done behind the scenes that neither the user nor the programmer needs to worry about.

Web Services Walkthrough for Antoine's Pizza Business

The following scenario is an example of how Antoine could use Web services to improve his business and business processes.

Antoine wants to find some cheaper toppings. He asks Floyd to find some new toppings suppliers, get their wholesale prices, and then arrange for orders to be placed as the need arises. (Antoine trusts him to do this kind of thing more than coding.) He can then analyze the prices and decide which toppings he wants to use and which companies he wants to buy them from.

Discovering New Distributors

Floyd decides that the best way to locate new toppings suppliers is to search a Universal Description, Discovery, and Integration (UDDI) registry, where Antoine has already registered his pizza shop. (The UDDI registry was the Central Tree o' Information, in the treehouse analogy.) Floyd uses JAXR to send a query searching for wholesale toppings suppliers. The JAXR implementation uses JAXM behind the scenes to send the query to the UDDI registry, but it's all under the covers and Floyd has no clue it's going on. (As usual.) The UDDI registry receives the query and applies the search criteria transmitted in the JAXR code to the information it has about the organizations registered with it.

When the search is completed, the registry sends back information on how to contact the wholesale toppings distributors that met the specified criteria. Although the registry uses JAXM behind the scenes to transmit the information, the response that Floyd gets back is JAXR code.

Requesting Price Lists

Floyd's next step is to request price lists from each of the toppings distributors. He's got the WSDL description for each one, which tells him the procedure to call to get prices and also the URI where the request is to be sent. He writes code to make the calls correctly using the JAX-RPC API and gets back the responses from the distributors. Antoine's been doing business with one distributor for a long time and has made arrangements with it to exchange JAXM messages using agreed-upon XML schemas. Therefore, for this distributor, the code uses the JAXM API to request current prices, and the distributor returns the price list in a JAXM message.

Comparing Prices and Ordering Toppings

Upon receiving the response to the request for prices, Floyd processes the price lists using SAX.

He uses SAX rather than DOM because for simply comparing prices, it is more efficient. (To modify the price list, he would have needed to use DOM.) After his application gets the prices quoted by the different vendors, it compares them and displays the results. Antoine takes the results home over the weekend and uses them to decide which suppliers to do business with. He puts together some new orders and Floyd sends them to new distributors using JAX-RPC; he sends orders to the established distributor using JAXM. Each supplier, whether using JAX-RPC or JAXM, will respond by sending a confirmation with the order number and shipping date.

As you can see, this wasn't done in an afternoon. However, once the service was written it was easier to find the cheapest toppings wholesaler. And as an added benefit, thousands of people around the world are now sitting down to a nice meal of high-quality, nutritious pizza at less than you'd expect to pay.

part III

J2EE Services and Architecture

"She was old enough to know better
And she was strong enough to be true
And she was hard enough to know whether
He was smart enough to know what to do."

Lyle Lovett, When It Happens to You

We talked about all those services two or three times: resource management, security, and data integrity. Didn't give a whole lot of detail, though. That's what we're going to do in this part. This part is all about how to put together a good J2EE system that runs well. Taking advantage of the container services is one aspect of making a good system.

What we haven't really focused on so far is that these are generally the services of the EJB container. The Web container doesn't do transactions or other data integrity, though of course it doesn't go out of its way to goof things up. And it doesn't do resource management except for what you automatically get from the JVM because servlets and JSPs are Java. The Web container is there to communicate with the Web server and to enforce security. So if you want to understand the Web container services, head to Chapter 17, *J2EE Security*, on page 207.

Another aspect is just making the right choices when you're planning. You know *what* goes into J2EE, but how do you write a *good* J2EE system? How do you figure out whether to use servlets or JSPs for a function? How do you know how many servers to use? And how do you plan for internationalization? All very good questions, which we answer here.

Here's what you get in Part III.

chapter 15

Resource Management

Prince Humperdinck: "Tyrone, you know how much I love watching you work. But I've got my country's 500th anniversary to plan, my wedding to arrange, my wife to murder, and Guilder to frame for it. I'm swamped!"

Count Rugen: "Get some rest. If you haven't got your health, you haven't got anything."

The Princess Bride

Resource management is one of the three big types of services J2EE gives you. Sounds good. You wouldn't want resource *mis*management. What does it actually mean, though?

The big resource in real life is time and/or money; a big resource when you're running an application is memory. There's never enough. So how does that get managed—does the container have a little book called *The One-Minute Memory Manager* to consult?

We've also talked about connecting to the database. Is this a trivial little matter to be done whenever needed, or is this something one can do more efficiently?

The Chapter in Brief

If you're not smart about memory management, you risk slowing to a crawl or crashing. Resource management is being smart about memory and using only what's actually needed at the time. The features that accomplish this are garbage collection (getting rid of objects not needed anymore so the memory they're using can be freed up); connection pooling (having connections to the database already created and reusing them); bean pooling (having session beans around already created and reusing them); and activation and passivation (making stateful session beans to nap if they're not doing anything at the moment).

Here's what we talk about in this chapter.

- *What's Resource Management and Why Do You Need It?*
- *Creating a Bean*
- *Four Kinds of Resource Management*
- *Garbage Collection*
- *Connection Pooling*
- *Bean Pooling*
- *Activation and Passivation*
- *Server Configuration Tools for Setting Up All This*

Note: The services in this chapter are provided only by the EJB container, with the exception of garbage collection, which applies to all Java applications.

What's Resource Management and Why Do You Need It?

To understand why resource management is needed, you need to understand why the management is necessary, and what the resource is.

Beans Are Selfish Little Creatures

When you've worn a pair of jeans, you take them off and put them in the laundry basket and wash them; you don't just keep wearing them under your other clothes, and you don't throw them out. When you rent a car and you're done using it, you return it to the car rental agency so someone else can rent it. (And so you don't get arrested for stealing, of course.)

All of which is very sensible and a logical way to behave. When you're done with something valuable, let someone else use it, or else prep it so that it can be reused. In short, don't bogart the resources; and reduce, reuse, recycle.

EJBs, and Java code in general, are not so responsible and not so smart. When they're done using a resource, they just sit on it, hogging it so no one else can use it, unless Someone Does Something. That resource is memory, and that Someone is the container or the JVM.

Memory Is a Valuable Limited Resource

You only have a certain amount of physical memory. Now, Jeannie logging onto www.antoinespizza.com and looking at the specials is not going to tax your system. Even if she and a hundred of her closest friends do it at the same time, your application can probably handle it without too much trouble. But think about every June when the whole world is celebrating Saint Antoine's Holy Festival of the Calzone. Thousands or potentially millions of customers will be accessing www.antoinespizza.com at once, and they're going to be annoyed if they have to wait five minutes between page reloads. How do you deal with enormous demands for memory? One of the ways you do it is through resource management. Resource management is essentially just being smart about who gets memory and how long they get to hold on to it.

Imagine that you live in a house with 20 of your closest friends in a rainy climate. But there are only 10 rain coats in the house. Resource management applied to this wardrobe issue means that anyone who's going outside in a rainstorm gets a raincoat. But once you come back inside, the House Leader makes you take it off and hang it on the coat rack.

Database Vendors Have MBAs

A common way to price databases is based on the number of connections allowed to it. Obviously, the fewer database connections you can get away with using in your application, the less you have to pay, but the more business you get the more database connections you need. Database connection pooling, one of the types of resource management, helps you be economical with your database connections.

Creating a Bean

We've mentioned this before but it's important to remember. When you need a real live bean instance to rise up and do stuff that's in the bean code, the container actually creates the bean instance. You don't have to.

Because of this, the container has a lot of control over the bean's lives. When they live, what they do when they live, and when they die.

Geek Note on Bean Creation

If you
really want
to know

By the way, just because the container creates all these bean instances doesn't mean the programmer never creates a single object in a J2EE application. There might well be some plain Java code floating around; you might have some Strings that need creating, and so on. You're still in charge of regular Java code. But you have to keep your grubby programmer mitts off of any of the container's pet things—beans, servlets, etc.

The container creates the bean using the `create` method in the bean's Home interface.

Four Kinds of Resource Management

You get four basic kinds of resource management:

- Garbage collection (in J2EE because it's in Java)
- Connection pooling (for database connections)
- Bean pooling (so you have a lot of stateless session beans and entity beans around ready to do your business logic bidding)
- Activation and passivation (so your stateful session beans don't bogart the memory)

Garbage Collection

Garbage collection is one of the things in Java that made former C++ programmers who switched over happier and less stressed-looking.

How Garbage Collection Works

The folks who created Java did in fact take that memory management task and assign it to a part of the Java platform that they call the garbage collector. The garbage collector is just built right into any JVM, and goes around like a little memory bot, looking for memory that no longer is being used and throwing it into the Memory Recycle Pile, ready for some other process. The Recycler might have been a more accurate and more positive term but as we might have mentioned before, techies aren't that great at naming things.

In J2EE, the container takes care of cleaning beans for reuse, avoiding the garbage collector entirely for these components.

The container does reuse; the garbage collector does recycling. Reuse is like washing dishes; recycling is like taking some dishes you've thrown away, putting the through the dish chipper, and making new dishes out of them.

Connection Pooling

Let's say Jeannie is using Antoine's online pizza application and asks to see what kinds of pizzas are on special today in her area. To get the latest information, the application has to check the database.

In order to do that, the application's container needs to create a *connection* to the database. Entity beans can't just walk down the hall to the database room, knock on the door, and say, "Hey, we got any meatlovers' specials going on today in Albany?" It's a bit more complicated.

A connection to the database is needed as long as Jeannie's getting info out of the database.

This is expensive in terms of CPU resources and memory, both on the system where the container is, and for the database. And, if you've got a database where the cost of the database is based on the number of users that can connect to it at the same time, then not only is a connection expensive in terms of memory, it's expensive in terms of cold hard cash.

But, you know, it's just Jeannie trying to find out about the pizza specials so how expensive could it be?

Very, because it's never just Jeannie. (Sorry. We gave you a fallacious premise.) Antoine's got a huge following among the pizzerati and at any given time a hundred or a thousand other people from across the country are going to need a connection to the database too. You've got all these people trying to do stuff that requires a connection to the database. If your container is creating the database connections when they're requested, along with all the other normal work it has to do, your performance is going to be downright pitiful.

So what you do is you create connections ahead of time, like when you first start up the container, and keep them around. Then when Jeannie and her hundred closest friends ask for connections, you hand out your fifty pooled connections, make the other folks wait a couple seconds, then hastily take those fifty "used" connections and hand them over to the other fifty people who are waiting. That means you don't drag down performance creating the connections when they're requested, and you don't drag down performance by creating more than you need; you make some customers wait a little while but it's not too bad.

You can control just how many connections are created when you configure your container. Any application server worth its salt is going to come with some nice GUI configuration tools.

If I Had a Hammer: Analogy for Connection Pooling

You're a contractor and you're building a house. You have ten people but things are a little tight moneywise right now and you only can afford five hammers. Could you do it? Sure. Are you going to be using everyone's time efficiently? Well, it all depends on how you manage all your resources.

Here's how it might work if you didn't apply any logic to it. You'd tell workers one through five that they can each go to the hardware store for a hammer each day when they discover they need one. The other five workers find that they're just out of luck since you can only afford five hammers. The first five people get to use their hammers all day but the other five people wouldn't get to use those hammers. They'd stand around eating donuts and gossiping, all the while getting paid those high union wages. The other annoying thing is that when the people with hammers went to lunch, or were sanding or taping sheetrock, they'd still be bogarting the hammers. And the nonhammer people are still eating donuts. Doin' nothing.

Another approach might be more efficient. You could just go buy five hammers all at once at the beginning of the day. You put the hammers in a box at the center of the work site and you say, "All right, folks. Whoever needs a hammer can take one from this pile. But when you don't need it anymore, you have to put it back." Then when someone who doesn't have a hammer needs one, then they just pick a hammer off the pile. Then everybody still isn't going to have a hammer when they need one, probably, but the hammer resources will be far more evenly distributed among the hammer users.

Plus, it's easier and less time- and money-consuming to reuse a hammer than to get brand new ones.

Bean Pooling

Bean pooling is different from connection pooling. There's a similar effect of reuse, but the mechanics are different and the things being pooled are quite different. The reason for the pooling is different too.

- With connection pooling, it's expensive to create connections, so you create them ahead of time.

- With bean pooling, it's not expensive to create the beans but it's expensive to maintain the memory assigned to the beans. So you take the ones not currently doing any work and you assign them to a new task.

When anyone talks about just plain "pooling" without a context, they're being annoyingly vague. Ask'em what they mean.

Why Have Bean Pooling?

So let's take a look at that statement again. It's not expensive to create beans. What's up with that? So putting aside for the moment the issue of the memory a bean takes up when it's not doing anything useful, why pool beans?

It's not so much the creating as the destroying that takes up time and energy. Destroying the bean is a big deal because that's the nature of garbage collection. Garbage collection is how you get rid of beans that you don't need anymore but it's not the fastest process on earth.

So just as throwing stuff out in real life instead of reusing and recycling is expensive and bad for the environment, destroying perfectly good beans is a drain on your J2EE application resources.

Geek Note About Garbage Collection

If you
really want
to know

Be careful how you use this knowledge. Only three people know about it: one of them is dead, and one of them is in an insane asylum in the Cotswalds.

It's time to open a debate on the issue of whether garbage collection is actually all that expensive. It definitely was for a while; however, huge improvements in garbage collection performance have been made between JDK 1.2 and 1.4. (How garbage collection is done varies from one JVM to another. However, in general many of the JVMs have made considerable improvements.)

The improvements are related to how long an instance was in use. If you've just been using a bean instance for a half a second or so, the new garbage collection techniques are quite fast. If the instance has been around for an hour, though, the improvements aren't as effective. Just what the garbage collection does well and not so well is also tunable in your JVM so you're not entirely stuck with how your JVM was when you brought it home from the shop.

Bean pooling was developed back when garbage collection was always slow; you can think of bean pooling as Slow Garbage Collection Compensation. But now that garbage collection can be a lot faster, the whole issue of whether you need bean pooling at all is up for debate.

Analogy for Bean Pooling

Bean pooling in its simplest form is just reuse. It takes CPU power to create and kill a bean instance (more on that killing later) and it takes memory to keep it around and awake. So you reuse them.

Bean pooling is kind of the same thing you do with a whiteboard in a classroom. Say you're Antoine, you're on a pizza fellowship at the Culinary Institute of America, and you're teaching the class the finer points of sauce-making. You've got a white board up at the front so as you go along, you draw illustrations, you write recipes, etc. Sooner or later you're gong to fill up the white board. What do you do?

It would be a big pain if you had to take down that white board and have it hauled out to the trash.

Besides, the ideas on the white board aren't really that important anymore. Using that information, in response to questions from students or just because you wanted to say it, you've conveyed the main points: that sauce is composed of three key ingredients or that clearly Roma tomatoes are the best. That information has been copied down by the students.

So the most logical thing is to just erase the white board and start over. That's what the container does to beans instead of destroying them; it wipes out their memories so they can be reused.

If it's an entity bean rather than a stateless session bean, that means that just prior to erasing the bean, the container makes a note of whatever information it actually needs to keep, and stores the information in the database.

What about the stateful session beans, by the way? Don't they get to participate in the Recycling Circle of Life? Are they just leeches on bean society since they can't be pooled? Are they shunned and spat upon as they walk around, shoulders sagging under the weight of the data in their fine leather data-stuffed briefcases?

Luckily, such an unkind fate does not befall stateful session beans. They get *passivated.*

Activation and Passivation

Activation and passivation are what the container does to stateful session beans so they can participate in the effort to reduce unnecessary memory usage.

Why You Need It

Let's say you've got a bunch of stateful session beans, all awake and alert and keeping track of their info. They're all shopping carts on Antoine's pizza site but twenty of them aren't being used right now because it's Super Bowl Sunday. A bunch of people watching the Super Bowl started ordering pizzas but then somebody made some sort of play and everyone's riveted to the screen, their online shopping carts sitting alone, bravely keeping up the illusion that their clients will come back...some day...

Meanwhile perfectly good customers who only watch PBS and never to excess are trying to order pizza but can't.

What should the pizza application do? You can't just erase the cart and put it back on the pile, nice and shiny and ready to reuse. You might eventually but your timeout for shopping carts is set for an hour and it's only been ten minutes.

So you *passivate.* You take the data out of the stateful session bean, or rather the container does, and you put it on the passivation pile. The stateful session bean, relieved of its load, falls asleep and stops using all that memory. Now there's enough memory to create shopping carts for the hungry non-football fans.

Analogy for Passivation and Activation

You're now the owner of a grocery store. You've got ten shoppers in the store but only eight shopping carts. (Real shopping carts this time.) What do you do?

You could let eight of them shop and make the other two wait until the first eight are finished. But people don't like to wait, and it might be hours before these people are done shopping. (Your store makes CostCo look small, so these people might be in here shopping for *weeks*.)

The thing is, most of the time the shoppers are just pushing the carts around fruitlessly looking for nonfat donuts and tofu sausage so they aren't really using the cart. And, key point number two, there's a coffee shop in the grocery store where you can send people to hang out for a while. (And, OK, key point three, you can tell these shoppers exactly what to do and they'll do it, and not be mad.)

So here's what you do. Eight shoppers a-shopping, two shoppers sitting there without shopping carts. You cruise the store and look for the shoppers with carts who are just zoning out, staring at the dried milk. You find three. So you give each of them a mighty push in the direction of the coffee shop. When they get there they just sit back in some nice comfy chairs and zone out. You dump their groceries beside them, you steal their carts, whiz the carts back to the people who need carts, and you have one leftover for the next person.

When the three shoppers in the coffee shops wake up, let's say because their spouses call asking them to pick up cat food too, you quickly whiz some empty carts back to them and put their groceries back in the carts.

(You have the empty carts to spare either because they're just spare or because you pull the same cart-stealing trick on some other shoppers.)

Stealing the cart, making the customer zone out in the coffee shop, and piling their groceries on the floor, *passivation*. Returning the cart and filling it back up is *activation*. The container does this automatically for stateful session beans.

You can also compare passivation to furloughs, or limited-time layoffs. If your company has way too many demands on its money and doesn't have enough to pay all the employees, the company will tell the employees who aren't all that critical, "Take a vacation. We'll, um, hire you back when times are better. Yeah." (In the container, reactivation actually happens.)

Server Configuration Tools for Setting Up All This

OK, so this is all great. But how do you set up how many connections to make? How long to wait before passivation? It's all up to you, your genius J2EE architect, and your server configuration tools.

Tools to set up pooling, passivation, etc. come with your J2EE server. Figure 15-1 shows one of the configuration windows for WebLogic Server. You can go through the documentation, tutorials, etc. on the BEA WebLogic Web site, www.bea.com. Other servers have online documentation and screen shots, as well.

See *J2EE Products* on page 279 for application servers current at the time of writing.

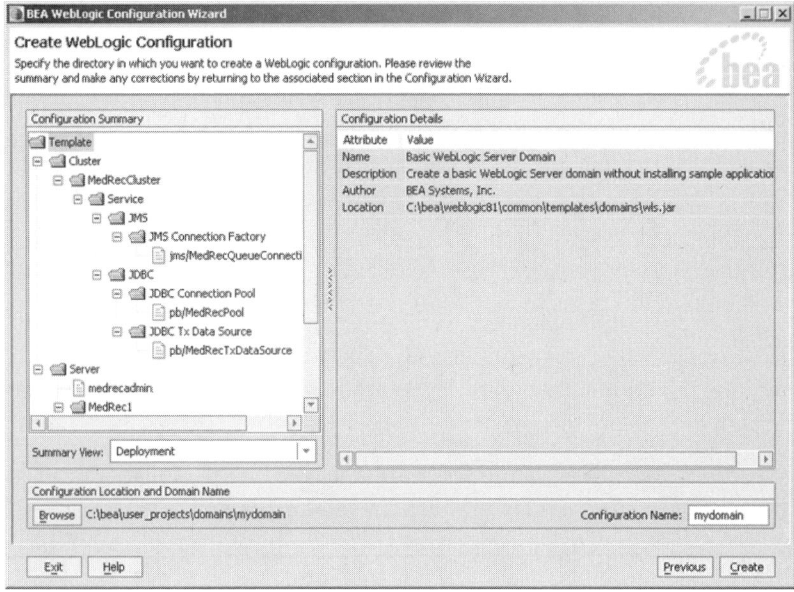

Figure 15-1 A resource management configuration window for WebLogic Server

chapter 16

Data Integrity, Transactions, and Concurrency

"I'm just a bill, Yes, I'm only a bill, and I'm sitting here on Capitol Hill. Well, it's a long, long journey to the capital city, It's a long, long wait while I'm sitting in committee. But I know I'll be a law someday...at least I hope and pray that I will, but today I'm still just a bill."

Music and lyrics: Dave Frishberg, sung by: Jack Sheldon I'm Just a Bill, School House Rock.

We've gone over a lot of the mechanics of the code: the JSP to the servlet to the bean to the database, all with the helping hands and wisdom of the container.

But let's think about this. You're sitting there shopping online for old Schwarzenneger campaign memorabilia. You've selected your items, you've entered your credit card, you're clicking the button to place your order, when Eugene from Accounting comes running through and trips over your power cord. Everything goes black onscreen.

What happens to your order?

The Chapter in Brief

Some things need to be done all together, or not at all. If you're withdrawing money from your account at an ATM, you want to eventually get the money. Stopping halfway through, after deducting the money from an account but before receiving the bills, would be bad. The steps in an ATM withdrawal are a *transaction* composed of smaller steps that are related and really need to stay together. J2EE helps to define and protect transactions.

Transactions are one of the things that are so hard to write, anyone doing it themselves should be committed. Transactions are also vital to making sure that in an imperfect world, your business operations can be as perfect as possible.

Here's what we talk about in this chapter.

- *Data Integrity Overview*
- *Three Aspects of Transactions*
- *How Transactions Work*

Note: The services in this chapter are provided only by the EJB container.

Data Integrity Overview

Antoine is by now a phenomenally successful Pizza Man. One thing that means is that he has a lot of orders coming through. And that means he has a lot of customers, a lot of data in his databases, and a huge underground lair of drones who work in his pizza lair where all the toppings and cheese are kept.

Let's think about those orders for a bit. Let's say that Victor and Jeannie are placing pizza orders online at the same time.

> Hi, I'm victor@nextstep.com.
>
> *Hi, I'm jeannie@vacation.com.*
>
> *I'd like a large pepperoni pizza.*
>
> I'd like the Super Bowl Special, the calzone ten-pack.
>
> *Wait, make that three.*
>
> *With mushrooms.*
>
> Delivered to 110 Harrison Drive tomorrow at 1 PM.
>
> *Delivered in the next hour to 42 Pearl Street.*

Now, with each request from the client (Jeannie in Colorado and Victor in California), eventually some session beans and entity beans are involved. They'll need to look up Jeannie and Victor's records, look up addresses, and when the orders are placed, send orders, reduce inventory for the appropriate amount of mushrooms and other ingredients, and so on. But in the end, Jeannie will get three pepperoni and mushroom pizzas within the hour on Pearl Street, and Victor will get ten calzones tomorrow for his Super Bowl party on Harrison Drive.

(Thunder clap, with creepy music.)

Or *will* he?

There are a lot of things that could go wrong in this scenario.

How would the beans know for sure that Victor's the one who wants the calzones and Jeannie's the one who decided to say "no, make that three"?

If Sharon from the cube next door suddenly unplugs Jeannie's computer halfway through her order so she can plug in her CD player instead, though, what happens?

Will the order go through? Will the orders be ordered, will the credit card have already been charged? Will Jeannie get charged for pizzas she never gets?

Or worse?

Just having a plain old application doesn't necessarily mean that all those things happen correctly. All those requests from Jeannie, Victor, and the 420 other people sending in orders at the same time might easily end up confused in one big lump with no ability to tell where each order starts, where each ends, and who wants what. And of course since the Online World of the Internet is fraught with peril, wackiness could ensue at anytime, interrupting someone's order.

So without taking the Proper Precautions, something like this might happen.

Hi, I'm jeannie@vacation.com.

Hi, I'm victor@nextstep.com.

I'd like the Super Bowl Special, the calzone ten-pack.

Wait, make that three.

With mushrooms.

Delivered to 110 Harrison Drive tomorrow at 1 PM.

I'd like a large pepperoni pizza.

Delivered in the next hour to 42 --AGH!!! [Lenny Down the Hall Trips Over the Cord]

So Victor gets thirty calzones, with mushrooms (he hates mushrooms). Jeannie orders her pepperoni pizza but without mushrooms and the order goes through to inventory and the cooks make it but nobody delivers it because of Lenny interrupting the order.

Imagine now that this happens a whole bunch of times a day. You've got pissed off customers, inventory being debited when the ingredients weren't actually used, and all sorts of payments being taken when no product is given.

Antoine would have to call up Floyd and Jennifer and use some choice expletives. Primarily expletives that his customers would already be using on him.

Fortunately, Antoine can save his expletives for another time because any J2EE application server supports *data integrity.* And since Jennifer took advantage of J2EE's data integrity mechanisms, Antoine should never run into these problems. Phew. (It's about time Antoine caught a break.)

The primary way that J2EE supports data integrity is with transactions. Every J2EE server has a transaction manager whose job it is to create and monitor transactions.

Transactions encompass two aspects of keeping things straight:

- Making sure a transaction is done with all its atomic subparts or not at all (the transaction is committed or rolled back)
- Making sure a transaction is done with only its own atomic subparts and not accidentally mixed up with the atomic subparts of another transaction

Three Aspects of Transactions

There are three aspects of transactions, which we covered in the tragic tale of Jeannie and Victor's orders.

What a Transaction Is Made Of

A transaction is atomic. *Atomic* just means a single unit of work, composed of one or more steps that realllly need to be done together, or not at all. That's the definition; the next two are characteristics that transactions should have.

What Qualities a Transaction Has

A transaction should have these two qualities. It should be:

- Consistent – Making sure that each person's order gets completed, or else rolled back (all steps undone as if nothing ever happened). When Lenny tripped over the power cord, everything Jeannie had done to that point regarding pizza should have been wiped out, rolled back.

- Isolated – Making sure that each person's order is composed only of requests they've made, not mixed up with requests from other people. This is what went wrong when Victor got three of his calzone orders, instead of Jeannie getting three of her pizza orders. That was not good isolation.

Transactional Consistency

When you withdraw money from an ATM, one of two things should happen. The bank should deduct the money from your account and the ATM should spit out that money. You wouldn't like it very much if the bank deducted the amount but the machine didn't spit it out, and rightfully so. Likewise, the bank would go out of business rather quickly if the ATM spit out the money but didn't deduct it from your account. These two separate steps should count as a single step. In other words, these steps are *atomic*.

Consistent means that there is one of two possible outcomes, commit or rollback. A commit means the steps created some valid data. If the money gets deducted and the ATM spit it out, you'll have cash in hand and new account balance. A rollback means that the data returns to its original state. If the money doesn't get deducted or the ATM doesn't spit it out, then you get no cash and your balance doesn't change, just as if you hadn't visited the ATM at all.

Transactional Isolation

Isolated means that the steps within a transaction run independently from any other transaction. The completion of your transaction does not depend on another transaction outside of your control and doesn't get muddled with bits of other transactions.

If your spouse tries to check the account balance as you're doing the deduction step of your withdrawal transaction, your spouse's check account balance transaction will run as if no other transaction is running. If you walk away with cash and the amount is deducted from your account and then the bank's computers crash or they restart their systems, you'll still have your cash and the amount will remain deducted from your account.

Geek Note on Transactions Versus Sessions

If you really want to know

Transactions aren't to be confused with sessions. If you weren't confusing them, never mind. If you were, sessions have to do with the Web container tagging requests so that they're all recognized as coming from the same browser. Transactions mean that all tasks between the starttransaction *and the* endtransaction *are all done sequentially. Transactions mean recognizing that all your body parts should remain attached. Sessions mean recognizing that you are named Bob and it's you who keeps asking for the names of each of the aerobics instructors.*

How Transactions Work

Let's look a little closer at just how you take those things and hook'em up in that All Or Nothing mode. Commit or rollback.

How You Make Something a Transaction

How do you make something a transaction? Does the transaction fairy come along and wave a wand? Pretty much; the J2EE server is the transaction fairy, and your programmer who's hooking up your program to the server just shows the fairy where to go.

All the actions that are part of that main task are put in a sort of holding pen, and not actually written to the database until everything's been completed successfully. The data just hangs out in a bean until it's all done and done right. Once that happens, the container shrieks "Whoohoo!" and commits it all to the database.

The code itself is a little more complicated, but basically the programmer just types something that accomplishes this:

Example 16-1 Transaction pseudocode

```
log in the customer
get his name and address
transaction start
        record what they want to buy
        take their money
        send an email to the chair shipping department
        subtract the right amount from the inventory table
        give the customer a confirmation email
transaction end
```

Types of Transactions

This might not come up a lot but it's quick and easy just to learn the terms. There are three types of transactions: flat, nested and chained. Before you get too overwhelmed, or alternately get too excited, J2EE only supports flat transactions.

- With *flat* transactions, only one transaction can run at a time. If you (or the container) starts a second transaction the first transaction suspends and neither transaction affects the other. Flat transactions have either commit or rollback at the end only.
- With *nested* transactions, a second transaction will run as an inner transaction. Inner transactions do not effect other inner transactions. However, the inner transactions do affect the overall result of the outer transaction.
- *Chained* transactions are a lot like flat transactions except that commits can occur at various breakpoints within the transaction.

Transactions, the Transaction Manager, and the Database

The transaction manager, a part of every J2EE server, is dedicated to overseeing transactions. The transaction manager has no idea which parts or steps should run within a transaction, so you need to specify which parts of your application should go in a transaction. For example, should the transaction start in a servlet and then hand over a request to an EJB, or should the transaction be fully contained in the EJB?

You also have to decide whether you are going to bean-managed transactions (BMT), also known as *programmatic transactions*, or container-managed transactions (CMT), also known as *declarative transactions*.

- With BMT or *bean-managed transactions*, you write code to start and commit or rollback a transaction, wherever you need it. BMT offers the programmer more control but involves more work and tends to be harder to debug. Also changing the way a BMT bean handles a transaction requires changing your code, recompiling and redeploying.
- With CMT or *container-managed transactions* you mark each method with an attribute that tells the container what it should do when some client says hey, blah, invoking that method.

Note: It's easy to confuse all the container-managed things and bean-managed things. There's container-managed transactions, relationships, fields, and possibly in the near future container-managed hair salons or coffee shops.

Here in glorious technicolor detail are those very attributes. They cover all possible behaviors for transaction support on an EJB. The information is a little techy for this book but we're including them because they'll give you a sense of the kinds of things that you might or might not want to have happen in transaction. You apply them to methods in EJBs to make them work the way you want.

CMT allows you to change the attribute at deploy time. So you don't need to change the code or recompile like you did with BMT. You can just change the attribute in the deployment descriptor and redeploy.

In either case (CMT or BMT), the container takes care of the details of actually starting, committing and rolling back the participants involved in the transaction.

- The Required attribute – The container ensures that the method is invoked with a transaction. If the calling client does not have a transaction, then the container starts a transaction. If the calling client has a transaction, then the container passes the transaction to the method.

  Despite the wide array of attributes, most bean methods are labeled Required. This means that a transaction starts with the first call to a bean, is used by all other beans in this process, and the transaction ends when the original method runs.

- The Requires New attribute – The container always starts a new transaction when invoking this method. If the calling client has a transaction, the container suspends the transaction and starts a new one. This is not a nested transaction because the outcome of the new transaction has no impact on the suspended transaction. If the calling client does not have a transaction, then the container creates a new transaction and invokes the method.
- The Not Supported attribute – The method cannot handle a transaction. If the calling client has a transaction, then the container suspends the transaction before invoking the method. If the calling client does not have a transaction, the container invokes the method.
- The Supports attribute – The bean method accepts a transaction if available, but does not require the application server to create a new transaction. If the calling client has a transaction, the container propagates the transaction to the method. If the calling client does not have a transaction, then the container invokes the method.
- The Mandatory attribute – The calling client must have a transaction. If the calling client has a transaction, the container propagates the transaction to the method. If the calling client does not have a transaction, then the container throws a `javax.transaction.TransactionRequiredException`.

- The Never attribute – The bean is not expecting a transaction. If the calling client has a transaction, then the container throws `java.rmi.RemoteException`. If the calling client has no transaction, then the container just invokes the method.

Dirty Reads and Other Transactional Naughtiness

As any married person will tell you, or more so someone with kids, having other people messing with your stuff can be really annoying. There was plenty of milk around when you went to the grocery store, but now two hours later it's almost all gone. Your hairbrush is never where you left it. And so on.

Having multiple people accessing a database is kind of like that. You run into problems because lots of people are messing with the data all at the same time.

Here are the main things that go wrong. You can have dirty reads, non-repeatable reads, and phantom reads. Why do you care about any of the types of reads? It's a good idea to understand the complexity involved in multiple people accessing the database. For one thing, it helps you understand the complexity in writing the code to do that.

- A dirty read occurs when transaction A is changing some data and transaction B reads the changed data. *But* then transaction A does a rollback to change the data back to its original value. Transaction B has read a value that does not exist in the database.
- A non-repeatable read occurs when some data value is read twice within the same transaction. (The reading twice part is fine; it's something else that causes the problem.) Transaction A can read a value, then do some other stuff. In the meantime, transaction B could change the value of the data. When transaction A does the second read, it will get a different value for the same data.
- A phantom read is similar to non-repeatable reads. They can occur when transaction A does a select and gets no results, then does some other stuff. In the meantime, transaction B inserts rows that satisfy the select statement. When transaction A does the same select again, it will get back some results.

chapter 17

J2EE Security

Joe: "Why would a guy want to marry another guy?"
Jerry: "Security!"

Some Like It Hot

"The more they overthink the plumbing, the easier it is to stop up the drain."

Scotty, Star Trek III: The Search for Spock

Freedom and security. Always the big tradeoff, huh? It can slow things down, a lot, too, just like the line at the airport during the holidays, but all in all you probably want at least a little bit.

How do you decide how much security to have...and while we're at it, what does security mean? Is it just "yes you can" or "no you can't"? Do you have to log in for the security system to apply? Can't a big firewall and some nice McAfee software just take care of everything?

The Chapter in Brief

Authentication and authorization are a major basis of security. It means who are you, and now that we know who you are, what are you allowed to do? You can implement those two things *programmatically*, which means you just roll your own, or *declaratively*, which means you list what needs to happen and let the container figure out how to enforce it. You can also use firewalls to enforce security, which are basically an access control list for anything that wants to go from you to the outside world or vice versa. Encryption also helps; it makes it hard for people to peek at the data going to and from your system and see what it is.

Here's what we talk about in this chapter.

- *Authentication and Authorization*
- *Encryption*
- *Firewalls*
- *How J2EE's Component Structure Helps You Make Things Secure*
- *Complexity Means Less Security*
- *Security Is Hard*
- *Security and Tradeoffs*

Authentication and Authorization

The key phrase that comes to mind for security, going way back, is a guard yelling out "Who Goes There?"

Then the person who goes there responds, "Just me, John," or "Tis I, Tanya, Queen of the Elves," or whatever. The person might also provide a pass phrase, such as "The white owl flies at night" or "layoffs are just another word for nothing left to lose".

This is basically just an ID and password.

It's also *authentication*.

Authentication

Saying who you are is identification, and proving it is authentication.

But what does that get you? What does that get Tanya, Queen of the Elves? She already knew who she was, and now the guard knows it, too. That and $4.75 will let them share a mochalattecino at Starbucks.

Authentication isn't much fun without *authorization*.

Authorization

Now that the guard knows who Tanya is, there's Stuff He Can Let Her Do. Tanya, Queen of the Elves among other things gets to go upstairs to do anything she wants with the Elf King, Harry.

If the visitor had said, "I am but a poor foot soldier seeking shelter for the night," the guard might have said, "OK, fine, but you have to sleep inside the gates here but you can't go in any of the buildings.

That's *authorization*—where you're allowed to go and what you can do when you get there, based on who you were authenticated as.

When you log into Amazon with the right *authentication*, Amazon *authorizes* you to edit your reviews, your So You Want To lists, to add reviews to all products, to make recommendations if you've placed orders with Amazon before, and to just see everything else on the site. But you're not allowed to vote for your own book reviews or totally change the Amazon interface.

Much of security is simply about authentication and authorization. Well, perhaps not simply, but a lot of security is most definitely about those two things.

How This Is Applied in J2EE

You've got three things you need to secure in a J2EE application: the code on the Web tier, the code on the EJB tier, and the database.

Don't worry about the database right now. The database management system has tools of its own, and not J2EE specific. Essentially you can specify read, write, delete, and other rights for any table, field, and so on in your database.

So, moving on to J2EE security for the Web tier and the EJB tier. They both use the authentication and authorization system we've been discussing. Each sets up the system a little differently, but the same rules apply:

1. A system of authorization, which is called a *security realm*, and specifies what users there are, their passwords, and what roles they have. LDAP is a type of security realm.

Mark	qflioreref	Honcho
Jeannie	536oljifj	Minion
Simon	GGRgfrerw	Minion

2. A system of authentication, specified in the deployment descriptor. The following examples show the gist; the deployment descriptor format is a bit different and more complex.

   Web authentication specifies directories a user or role can go to

Admin	/wholewebapplication
User	/jsps/harmlessjsps

   EJB authentication specifies EJB methods a user or role can run

Admin	getShoppingCart, buyItems, deleteOrder, changeAllRights
User	getShoppingCart, buyItems

3. And third, a system to tie the systems together, since as you've probably noticed, the roles are Honcho and Minion in one file and Admin and User in another file.

Admin	Honcho
User	Minion

That's actually a good thing; it means that both systems, which you might have acquired at different times, and perhaps when your company was run in two different countries or under two owners, don't have to have exactly the same systems of roles. It also means that if you have a lot of different roles for your company intranet, like Minion, Peon, and Grunt, but that when it comes to the J2EE application they all have the same rights, you can just say

Peon	User
Grunt	User
Minion	User

and be done with it instead of setting up Peon, Grunt, and Minion in the J2EE application.

So, to sum up.

- The security realm included with the EJB container takes care of authentication. "This person says she's Jeannie and her password is ereWWWfdfds...yep, she's on the guest list and she's got the right password. And by golly, she's another one of those Peons."

- The container itself enforces the authorization that's set up in the deployment descriptor. And uses the mapping file between the security realm and the deployment descriptor to keep things straight.

The Web server says "Peon, Peon....oh right, that's a User. Good. Well, then, I'll let her go to that JSP she's heading for but she's in for some resistance if she tries to get to any of the JSPs in the /goldusers directory.

And the EJB container basically says the same thing, but finishes up with "I'll be damned if I'll let her run that changeAllPrices method. She's going to get that error page I love to show." Or, if Jeannie isn't trying to do anything naughty, "Sure, you can shop for pizzas. Go right ahead."

Note: Security *realm* is a pretty poor term for it. At least, it seems like that to use. Realm is a place you go, in real life, whereas realm in this context is just a list of logins and passwords. If the word realm is confusing you, then that just means you have a normal person's non computer science vocabulary.

Application server vendors like BEA and IBM provide their own security realms, which are recommended over the security realm included with the J2EE download.

Programmatic and Declarative Security

In general there are two ways to use all of this security stuff. There's programmatic and declarative. With either one, you need to set up roles and map the roles to users using the container's security tools. For instance, manager is a role, Antoine is a user, Antoine is a manager.

- Programmatic means you write code to check the role in the code and either allow the action or generate a security error. You're the one checking all the authorization. You wrote code to check to see if Fred is allowed to enter the kitchen and make pizzas.
- With declarative security, you list each servlet and JSP or EJB with the roles that are allowed to use them and the container does the rest.

The difference between declarative security and programmatic security is kind of like the difference between using basic body language gestures to communicate, and using language. Nodding, waving, and so on will definitely communicate some things, but if you want to be precise, you need spoken language.

Let's say you need to specify what kind of security Fred has in Antoine's application. With declarative security, you can say whether or not Fred can run the methods in the application. But one of the methods is getAccountBalance. If Fred is allowed to run that method to get his own balance, he can also run that method to get anyone's balance. That's where programmatic security needs to be used.

Encryption

Encryption keys, Secure Sockets Layer, HTTPS, and other technologies are big iron. Their goal is to make it unlikely that people hanging out, looking at that data going in and out of your site, will be able to tell what it really means and steal your customers' credit cards.

The simple definition of encryption (which is like mentioning the simple definition of string theory or quantum mechanics) is a way to make sure data going to and from your site is so goofed up that nobody except someone with the Goofy Decoder Ring can figure out what the data says.

There's more to it than that, of course, If we could cover encryption in a couple pages, we would be far too smart and full of ourselves to do anything but sit staring at our navels all day. That said, here's a very small gist of what encryption is.

When you were in grade school, multiplication came pretty easily, right, but division was a little harder? Likewise, getting the square of 5 is easy; getting the square root of 5 is harder. And integrals are a whole lot harder than derivatives. The common thread among these statements is that, with software and math as with toothpaste and gossip, things are typically harder to undo than to do. So we count on that and hope that undoing the encryption algorithm is just too hard to bother doing.

You've probably ran into references to 56-bit or 128-bit encryption. This refers to the length of the keys, the two encrypted "answer keys" that let you encrypt and decrypt the message. The longer they are, the longer it takes to hack. Longer doesn't mean it's unbreakable, but longer means you need to spend more time trying to break it.

Movies About Encryption

Rent Enigma. It's got Kate Winslet and some other people, and the story is a fictionalized account of the breaking of the German code in World War II. It's a lot like modern-day encryption but on big, big machines.

So yes, by all means, make sure that data sent to and from your site is encrypted in some way. All very easy to say, but how do you do encryption? Here's the short description of how to do it in J2SE and J2EE.

- In J2SE, you'd use the `Cipher` class to do the encryption by hand.
- In J2EE, you tell the deployment descriptor that you want encryption.

Firewalls

Firewalls aren't an inherent part of J2EE but they're a good idea so we're providing an overview of them here.

A firewall is essentially just an access control list for anything that wants to go from you to the outside world or vice versa. There are personal firewalls you can buy for your new XP machine, and big ones for an enterprise application. They operate on basically the same principle: keep everything out that doesn't have a legitimate errand.

You want a firewall between your enterprise application and the rest of the world. Not to keep your employees from emailing things out or going to the wrong Web sites. If they want to send out information, they can print it and stuff it in their lunchbags. You can't prevent information from leaving via your employees. Nope, what you need the firewall for, and what it can do, is to prevent people with Dishonorable Intentions from getting into your system.

Imagine that your application is a castle with the usual rooms. The torture dungeon is in the basement, the ladies in waiting hang out in the Green Room on the third floor, the mail room is supposed to be Turret 25, Turret 30, or Turret 125. The weapons room is Turret 12, Turret 15, and Turret 8080. And the thing about this scenario is, everyone knows where all of the rooms are. All the people building castles build them the same way; Turret 12 is always a weapons room.

Ivan the Terrible, your sworn enemy, knows this. He can knock at the door, carrying his big lance, and say, "Hi, I'm the new weapons manager. Let me into Turret 12, please." And without a smart gatekeeping sort of firewall guardian at the door, the idiot who's there instead will just say, "Um, OK." Ivan shows up at the door of Turret 12, shouts at the serfs and tells them to give him three cannons, seven swords and a nice big petard. And, being serfs, they just give it to him. And before you know it Ivan's shooting at screaming ladies in waiting running down the hall from the Green Room.

Here's one way around that. Turret 12, if unused, should never have been built in the first place, or should have been filled up with gruel and boarded up.

However, if you've got enough weapons activity to need it, then the gatekeeper should have been taught how to tell the difference between those who should get in, with legitimate business, and those who shouldn't.

You can do this teaching in two ways.

- Set up a way for the gatekeeper to know that Ivan is, in fact, Terrible. The multiple facial scars, the human bones woven into his hair, or the "Kiss Me, I'm Terrible" tshirt. Something like that. That's called, in the ancient feudal terms, a packet-filtering router. It checks out requests based on where they're from. This doesn't mean you don't let people in; you might let Ivan visit the Anger Counselor. But not the weapons room.
- The other approach is to say, "OK, Ivan, what do you want?" And when he responds, you just pass on the request to the other gatekeeper within the gates. That gatekeeper evaluates the request for reasonableness and safety with great deliberateness (which of course takes time and Ivan is getting impatient). Then that person, if the request is reasonable, handles the request and then hands it back. This person, again in the ancient feudal terms, is a proxy server. Ivan thinks he's already at the weapons room, but in fact someone else is taking care of things for him.

  A proxy server is particularly useful for protecting against a sneaky attack where the attacker pretends to be legitimate. For instance, let's say Ivan discovers that if as a legitimate user he asks the serfs for ten thousand sword tassels, one at a time, they get really confused and end up giving him a sword, to boot. Because of a weird mental bug or something in the serfs, or just from being really stupid. The odds of the serfs and the proxy server both being confused in the same way by the same request are really low, however, so a proxy server is excellent protection against this type of attack.

Here's how this applies to a firewall and protecting your application. There are servers in your enterprise, like email servers, that have standard ports, just as the turrets in the example were always assigned to certain things. Mail is always on a specific port, POP is always on a specific port. Someone can send a request to your application, ask for port XYZ, and potentially be admitted if there's no firewall. Your firewall, however, knows that there's nothing happening on that port and no one should be using it. And if the unauthorized request tries to get to the actual port being used for mail, then the mail server, seeing what this request wants to do, knows that's not allowed and whacks it.

How J2EE's Component Structure Helps You Make Things Secure

Think about trying to get your life together and accomplish all those goals you have including losing weight, starting your own business, and getting on Jeopardy.

A little overwhelming, to say the least.

Now, think about going to that seminar on starting your own business.

That's a little more manageable.

As with life, so with security. It's easier to secure a bean than an application.

It's easier to focus on a small task. And since any J2EE application is broken up into nice little components (when you do it right), therefore security for a Java system is a bit easier because of that.

J2EE applications are very *componentized*, due to the whole separation of concerns thing, the EJB structure, and the object-oriented nature of Java. This means that, if you've followed these guidelines and made an application that's got a lot of separate components working well together, you can build differing levels of security around different parts of the application. Kind of like how there might be just a big wall around a particular fiefdom but a moat around the castle itself, or only Very Authorized People can use the executive washroom.

This is another good reason for separation of presentation and business logic. Because, in the end, does it really matter if someone hacks your JSPs and writes "Antoine's Pizza sux!" on your main login page? Loss of dignity of course, and it means that those jerks over at Vinnie's pizza need to have their corporate van egged, but other than that, not a big deal. You haven't lost any data, and you also haven't been slowing down performance with an unnecessary level of security on your JSPs. You don't need as much security on your presentation logic as on your business logic. All in all, the lighter security on the presentation logic of Antoine's site was a decent tradeoff of convenience and performance against the loss incurred.

If you
really want
to know

This would be a good time to talk about granularity, component model, *and related buzzwords. J2EE uses the component model approach to things, where there are a bunch of separate things that go together in a bunch of different ways, kind of like the Garanimals approach to clothing. (Garanimals is a brand of children's clothing that offer separate shirts, shorts, skirts, etc. that all coordinate.) Only with even more granularity, meaning you'd be able to pick a sleeve, a collar, and a body, and mix and match. The more parts in a whole, the more granularity, and having a bunch of parts in a whole is a component model.*

An application that's made up of a bunch of distinct components would have a high degree of granularity for security. Instead of one big wad of security that you throw at the system, you can have different security settings for every bean.

Another reason that componentization is good for security is that just because someone might get into bean A when they're not supposed to, bean B is secured too. So getting to A doesn't necessarily mean they get to B. Components mean extra lines of defense.

Complexity Means Less Security

If you always know where your keys are, then that's secure.

However, if you have five sets of keys and seventeen purses and two houses, then it's hard to know where you might have left your keys.

Let's say you've got a really complicated automatic snow removal system in your house in Aspen. It's really, really complicated. Boilers and sliding driveways and all that. And you're supposed to let some of the security guys get to the snow removal control room. But what you don't realize since the snow removal system is so complicated is that once you're into the control room, you can get into the whole house.

Now expand that several orders of magnitude. You have a complicated J2EE application that Floyd designed for you and which he really doesn't understand.

How are you going to secure something when you don't really know how it works?

So simplicity is good. You might get some ultra uber alpha geeks who like to be complex and do complex things so that everyone else will think they're amazingly smart. Well, no. Not might. You will run into these people. But they're Bad. It's easy to be complicated. Simplicity and clarity take work.

If you
really want
to know

Geek Note: Security by Obscurity

You might have heard the phrase security by obscurity. *OK, it rhymes, and that's fun but it's not a good approach to security. It just means the attitude toward security is that if something's complicated, surely no one will figure out how to infiltrate it, right? This statement is usually accompanied by a naive smile.*

Security Is Hard

Security is hard. It just is. Keep that in mind whenever you feel a little overwhelmed. People who are incredibly techy, who carelessly do differential equations in their head or throw together a little content management system on their coffee breaks, blanche and make up lame excuses when told that they need to work on security.

Security and Tradeoffs

Your application can never be absolutely secure, and still be running, just as you can never be absolutely secure unless you live in a locked room and never leave it.

Really high security also really slows things down. At airports and in J2EE. So consider what's important to you.

In general, keep things secure *enough* so that the effort required to break in and take or damage the information and systems you're protecting, exceeds the benefit of obtaining control of the information and services.

chapter 18

Internationalization

"It's like those French have a different word for everything."

Steve Martin, Wild and Crazy Guy

Depending on how much you're learning at this point, you're probably not thinking much about internationalization. That's how it often goes, and then when things get going bigtime with your business, and you want to expand to Belgium, it's like pulling teeth to get your application reworked to function internationally. But you know, no matter what country you live in, there are more people outside it than in it. So it's probably worth thinking about ahead of time.

Given that, what does J2EE give you? Does the spec just say "think about internationalization" or are there some actual tools or processes to use?

The Chapter in Brief

With luck, someday all of us will be big in Japan. Or Norway or Canada or somewhere that's considerably different from where we are now. J2EE gives you tools for internationalization, including ways to package up a whole different user interface or at least a bunch of different labels for fields. (The label for the OK button is usually the same but the rest needs translation.)

Planning ahead will make accommodating international differences, whether in language or currency or fundamentally how text is represented, less painful.

Here's what we talk about in this chapter.

- *Getting That Certain Je Ne Sais Quoi When You Don't Know What It Is*
- *What You Might Internationalize*
- *Bundles of Tools and APIs for Internationalizing*

Getting That Certain Je Ne Sais Quoi When You Don't Know What It Is

Antoine wants his pizza shop to go international. He can ship flash-frozen pizzas all over the globe. But can his application handle it? Well, only if his international customers can read and understand English. The application, including the GUI (labels, buttons and text), is all in English. Antoine wasn't thinking about selling his pizzas all over the globe when he first started. The developers hardcoded this information and it won't be easy to change.

Internationalization means that the application can automatically display the correct language based on the computer's configuration. That is, if you were on a computer in Italy and the application supported Italian, then it would automatically display in Italian. It is also quite simple to later add support for additional languages without having to change the code.

Geek Note in Internationalization Jargon

If you
really want
to know

Programmers with their eye for abbreviations often write I18n *instead of* internationalization.

The decision to internationalize an application needs to be done long before coding. If a customer doesn't decide one way or another then the decision usually falls to the architect. The architect would do a cost-benefit analysis. In other words, would the gain in flexibility be worth the effort, even if the flexibility is not used for internationalization? If the answer is yes, then you'll be happy to know that Java technology provides easy to use and powerful internationalization tools and APIs.

You could even use Java's internationalization tools if you weren't going to support multiple languages. Instead of using internationalization for language or cultural support, you could use it to easily create multiple sets of functionality. That is, using the capabilities of internationalization, you could change the user interfaces within an application without having to change existing code. Using Java's internationalization tools this way, would allow you to create multiple products for a lower cost.

What's Localization?

If you
really want
to know

You might have heard the term localization. *Internationalization is not the same as localization although they are related. Internationalization refers to creating a program that does not have information cultural or language information hard coded into it. Localization, on the other hand, is the process of taking an internationalized program, and configuring it to run in a particular regional or cultural environment.*

The application you're internationalizing would contain code to select a resource bundle at runtime. It can search for the bundle for a particular region and if it doesn't find the one that it is looking for, it can default to whatever is available. So if you were to run the application in Italy and it didn't support Italian (that just means it didn't have a resource bundle with the Italian translations) then it could still run and display English.

What You Might Internationalize

What things within the application should change when it runs in another country? The most obvious thing that needs to change is the language. The application needs to display any text (labels, buttons, messages, etc.) in the language within the region it is running. This includes not only text messages but also numbers. If you are the international sort, you'll quickly realize that numeric formats also need to change.

For example, 1,000 means one-thousand in the US but in other countries it may mean 1 with three decimal places of zero (or 1.000 if you are in the US). And what does 10/1/2003 mean to you? Well that all depends on where you live. It could mean October 1, 2003 or January 10, 2003. So you'll need to internationalize date formats. Currency symbols are another area that needs internationalization; not only the symbol but also the position of the symbol. Other countries use different symbols and some countries put the currency symbol after the number.

You might even choose to internationalize things like colors and other symbols to match cultural preferences. Even the code itself may need to be internationalized. Another, less obvious, thing to internationalize is algorithms. Tax systems and legal rules differ rather considerably from country to country.

Bundles of Tools and APIs for Internationalizing

You get quite a few tools in Java, just plain old Java, for internationalization. Lots of classes. The major ones are the ResourceBundle, Properties, Locale, java.text package, InputStreamReader and OutputStreamWriter classes. You also get Unicode, which we'll explain later.

ResourceBundle

You'll find ResourceBundle described as a way to put together a bunch of unique keys and values, or as a way to put together *key-value pairs*. For instance, you could internationalize the *key* okbuttontext and the corresponding *value* OK. When you're internationalizing, you'll need to put a lot of things in your resource bundle. OK might fly as the label for your OK button but the words for the Cancel, Enter, First Name, and other buttons and labels will likely be entirely different.

Put more simply, ResourceBundle is just a big empty Java class that you fill in with the international values you need. Then you just plug it in and boom, your application is internationalized.

If you
really want
to know

Geek Note on What You Can Put in Resource Bundles

The resource bundle doesn't have to contain strings (text) only. The key will be text. However, the resource bundle can hold any object, including entire user interfaces. In fact, primitive types such as integers (plain old whole numbers) or booleans (true/false values) are the only thing that you can't put in a resource bundle.

You can get around that restriction by using the wrapper classes, but we're not going to get into that. Just know that it's not an actual barrier to a Savvy Programmer.

The Properties Class

The application you're internationalizing would contain code to select a resource bundle at runtime. It can search for the bundle for a particular region and if it doesn't find the one that it is looking for, it can default to whatever is available. So if you were to run the application in Italy and it didn't support Italian (that just means it didn't have a resource bundle with the Italian translations) then it could still run and display English. The APIs do this; you only have to ask.

The Properties class is simply a type of *hash table*. A hash table is a collection that consists of key-value combinations, organized into "buckets" for fast searching. It's the programming equivalent of things that, if you were writing about them in a document, you'd put in a Rolodex. Like lists of employee IDs and employee names.

The Properties class holds objects that you can retrieve using a key. It's similar to a resource bundle but with a different implementation. Although you can use the Properties class for your own purposes, at startup the Java virtual machine (JVM) creates and initializes a single instance that contains system properties that you can use to help in your effort to internationalize. With these properties you can retrieve a number of known values. These values are things like the host platform operating system, version of the JVM, the vendor of the JVM and lots of other useful information. You can also use the system properties to set your own values at the command line or read them from a text file. This feature makes the Properties class especially useful for configuring local machines.

The Locale Class

A *locale* represents a set of cultural and language preferences. The locale has either two or three parts.

- The first and most significant part is the language code.

- The second part is the country code. The country code fine tunes the language. For example, both the US and Britain would have a language code of English but because there are a number of variations between each you can supply additional localization information (like spelling and currency) with the country code.
- The third part describes the host machine: UNIX, Windows, Macintosh, etc.

When your application supports and uses a Locale instance, other Java classes automatically benefit from this because they rely on a locale object to provide the most appropriate information. For example, the Calendar class uses the locale to decide what default behavior is required when presenting dates.

Unicode

The Java platform uses Unicode to represent text. Unicode is not class. It's a standardized way to represent textual information. Java uses Unicode because it can support almost any modern language, and quite a few ancient ones. Just because Java can support Greek text doesn't mean that your operating system can. In other words, the host operating system must be able to display the characters that your application represents. If your application uses a character that represents a Greek character, it will only display correctly if the host operating system supports the correct font. As long as the users set up their computers to work with their languages, this shouldn't be an issue.

One exception is that you might receive a file from a user in a different country and your application will read and interpret it correctly. However, because you don't have the correct fonts installed, you wouldn't be able to read or edit the file.

We've talked about how there are differences in the presentation of dates, numbers and the currency symbols. The classes that address these issues are in the java.text package. These classes include MessageFormat, NumberFormat, and DateFormat to name a few. The classes in the java.text package reply on a Locale class. If you don't supply a locale class then a default locale will be used.

chapter 19

Good J2EE Architecture

"Logic clearly dictates that the needs of the many outweigh the needs of the few."

Spock, Star Trek II: The Wrath of Khan

"The needs of the one outweighed the needs of the many."

Captain Kirk, Star Trek III: The Search for Spock

"And did you exchange a walk-on part in the war for a lead role in a cage?"

Roger Waters, Pink Floyd: Wish You Were Here

We all had a good laugh at Floyd's expense in the example of Antoine's online pizza application, didn't we? The thing is, he's not *that* unusual, and he wasn't all *that* dumb. How do you make a good application that interacts well with other elements like the server, the firewall, the network? How do make sure that the application runs "fast enough" or that it's "secure enough"? At some point the code details fade away and you have to make sure that when this thing runs, it's *good.* To put it simply. And of course how do you make sure you write an application that lets you add on and expand as your business grows?

The Chapter in Brief

When you plan how to write an application, you need to consider how to get the characteristics out of it that are the most important. And you need to let go of characteristics that while appealing are less important. For instance, you can't be really, really fast and really, really cheap. In life or in an application. You need to choose. Some of the things that help you do the planning and implement your planning decisions are design patterns, problems and solutions that recur a fair amount in applications, and UML, a standard set of diagrams for writing down exactly what the application will look like, from the top level on down to the methods and attributes. These help you think about the application and discuss it with others. The more accurately and more quickly you can communicate with others about software design, the fewer horror stories your development process will be. Or if you're trying to understand how an existing system works, being able to read the design schematics will help tremendously.

Here's what we talk about in this chapter.

- *There's More to Life Than Performance*
- *Qualities of Service (QOS): What's Most Important in an Application*
- *Getting the Right Qualities of Service Through a Good Architecture*
- *If you think that the answer to both of these questions just might be yes, turn to the next chapter to be not at all surprised.So Now That You Know What To Do, How Do You Communicate It?*

There's More to Life Than Performance

We talked before about the whole decision-making thing, in Chapter 7, "Does a Cup of J2EE in the Morning Always Smell Like Victory?" on page 79. How do you decide whether to use J2EE, and if you do use it, what elements do you use? One point we touched on there in the discussion of stateful session beans is that it's not always about performance. Just doing it fast isn't always best, especially if you can't do it reliably. There's a whole big world of qualities of service to evaluate, and performance is only one of them.

Let's say you've more or less decided *how* to code your application. Servlets and JSPs with the occasional stateless session bean. Your how is decided. Are you done planning?

Not so much. You need to decide how *well* should your application do its job.

That sounds kind of stupid, at first. You want it to do its job well. Duh. That, however, isn't really possible when you take a closer look. There are a lot of different qualities of service that your application can maintain more or less well. For instance, do you decide to have a really secure J2EE application, by implementing the J2EE security support features? Do you want your application to be really fast, too? And always be available no matter what? And incredibly reliable so that it's always absolutely correct?

Sorry, that's not an option. You want performance? You might have to sacrifice a little reliability. You want security? Get ready to sacrifice some performance.

It's similar to the process you go through when you decide to buy a car. You know it's going to transport you and baggage while burning fuel. But how's it going to perform those functions? You determine that by figuring out what's important: low price? gas mileage? room? power? status symbol? Those are a car's quality of service requirements. If gas mileage is the most important, then power drops lower on your list; if status symbol is the most important then low price drops off your list. Some of the items aren't mutually exclusive, of course; there are some cheap largeish cars with decent gas mileage. But a $12,000 high-mileage status symbol with an incredibly smooth ride and a V8 doesn't exist.

Qualities of Service (QOS): What's Most Important in an Application

Note: Qualities of service are also referred to as *service-level requirements.*

What qualities of service you choose depend on what's important to you. In general, what you *have* to have takes priority over what you'd *like* to have. A J2EE architect can talk to you or the end user of the application to get these priorities and translate the results into a blueprint for the application, for your development team to implement.

These qualities of service are sometimes referred to by the J2EE In Crowd as the "ilities." Because they're scalab*ility*, extensib*ility*, etc. They aren't all the exclusive domain of J2EE, but they're all things a good application needs that J2EE helps you achieve, from providing a good set of tools to enforcing through services from the server.

Here are the options you have with a J2EE system.

- Performance – Speed, of course. However, you can measure it in different ways. You can measure how long it takes one user to do her job, or how many users can be processed per hour. Not the same thing.
- Scalability – The application can handle increased load without rewriting the application, and ideally without buying new hardware.
- Reliability – The system won't gack on you or your customers periodically, such as not processing some orders, and leaving the accounts with the wrong balances.
- Availability – The application is up and running all the time, or as much as it needs to be, and the users can get to it.
- Extensibility – You can add new features without rewriting the entire system. This includes flexibility and portability: how easy is it to change the platform, switch to another operating system, cluster it, scale it, change databases.
- Maintainability – You can just go into one part of the system and fix it without breaking the entire system.

  This is kind of a catchall but given the rapid development and huge amount of postrelease development these days, maintainability is more like normal development.
- Manageability – This is more accurately called monitorability, but nobody calls it that. It means your system administrator can keep an eye on the application's CPU usage, memory usage, etc., and accurately add memory, machines, extra servers, or whatever else is necessary when the system needs better performance, scalability, and other characteristics.

  It also means that when your server vendor sends out service packs, patches, and so on, that you need to be able to make those updates and keep your application running too.
- Security – Code with Dishonorable Intentions can't get in and do nasty things, and Susie Peon can't get to the `changeAllPrices` method in your `Price` session bean.

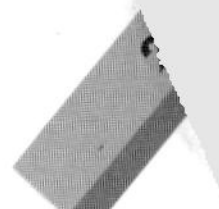

Performance

What it is This is easy to understand: how fast after clicking on "put this in my shopping cart" do the socks get put in the customer's shopping cart? It's usually measured in terms of how many simultaneous users a system can handle and still give a response in a reasonable amount of time; you specify your requirements for X simultaneous users and Y maximum response time; you might require that the system be able to handle 100 simultaneous users and always give each user a response in three seconds or less.

For a pizza shop you might want to be able to handle 5 simultaneous customer orders and get them their pizza in 15 minutes or less. You will need 5 people at the counter, enough ovens, pizzamakers and ingredients to make at least 5 pizzas at a time (assuming the average customer orders one pizza).

Then you figure out what you need to do in terms of hardware, software, network functions, etc., to achieve that.

How to get it Really good coding and design! (Is that all?) Anything can affect performance. Key factors of course are memory and CPU processing speed.

Another iffy angle for increasing performance that you'll hear about is using bean-managed persistence (BMP). Your programmers should be pretty good at their jobs to pull this off better than the container. Containers are getting smarter and faster all the time. You might want to think long and hard about using BMP since it means you lose the flexibility of changing databases without changing code. It's not generally a good idea unless the performance tradeoff is really huge and can't be achieved any other way. Or you might go with BMP if the goal is performance at any cost and you don't give a rat's posterior about database flexibility and maintenance.

You can also achieve performance, as well as scalability and a few of the other qualities of service coming up in this section, through the resource management built into J2EE:

- Bean pooling means you've always got an entity bean sitting there waiting to service your session bean, so there's no expensive performance overhead in doing the work on the spot and waiting for it to be done.
- Connection pooling means the same thing; there's always a connection to the database waiting, ready for the container.
- You also have passivation and activation, which is kind of like when, on "Who's Line Is It, Anyway?" one of them smacks the other and says "Sleep!" and they lie down and don't have to improvise for a while.

Getting it means you might not get as much Anything else. Performance is always a tradeoff with the rest of the *ility* crowd.

Scalability

What it is Scalability is the ability for the application to handle additional user load *without modification*. That means you don't touch the code itself, you just install more hardware or instances of the EJB container and boom, you're back up to standard performance speed.

Scalability also means, ideally, handling increased load without throwing away the existing hardware and getting something enormous instead. You don't want to have to throw away perfectly good hardware just because your total need is higher; you want to be able to just add to your current hardware.

How to get it J2EE is structured so that you can do this just by doing J2EE right. Using the right application server helps. Some support using multiple copies of themselves on multiple machines; others don't.

The deployment descriptor helps. Many of the issues that affect scalability are set up there, like the number of database connections you keep around. Just edit that deployment descriptor in a text file and you're scalable.

Passivation and activation, mentioned earlier, also help.

Another aspect of J2EE structure that enables scalability is that objects—servlets, beans, whatever—can be on different machines, communicating with each other via RMI. So you can bring in more hardware, take a sackful of beans and put them on that new machine, and your performance goes up again without your having to rewrite the application.

Getting it means you might not get as much Money. It adds to complexity, thereby reducing maintainability and manageability. Complexity is the negative result of taking advantage of scalability.

Reliability

What it is It means that as the demands on your application increase, as much of the time as possible, it does all tasks absolutely correctly, and always completes them. You want extremely high reliability in things like air traffic control systems. It's not so important for online chess games. (It would be annoying to have your whole game go up in flames, of course, but you would still be alive.)

How to get it Absolute reliability typically requires a very uptight approach to transactions (pessimistic locking). You also need a whole bunch of "back it up as you go along" work, so that if the system crashes it can pick up from where it died when it restarts. Both of these can really hammer performance.

Getting it means you might not get as much Performance. As you can tell as you stand in line to get on your plane, around the holidays. But if security is important, then that's the tradeoff you choose to make. You can add servers and hardware and other techniques explained in the scalability and performance sections to alleviate the performance reduction.

Availability, or Being Highly Available

What it is This means the system is never down for maintenance, or at least it never appears to be, even at 3:00 in the morning.

How to get it Clusters, clusters, clusters. This means that you can pull out the BEA WebLogic Server CD from the box and install the server two or three more times, each on separate machines. And when one of the running instances of that server application gacks, one or more of the others take over. The official term is failover.

This isn't the same as scalability, where the servers all working at once. This is all of them waiting to do just one job; when one fails, another one takes over that server's job.

Getting it means you might not get as much Well, you might have to buy extra licenses to run those extra instances. You'll also need to buy those extra machines.

Extensibility

What it is This is the ability to add functionality without impacting the system, kind of like adding a CD player or a ski rack to your car. Wouldn't it be annoying if you had to do significant engine and body work just to put in a tape player?

How to get it A good J2EE system is very componentized; lots of little bits of code, all doing very small things and being managed by the container. You can also enable extensibility with a good design pattern. Basically, just write a good Java program. Appropriately use multiple tiers, object orientation, separation of concerns, and so on.

Getting it means you might not get as much Random fun cowboy coding. It means you have to plan well, in detail, and you can't let the programmers just dash off cool bits of code any way they like. It means you're a team of obedient synchronized swimmers, not a bunch of Michael Jordans. It might also reduce performance.

Maintainability

What it is Correcting flaws without impacting the system.

How to get it Again, just by doing nicely componentized planning and coding, as with extensibility. Following the guidelines of separation of concerns and multiple tiers gives you good maintainability.

The deployment descriptor also helps here. There are lots of things that you can change about an application by making adjustments to the deployment descriptor. This helps with maintainability because you may not have to recompile and redeploy an application to make changes. Depending on what you want to change, you might only need to change something in the deployment descriptor.

Getting it means you might not get as much Scalability. If you need high maintainability, you'll want to think twice about what machines and servers you add in the cause of scalability. Complexity reduces maintainability.

Manageability

What it is This is really about monitoring; it's monitorability rather than manageability.

How to get it Just use the monitoring application that you get with your J2EE server. Most server vendors have a program with a graphical interface that lets you set the number of database connections you keep around, see what performance is like in various conditions, and so on.

Getting it means you might not get as much If you need high maintainability, you'll want to think twice about what machines and servers you add in the cause of scalability. Complexity reduces maintainability.

Most application server vendor system have built-in controls for their systems. See *Server Configuration Tools for Setting Up All This* on page 201.

Security

What it is Everybody's doing what they should and nothing's doing what it shouldn't.

How to get it Again, you can get some of this just by writing good Java code. You can also implement systems like security realms and firewalls that were covered in the security chapter.

Getting it means you might not get as much Performance. See the performance section for ways to address this.

Getting the Right Qualities of Service Through a Good Architecture

So you've evaluated your qualities of service and now you know that you want a cup of performance, a quart of reliability, and a pint of maintainability.

How do you get it? Do you mark the "high reliability, medium performance" checkbox in your server configuration setup window?

Well, that would be nice. But until that feature is implemented, you get a good architect to plan your application at a high level. Then you just implement it according to that plan.

Good Architects Make Good Applications

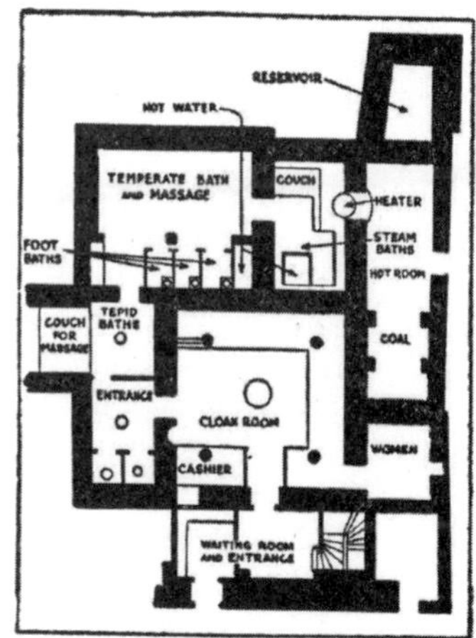

An architect is most concerned with the overall system, and focuses on qualities of service. The architect answers questions like: How many servers are needed? What kind of hardware can be used given the budget and requirements? How can I get the system to support thousands of users with 24x7 availability given this hardware? The architect needs to know the *capabilities* of many different technologies but not necessarily how to code.

A regular architect is going to figure out what kind of walls you need to support the weight of a roof for a Colorado ski condo that might be under 6 feet of snow at a time. A software architect is going to figure out what hardware and software and networking will handle the load of a business that does most of its business at Christmas with spurts in June and August, and doesn't really care if some orders get goofed up because Christmas ornaments are not a life and death situation.

What's Design, and What's Architecture?

A lot of very smart experienced people are very fuzzy on the difference between design and architecture. Here's our take on it.

We already defined an architect. Here's what the designer does. The designer is concerned with the details of the system. The designer works with the plan the architect creates, and must create the software that works within the system. Designers know the APIs that are going to be used and create the class diagrams (see Chapter 20, "Design Patterns and UML," on page 235). The designer creates classes using those APIs and determines how they will interact to create the application. The designer answers questions like: When a user clicks a button which class will respond to that event? What role will servlets play in the application? Which classes will interact with the database?

Architects don't necessarily know how to write code. It doesn't hurt, but they're big picture people. Designers, on the other hand, should be darned familiar with the Java API.

So Now That You Know What To Do, How Do You Communicate It?

You've got a great architecture. You've got a fabulous design. How do you tell people what it is so that they can then go off and do it? Do you put together some notes on napkins, hand them off to your designers and programmers, and say "Make it like this."?

Would reams and reams of complex verbal descriptions be a good way to say how to do the work? That might do the job in the end but it'd be like jogging in molasses to read it or write it.

Might there just possibly be a way to communicate software architecture in, oh, a preexisting set of diagrams? A modeling language?

There just might be one.

Here's another question. You're putting together a call center application or an online shopping application. You might or might not be doing revolutionary projects but you're just writing code. You're making objects. You're dealing with the network. You're not on entirely new ground. And remember that no matter how fabulous your team, you will run into some problems somewhere in the development, testing, and/or deployment process.

Is it possible there are people who've made applications like yours, and had issues like the ones you will inevitably encounter? Absolutely yes. Is it possible that they've written down the problems and solutions for other people to follow?

If you think that the answer to both of these questions just might be yes, turn to the next chapter to be not at all surprised.

chapter 20

Design Patterns and UML

"When instructions are cryptic, people get hurt."

Xander, Buffy the Vampire Slayer

Given the trouble that a lot of people have just showing up for the right meeting at the same time, despite all those emails and the handy dandy electronic scheduling application, how in the world do you make sure everyone on your team knows what they're supposed to be doing on the big J2EE application you're writing?

Sending out an email in all caps saying MAKE SURE YOU DO THAT THING WE DECIDED LAST WEEK ABOUT RESOURCE POOLING is not going to be enough. Having some long-suffering techwriter take notes and send them out again is not enough.

You need two things: a common vocabulary for how to talk about software design and architecture, and a way to write it down using that language. Oh, and if you had the experience of thousands of programmers who've already come across the problems you're having and the solutions they used, that would be cool too.

How do you get that?

The Chapter in Brief

This chapter is about two things: first, it's about the *reusable solutions* that design patterns give you. It's also about the *shared vocabulary* for talking and writing about software design that patterns and UML give you.

Design patterns are reusable solutions to common coding problems, such as how do you deal with making lots of different objects without bringing performance to a crawl. UML, or unified modeling language, is used for many things but one of the uses is showing a software architecture design.

Patterns and UML aren't inherent to J2EE or to any particular technology. However, they're extremely useful. Going into a J2EE project or any other enterprise project without a well understood, well recorded plan is like going off into the mountains in winter without a good book on surviving in the woods, or without even knowing which way is north. It's a big project and you need to not only know what you're doing but how to tell other people about it.

Here's what we talk about in this chapter.

- *Design Patterns*
- *Meeting Room Wallpaper: UML Diagrams*

Design Patterns

Patterns aren't an inherent part of J2EE but given the size and power of a J2EE system and the certain horror of just heading into it without a plan, patterns are generally a good idea.

Design patterns are a set of general plans for building applications that developers, after many years of painful mistakes, have decided is the best approach for a particular type of application, or feature of an application.

A Real Life Design Pattern

How often do you go grocery shopping?

Probably not every day. You probably have a shopping list, maybe a small whiteboard on your fridge that you write on, and when you figure it's worthwhile to make a trip to the grocery store or you discover an item you really really need, you make a trip. You probably take a car so you don't have to lug everything back by hand.

That's a pattern. It's a pattern because it's a reusable solution to a recurring problem (you need to eat). And it's reusable because a lot of people do this despite living in different places, buying different groceries, going to different stores, and so on.

Software developers, while faced with problems somewhat more complicated than a grocery trip, also use patterns to put together applications intelligently.

Software Design Pattern: Proxy

Here's an example. A design pattern used in J2EE is the *proxy pattern*.

- In real life, a proxy could be an assistant who's authorized to do what you do (meet with clients, sign documents) while you're busy on the golf course or meeting with different clients.
- A proxy might be your personal ad on match.com. You personally are not going to walk around the greater metropolitan area handing out flyers about yourself and your turnons and turnoffs since that would take a lot of time and be kind of risky, but the virtual you online has all the time in the world and can't be harmed.
- Or you could look at a restaurant and see the waiters as the chef's proxies. The chef is busy chopping and grilling but designates a few of her functions like taking orders and grinding pepper from a BF pepper grinder to the waiters.

With the proxy pattern you create an interface containing the proxy methods. That just means you write up a list of the methods that a proxy class would have to have in it. (Bear with us; this'll make more sense in a bit.) You then create a proxy class and the real subject class which contain implementations of this interface. The client then calls the method on the proxy object which then calls a method on the real object.

The proxy pattern is more work to set up initially (as with most design patterns) but means more productivity and security when the application is running.

We'll go into a little more detail on that restaurant example. For example, if you the client are ordering a meal at a restaurant, you call the `orderMeal` method. You call this method on the waiter, a.k.a. the proxy. The waiter then walks to the kitchen and tell the Chef (real subject), "Hey, `orderMeal (tofuCurry, beefWellington)`. You eventually get your meal without ever knowing or caring where the meal came from or how it was created.

Patterns Are Not Just What to Do But Also How to Talk About It

If you wanted to talk about the concept of a proxy before you read the last page or so, how would you have done it? You would have had to describe it, talk about creating an intermediary who could do stuff while the main object was busy, and it might have taken the whole meeting. And at the end you might not even be sure that everyone knew what you meant.

However, you and the pattern-using world know the word and concept *proxy*. So instead of going on for hours you can just say "This is a job for the Proxy pattern," and your boss could say, "Good point; with a bunch of proxy objects we could really increase performance" and before you know it you've got the corner office and a new car.

Meetings are horribly long now. Just think how long they'd be if we didn't have the names of patterns to use. They're worthwhile just for that.

Learning About Patterns

All right, so there are patterns and they're good when used appropriately and the shared vocabulary helps reduce meeting time and risk of misunderstandings. How do you find out about what patterns there are? You buy a patterns book: *Design Patterns*, *Core J2EE Design Patterns*, or if there's someone you find interesting on your design team, *Dating Design Patterns*.

So How Do I Know Which Pattern to Use?

How do you know which pattern to use? Is there one most common pattern? Is it possible to apply different patterns or is there one that's always right?

That's the sixty-four million Euro question. Architecture is an art, not a science. You get smart people and you make them prototype and you hope it all works.

With patterns as with J2EE in general: use patterns only if you have a problem to solve that's more complicated than the pattern you use to solve the problem.

Meeting Room Wallpaper: UML Diagrams

Note: UML is used for things besides software, but we focus on software here.

The most common way to model design patterns and to do design in general is to use the Unified Modeling Language (UML). UML is to software as those musical notes and scores are to music, or as blueprints are to architecture.

You wouldn't write music with a lot of words, like "OK, now wait for four beats and then go up to D#." You write using musical notation. Likewise you wouldn't design a house by writing "when you go around the corner, there's some pipe about four feet in." You use blueprints.

So you use a notation system for software because writing it all up in words is painful and inefficient. And the same picture can be understood by people who speak different languages, whereas words need translation.

What Kinds of Things Are Shown in UML Diagrams?

There are a lot of things you can represent in a software diagram: classes, processes, computers, users, etc. Classes show up a lot, so we'll illustrate one here. Any class in a diagram has a name, and optionally its attributes and its methods. Figure 20-1 illustrates a class with both attributes and methods. Sometimes you might see the class name and attributes but no methods; methods but no attributes; or only the class name.

Customer
-ID:String -FirstName:String -LastName:String
+pay (CreditCard:CreditCard)

Figure 20-1 A class that might appear in a UML diagram

What Information Is Conveyed in UML Diagrams?

Here's some of the information you might want to know about an application.

- Where the machines are and what pieces of software are on each machine
- Exactly what classes the programmers will be writing
- What tasks users will be doing when they use the software
- What exact deep-down software processes will be running for any given situation
- When an object is created, what it does while alive, and when it gets killed
- And much more

For each type of thing you can describe about software, there's a corresponding type of diagram. Some of them are just a bunch of squares with attributes and methods inside; some actually have stick men and ovals in them and look like what might happen if a Silicon Valley kindergarten was doing a school project.

Class Diagrams

The common diagram is the class diagram. A class diagram represents all the classes and their associations within an application. Sometimes you see allllll the classes at once; more likely you'd see a diagram of a few classes at once to do a particular chunk of features.

Let's apply this to Antoine's business. He has to get paid at some point, so credit cards and customers are part of the online application at www.antoinespizza.com. Here's part of a class diagram, shown in Figure 20-2, that Antoine might use.

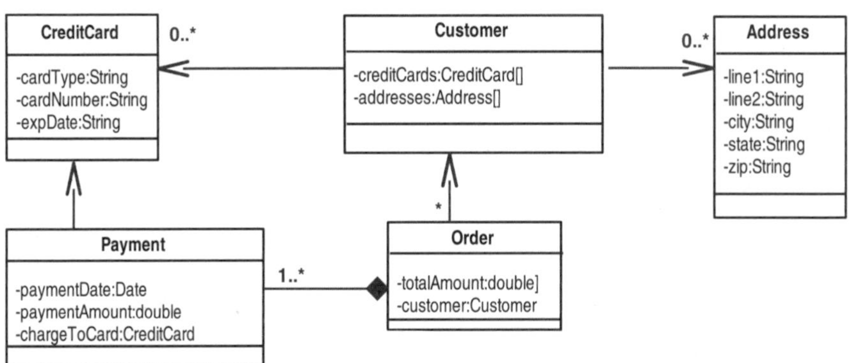

Figure 20-2 A class diagram for Antoine's online payment system

This class diagram shows a box for each class, lists the attributes that are in the classes (for this one, the methods aren't included), and the relationships among them. The point of a class diagram is so that the programmers will know at a high level what code to write. (Among other things.)

Use Case Diagrams

Here's another diagram, the use case diagram. These are very important since, after all, people are eventually going to be using the software and you need a use case diagram for every task they're going to perform. Here's a use case diagram for the pizza toppings wholesaler that Antoine buys his ingredients from. (And it's the one that looks like it came from a Silicon Valley kindergarten.) The gist is that the customer can do all the things in ovals, and that as a result the people running the catalog system, the people in customer service, and the people in the warehouse have to run around doing things.

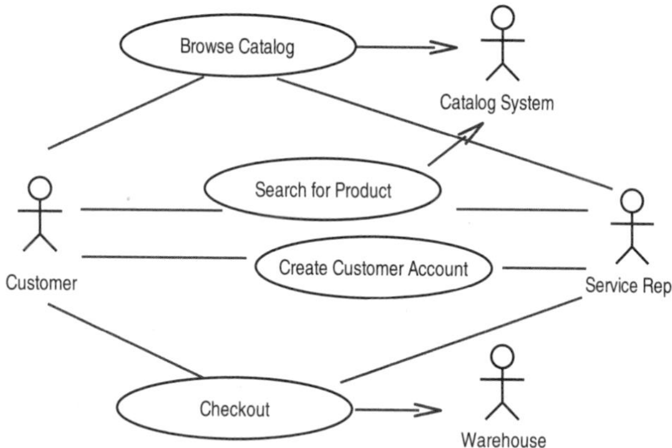

Figure 20-3 Sample use case diagram for Antoine's pizza toppings wholesaler

Reference of the Most Commonly Used Diagrams

Here's a quick reference for the most commonly used diagrams.

- A class diagram shows a set of classes, interfaces, and collaborations and their relationships. Translation: It's a guide to the code that the programmers will need to write.
- A use-case diagram shows a set of use cases and the actors and their relationships. Translation: It shows the tasks users complete and who's involved.

- A sequence diagram shows in very painful detail exactly what code runs, and in what order, and in response to what, for every process in the application.
- A component diagram shows the organizations and dependencies among a set of components. Translation: It shows what pieces of the system already exist, and what needs to be done. It's a higher-level class diagram, more of an executive overview sort of class diagram that might also include statements like "Oxygen is good."
- A deployment diagram shows the configuration of run-time processing nodes and the components on these nodes. Translation: It shows the machines you'll be using and what code is on those machines.

Should I Know Everything About UML Now?

Nope. And you probably don't need to ever, no matter how techy you want to be. It would be like memorizing every word in a foreign language when all you ever do is go to the coffee shop and order a drink and a pastry.

Of course, some people take weeks and weeks of training to be coming UML Studs. Some people find UML Gurus and follow them to India, Tibet, or San Jose to learn their wisdom. The main point is to remember that UML is just a language, a way to convey information. Take a look at *UML Distilled* by Martin Fowler to learn more about each diagram if you want to understand all the little arrows and * symbols and all that.

part IV

Big Picture Appendix

"So stack those chairs upon those tables, and stack those empties upon that bar
And count your money, and count my money
And hear those bottles ringing, you know where you are.
Closing time, unplug them people
And send them home, it's closing time."

Lyle Lovett, Closing Time

Sometimes the technical concepts aren't that tough to understand. It's the cloaked-in-mystery vocabulary used to describe the concepts that cause the problems. In this appendix, we defined all those terms that come up in meetings so it's easier to not only understand J2EE but to know who's talking about it without knowing what in the world they're saying.

There are also a few prerequisite concepts that help anyone to understand J2EE. If you were going to use this book in college in a *Survey of J2EE* course, you'd see these at the end of the course description:

Prerequisites:

***Java Programming* 101**

***Object Orientation* 110**

***Remote Communication* 301**

Survey of J2EE Vendors (no credit)

***Buzzwords and Vocabulary* 111**

So that's what this appendix gives you.

appendix

The Gist of Java in General

"I love coffee, I love tea
I love the java jive and it loves me
Coffee and tea and the java and me
A cup, a cup, a cup, a cup, a cup (boy!)"

The Manhattan Transfer, Java Jive

It's all very well to be learning about J2EE...but if J2EE comes from Java, shouldn't we know about Java first? If you're new to the whole Java thing—or Java™ technology as the Sun folks like people to say—spend some time with this appendix before hitting the rest of the book. If you're also new to object orientation, you'll want to review *The Attributes of Object Orientation* on page 261.

The Appendix in Brief

Once upon a time there were a bunch of other programming languages; some very powerful and exceptionally complicated, and some easier but less powerful. Java came along and, it might be said, is Just Right.

There are three kinds: small for devices like PDAs, medium for regular ol' applications, and large for enterprise applications, which of course is J2EE. Which kind of Java is Just Right for you depends on what kind of project you've got.

The five key benefits of Java are that it runs on any platform without rewriting; it's based on open standards; it's got more security capabilities, it's easier because of a few things including the garbage collector, and it's object oriented which is just a Good Thing Generally.

Here's what we cover in this appendix.

- *Three Kinds of Java*
- *Five Reasons to Drink That Big Cup o'Java*
- *What Makes Java Run*
- *JRE, JDK, and More Acronym Soup*

Three Kinds of Java

Some say, when asked where J2EE came from, that Ada Lovelace and James Gosling loved each other very much, and then nine months later J2EE came along.

Some will give you another explanation.

Here's that explanation. It probably wasn't lost on most of you that the J in J2EE probably has something to do with Java. So let's go briefly into Java to see where J2EE came from.

Java is a programming language developed by Sun. It does the same general kinds of things as other programming languages, like C++. Once upon a time there was only Java. Just plain Java, not J2EE or J2ME or J2SE or Java 2, Heroes' Edition.

But Java grew, and features got added, and more tools were developed, and people asked for more features. And the marketing people started to get twinkles in their eyes. So in a change that was partly code reorg and partly a marketing-related renaming event, Sun waved its wand, changed the name of Java to *Java 2*, and split the single Java entity into triplets: *J2SE*, *J2ME*, and *J2EE*.

If you
really want
to know

J is for Java, and 2 is for 1.2

*The J is of course for Java, and you'd think that the 2 would be an indicator of a version. However, that 2 is one of the most confusing numbers in Java. It's been Java 2 since **1.2**. Java **2** is now on version **1.4**, and before that Java 2 was on **1.3**. So if you're confused, that's the right way to feel.*

The splitting of Java resulted in what's shown in Figure A-1.

J2ME

Java 2, Micro Edition

A different toolset for writing Java applications for **handheld devices** and other items with limited resources.

J2EE

Java 2, Enterprise Edition

An additional set of tools that work with J2SE. J2EE is tools for writing **big distributed applications**.

J2SE

Java 2, Standard Edition

The core functionality of the Java programming language, for writing **regular run of the mill applications**.

Figure A-1 Plain old Java became three different types of Java

- **J2SE** – Java 2 Standard Edition. The basics for writing regular programs that probably aren't going to stray too far from their home computer. If you wrote a regular text editor application in Java that just runs on one person's local computer, you'd be using the Standard Edition, J2SE.
- **J2EE** – Java 2, Enterprise Edition. These are the big tools that are used to create servers and the applications that work with them. These are the tools for handling applications that have separate bits working together and distributed all over the world.

J2EE can't go anywhere without J2SE, but it adds on a whole lot. J2EE is like a trailer full of powerful tools being towed behind a J2SE SUV.

- **J2ME** – Java 2 Micro Edition. Java that does stuff that's similar to J2SE, but generally smaller cuter applications and on pagers, PDAs, smart cards, etc. If J2SE is an SUV, J2ME is a Vespa scooter. Now that you've learned what J2ME is, don't worry about it for the rest of this book.

Five Reasons to Drink That Big Cup o'Java

Java's a programming language you can do pretty much anything with. So far, no big deal. There were other programming languages before Java, like C++ and FORTRAN and Visual Basic, and there still are. However, Java came along in 1995 and even though there were plenty of experienced programmers coding in other languages, it took off like a house afire and has been adopted faster than any other language.

Note: The standard quote regarding this is from Bjarne Stroustrop, the inventor of C++, prior to Java's genesis. "Inside C++ is a smaller, more elegant language trying to get out." This is commonly considered to be Java, especially since its syntax is quite similar to C++.

Write Once, Run Anywhere™

Ask any programmer about the cross-platform issues of creating different programs for each platform, and they'll groan loudly and slump in their chairs. Or at least seem a little less fresh.

What Development Is Like With Most Programming Languages

Different operating systems evaluate and process instructions differently; otherwise you could just take that Windows Ms. PacMan game, throw it on your Mac, and not bother with buying a different version. That means that the programmers who wrote Ms. PacMan had to do a whole heck of a lot of work to rewrite the

Windows version for the Mac (or the Atari version). And a lot of companies don't have the time or resources to do it at all.

Most programs don't have to be redone from scratch to run on another platform, of course. The range is anywhere from recompiling the source code for another platform, to rewriting maybe 50% of the application (and retesting it, and maintaining it, and so on).

Pure Java code runs, as is, on any computer without changes. This in itself doesn't mean that the first time through is any less work, but when you're done writing the program, you run on all platforms, period. If you had only a Windows program three years ago that you wrote in C++, you might be wishing now that your code ran on Linux now. If you wrote it in Java, it already runs on Linux, just like that.

Code that runs on any platform with no rewriting means a lot of great things, including:

- All companies, but in particular small startup companies, can write in Java and sell a version of their program to anyone on any operating system, and get a lot more money for their effort.
- Any company can support every operating system, instead of just defaulting to one operating system.
- Subsequent versions on other operating systems are just as good as the first version, rather than suffering from being rushed to market and skipping a few steps in the QA process.

Note: Not to get excessively partisan, but the Write Once Run Anywhere aspect of Java seems to make it easy for all software companies to run on all operating systems, instead of writing one version for the most commonly used operating system. Gosh. Makes you start to understand why Microsoft, allegedly of course, tried to discourage Java use.

What Makes Java Like This

Java can run on any operating system because it's *compiled* differently. Compiling means changing from the Java programming language source code, what the programmer wrote, which is kind of English-like, into something with more techy and machine-comprehensible stuff.

Most programs are compiled from the source code into 0s and 1s, which computers understand very easily and can run fast. Of course, every operating system has a different way that it likes its 0s and 1s arranged. So once you've compiled source code down to Windows-style 0s and 1s, that code won't work for Macintosh 0s and 1s.

Java isn't compiled down to 0s and 1s. It's compiled down to something called *bytecode*, which is a little higher-level, a little less frighteningly techy and machine-specific, than 0s and 1s.

Then (and here's the clever part) there's a JVM, a Java Virtual Machine, that *interprets* that same bytecode to the right format for each operating system. There's a Mac JVM, a Windows JVM, a Linux JVM, etc.

So the Mac Java Virtual Machine, for instance, tags along with the bytecode as it's run, saying, "hey, Mac buddy, this bytecode instruction `fx0028e` means you should do 0100100." Or something like that.

There have been programming languages that did the interpreting part before, but they weren't compiled. And compiled programs didn't interpret. Java combines the two features to be faster than the interpreted programs and more multiplatform than the compiled programs.

Geek Note on JVMs

If you
really want
to know

A lot of different companies make Java Virtual Machines, or JVMs. Some companies make JVMs that are better than others—one called JRockit is rumored to be faster at telling the computer what to do than most anything else around. Also, different companies and Java programs specialize to run with different JVMs. The JVM that a Java program runs with is sometimes listed in the system requirements documentation, along with how much hard disk and memory you need. If you're working on creating Java programs, everyone should be thinking about what JVM is being used.

Open Standards

Sun publishes the rules for writing Java programs so everybody knows how to do it. This is just Good in general, it embraces the open spirit of ideal software development, not to mention full-on capitalism. Sun doesn't write your programs for you. Sun just tells you and anyone else who's interested, this is how you do it, and here are some extra pieces of code we've already written for stuff like telling time and make windows show up, so you don't have to write them from scratch. Plus, the Java Community process lets anyone with a good idea for improving Java submit the suggestion. For every release, they incorporate the best ones.

Java Is Secure

If you pick up a piece of fruit and throw it against the wall, what will happen?

There are a lot of possibilities. You might miss and hit your boss. Lyle Lovett might be walking by and, inspired, write a love song about it with a nice steel guitar solo. Very nearly anything could happen; or, at least, it would be hard to absolutely rule out a particular result.

Luckily, Java is not like throwing fruit. It is the only programming language where you can specify things that will *not* happen. Knowing what won't happen allows you to make sure that the program can't accept a virus's instructions to erase your hard disk, or to send your high school poetry notebook to USA Today.

This doesn't mean you can control what will happen; you still have to test up a storm with Java as with other applications.

Java Is Generally Easier to Write, and Write Well, than C++

Imagine trying to keep track of several thousand one-year-olds, and make sure none of them gets into trouble, and that all of them get their naps and snacks on time, and washing their clothes as they use them, including dealing with the diapers and washing them and making them ready to use again. (And if you lose track of too many diapers, well, you know everything goes straight to hell.)

That's kind of what programming in C++ is like.

Now imagine that there are only seven children, and they're ten-year-olds, old enough to get their own snacks and put on their pajamas, and they come with a little Gollum-like helper that picks up their discarded dirty clothes and washes the clothes and puts'em back in the right drawers. That's approximately the improvement you get when you switch from C++ to Java.

The specific features that give these benefits include garbage collection, which means there's a little Gollum-like creature going around collecting memory that's not being used anymore and putting it back in a pile to be reused. In other languages, programmers have to keep track of where all the memory is.

It's All About the Planning

If you
really want
to know

In the overall scheme of things, writing the code itself is usually about 15% of a project. Design and architecture and arguing about who caused the release date to slip take up the rest of the time. But the easier that is, of course, the fewer bugs you get, and it'll keep the developers happier if they can be more productive and succeed more quickly and beat their chests and shout "I am invincible!"

Java is Object Oriented

It's not the only language that's object oriented, but it does it and it's good at it. The gist of object orientation is as follows.

Imagine there's a wedding being planned.

- In an object-oriented wedding, there's a flower person, and the dressmaker, and the cake person, and a bride or wedding planner who tells them all what to do and when. But she doesn't have to know how to make the cake, just needs to say "make it 3 layers, chocolate and vanilla, and bring it by 11 AM Saturday the 8th." Also, the flower person doesn't hang out with the dressmaker, and neither of them hang out with the cake person. That's object orientation, more or less.
- Now imagine a non-object-oriented wedding where the bride has to take care of everything herself: has to know how to make the cake and make it, and ditto with the dress and the flowers, and how to make sure the bride's brother doesn't drink too much before the toast, and a million other things. She also might have to go back and change the chocolate wedding cake recipe to carrot cake in all 17 places in her wedding planner notebook where she wrote the recipe, without making a single mistake. (If she makes a mistake, she could end up with a wedding dress that's carrot flavored.)

  That's non-object-oriented, or *procedural*, development. It can be faster at first but tough to deal with if you want to change anything.

What Makes Java Run

Java's just a language, the specific language rules based on English words but a world of its own.

Note: Some of the general principles of rules and prewritten code apply to programming languages in general.

Main Java Components

The main things Sun provides to anyone who wants to write Java code, and sometimes to just run, are:

- The Java classes that you can use to just throw stuff together, like code that knows what time it is or can make a button; and included in that the rules for writing it right, like naming your class the same as the file.
- The compiler, which turns what you write into something the JVM can run.
- The JVM, which turns what the compiler gave it into something an operating system can understand.

Figure A-2 illustrates the prewritten code and the rules, and what you do with them.

What you get from Java **and what you do with it**

use semicolons...
capitalize classnames...

Java rules

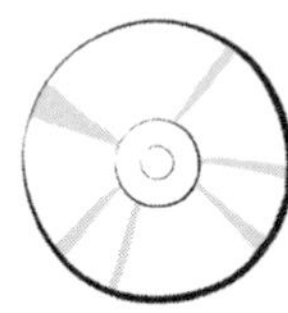

Quickly creating a Window
Automatically knowing the date
Timing how long something took

Java toolkit (classes, etc.)

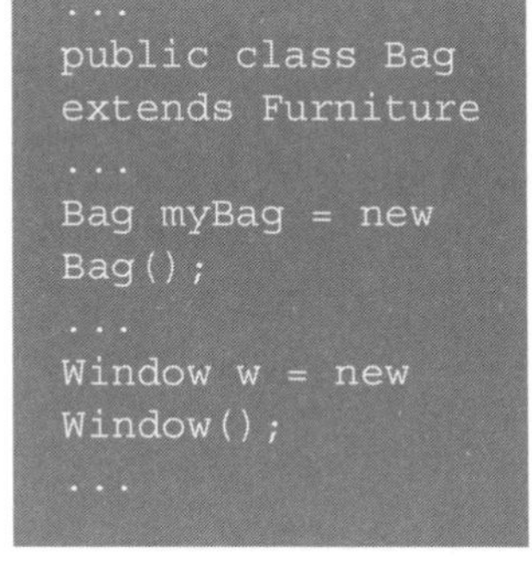

Write program source code

Figure A-2 Java tools for writing the source code for applications

Figure A-3 illustrates the compiler. Once the programmers have written some code in Java, then you run the compiler by typing javac in a terminal window and the compiler checks for errors. If there aren't any, it spits out a bytecode file for every source code file.

What you get from Java **What you do with it**

Java compiler

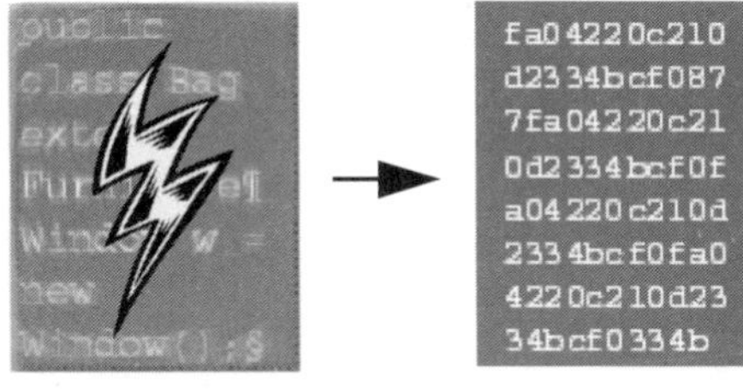

Compile the source code to bytecode

Figure A-3 How the Java tool, the compiler, turns source code written by programmers into bytecode the JVM can understand

Figure A-4 illustrates the different types of JVMs. JVMs come from Sun in the JDK or from other vendors.

What you get with Java

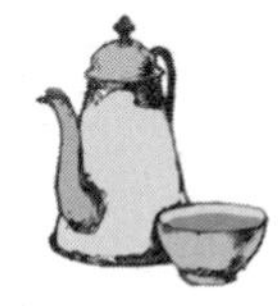

Mac OSX JVM

Linux JVM

Figure A-4 The JVMs

Figure A-5 on page 255 illustrates how the JVMs work with the bytecode and the different applications. You just put the bytecode on a computer, the JVM translates it correctly for its operating system, and your Java program runs.

More About the Rules: How to Write a Java Program

Any written language has to have a dictionary and grammar guidelines. Americans tried going without a definitive dictionary or grammar for a while, butf iyt dide noot well workk, and of course just look at how the national leaders speak.

Likewise, Java has a set of rules for just how you write the code. Here's how it might work with Antoine's pizza shop application.

- You use English spelling for the code—`Pizza extends ComfortFood` is English in spelling and, somewhat, in meaning. `xtends` will give you an error.
- You have to write it right:

```
public class Pizza extends ComfortFood;
```

not

```
Pizza is comfort food, obviously, so in this program give it all the characteristics and capabilities
that ComfortFood has.
```

- You need a set of definitions for what kinds of things you can do in the program, and how to write the code to accomplish them. If you want to make a window with the title **Get Your Piping Hot Pizzas Here**, you need to do it exactly the right way, or you'll end up with something very different.

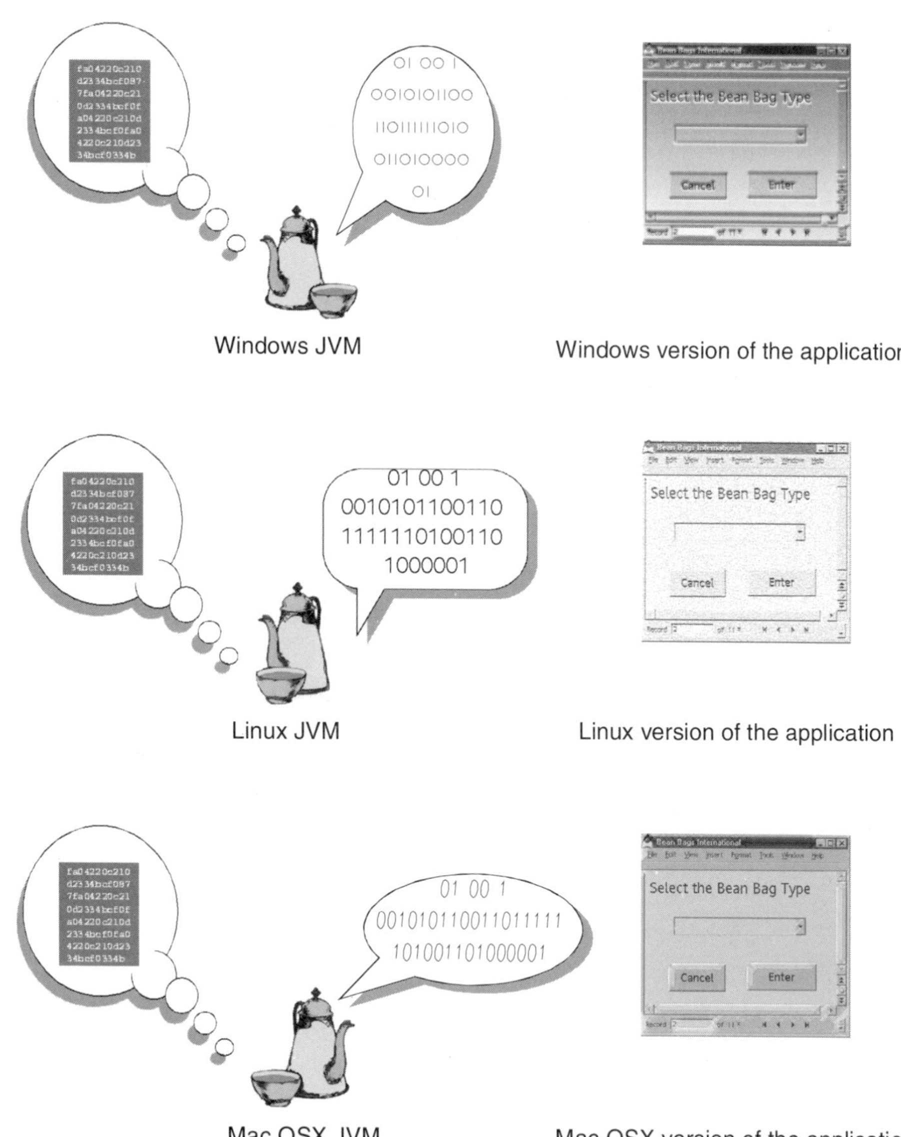

The JVM for each operating system reads the same bytecode and runs an application that works the same way but on different operating systems

Figure A-5 What the JVMs do

These rules, in general, are defined in the specification, which is the really techy-level set of rules about how the language works, written by people with heads the size of your monitor. The specification contains such gems as "A translation of Unicode escapes in the raw stream of Unicode characters to the corresponding Unicode character." (You definitely don't need to read this, just know it exists. Even programmers don't read the specification.)

The rules are also defined in the *API*, or *application programming interface*. (Which is annoying because "interface" is one of those words like "environment" or "paradigm" that can mean just about anything.) You might have heard people going on about the "API", referring to it as an idea, or a thing, or a book or Web site. Which one is it? All of them. It's just the rules, as concepts or written down.

The rules defining all of these things are written down at:

http://java.sun.com/j2ee/sdk_1.3/techdocs/api/

http://java.sun.com/j2se/1.3/docs/api/index.html

And just for fun, here's the language specification. Print it out and highlight random parts, and spread it around your desk just to scare your co-workers.

http://java.sun.com/docs/books/jls/index.html

More About the Toolkit of Prewritten Java Code That Makes Life a Lot Easier

Java has a whole bunch of predefined code, or *classes*, that are included in a Java Developer's Kit, the JDK. These classes have the same functions as *class libraries* in programming languages. You can use the classes in your Java applications, and it saves a huge amount of work. Huge. It's kind of like the difference between being able to make a casserole from a can of Cream of Mushroom Soup and some noodles, instead of having to plant and grow the mushrooms; raise, and milk the cow; plant and harvest the semolina; etc.

For an actual Java example, imagine you want to write code to draw a circle. You'd need to know about pi, you'd need to specify exactly where each part of the circle's line was positioned, and you would eventually probably convince yourself that circles are overrated and unnecessary, as you were carted away to the Programmers' Nervous Breakdown Ranch.

Wouldn't it be great if making a new button were this easy?

```
Button myEasyButton = new Button ("I'm an Easy Button");
```

And however shocking this might be, just *making* a new button is that simple.

Note: You still have to put the button in a window, make the button appear, etc. But once you've done that, the button you create in that single line of code will appear, will appear to go down and up when you click it, will have the label "I'm an

Easy Button," and will look like the right operating system. It's all built into the classes you get with Java.

You can get the J2EE predefined code, at http://java.sun.com/j2se/downloads.html and http://java.sun.com/j2ee/downloads.html

The download includes the stuff we're going to talk about next, as well.

More on the Compiler and the Java Virtual Machine

English or other spoken languages aren't much good if no one understands or cares what's said. Generally we do understand and at least react, if we don't obey; we listen to "There's pizza in the second floor kitchen," the consciousness in our heads turns it into meaning, and then we decide to head that way, or else we don't, we sit steadfastly at our desks, and to try to remember that pizza goes straight to our hips.

Same thing with Java—there needs to be some system that understands and reacts to Java code like Pizza extends ComfortFood. But computers (so far) aren't sentient, right? What makes it go when it receives Java code? Why in the world would the words "Pizza extends ComfortFood" make anything happen in a computer?

Good point. The computer has no clue what "Pizza extends ComfortFood" means and doesn't care. However, it gets very excited if you whisper softly into its hard disk, "0110011010100100 1101". Computers inherently understand and have an overwhelming urge to obey 0s and 1s. It's their native language.

The folks at Sun made two programs that turn Java into 0s and 1s: the compiler and the Java Virtual Machine. Don't worry about them now—the important thing to understand is that those two programs are what makes "Pizza extends Comfort-Food" have any effect on anything in the computer.

The compiler and the JVM both know all about the specification and the API, so they know how to turn the Java program code into just the right 0s and 1s.

You download the compiler and the Java Virtual Machine along with all the other programs and files that are part of Java.

http://java.sun.com/j2ee/download.html (J2SE—regular Java)

http://java.sun.com/j2ee/download.html (J2EE—Java for big systems)

Here's more on the two steps in the process of taking "Pizza implements ComfortFood" and turning it into something the operating system understands.

1. Compiling (compiler)

First, you write your program in Java code and run the compiler on it. The compiler turns your Java code into bytecode. Don't worry about what it is, exactly—it's just kind another form of the program, but less English and more Computery.

No other programs are compiled to bytecode; they're all either compiled straight to 0s and 1s, like C++, or else they're not compiled at all. The ones that aren't compiled at all need a hard-working translator to do all the translation work, all the way from the more or less English code that was written, all the way down to 1s and 0s. Which makes it platform-independent, like Java, but also freakin' slow.

2. Translating (JVM)

To run the programs, somebody eventually takes this compiled bytecode and puts it on a Solaris machine, a Mac, and a Windows machine, or whatever platforms are wanted. On each machine (and indeed on nearly any computer platform that exists), crouching in the corner ready to work, is a Java Virtual Machine for that platform. It's kind of like if you were going on a worldwide speaking tour, and having a French translator waiting for you when you get off the plane, a German translator waiting for you in Germany, etc. There's only one of you, but you can speak anywhere because of the native translators in each country.

Then on each of the different computers, the Java program, the bytecode, starts running, and the JVM starts translating that into 0s and 1s for that platform so that the computer can understand it. And boom, you've got your Java program running, on all the platforms, with exactly the same code on each platform.

JRE, JDK, and More Acronym Soup

You might have heard, in addition to the JVM, about the JDK and JRE and SDK. And the fun thing is that the JDK and SDK are the same thing, and that some of these things are subsets of others. There's a JDK for each of the types of Java: J2ME, J2SE, and J2EE.

Figure A-6 shows what they are and how they're related.

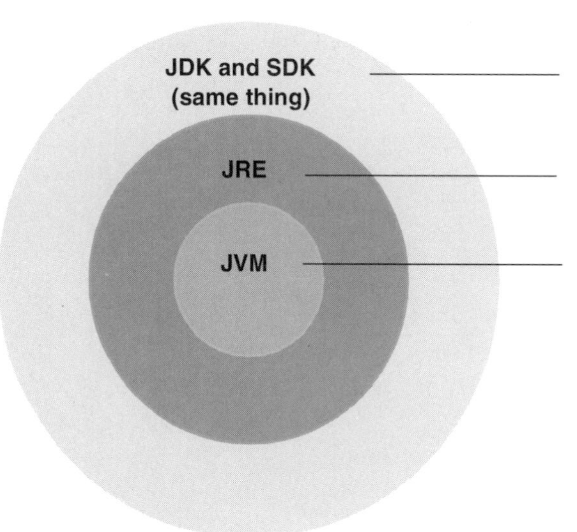
JDK and SDK
(same thing)
JRE
JVM
The essentials of what it takes to develop a Java program. The JVM, the compiler, and a bunch of other tools and prewritten code. It also has the Java source code the classes are made from—the source is the blueprint of the prewritten code classes.
The bare essentials of what it takes to run a Java program: the JVM plus the prewritten code classes.
Just the JVM, that translates instructions from bytecode to what the computer can understand

Figure A-6 Concentric circles of Java

appendix B

The Attributes of Object Orientation

"'Twas on the Monday morning, the Gas man came to call. ~ The gas tap wouldn't turn – I wasn't getting gas at all. He tore out all the skirting boards to try and find the main, ~ And I had to call the carpenter to put them back again. ~ Oh, it all makes work for the working men to do.

'Twas on the Tuesday morning. the Carpenter came round. ~ He hammered, and he chiselled, and he said "Look what I've found: ~ Your joists are full of dry rot, but I'll put them all to rights." ~ Then he nailed right through a cable and out went all the lights. ~ Oh, it all makes work for the working men to do.

'Twas on the Wednesday morning the Electrician came. ~ He called me 'Mister Sanderson', which isn't quite my name. ~ He couldn't reach the fuse box without standing on the bin, ~ And his boot went thru a window, so I called a glazier in. ~ Oh, it all makes work for the working men to do.

'Twas on the Thursday morning the Glazier came round, ~ With his blowtorch and his putty and his merry glazier song. ~ He put another pane in - it took no time at all - ~ Then I had to get a painter in to come and paint the wall. ~ Oh, it all makes work for the working men to do.

'Twas on the Friday morning the Painter made a start. ~ With undercoats, and overcoats, he painted every part, ~ Every nook and cranny, but I found when he had gone ~ He'd painted over the gas tap, and I couldn't turn it on! ~ Oh, it all makes work for the working men to do.

On Saturday and Sunday they do no work at all ~ So it was on the Monday morning that the Gas man came to call."

Flanders and Swann, The Gasman Cometh

Object orientation has been the underlying theme throughout this book. But if you don't know what it is already, well, that makes understanding it not as easy. Keeping everything separated into self-aware objects sure seems like a nice idea, but, after all, it's software. Aren't there some drawbacks? Why wasn't everyone doing it that way all along?

Would it really be so terrible if you wrote something that wasn't object-oriented?

The Appendix in Brief

One of the worst things you can tell a programmer to do is to go back into code that's been written, tested, and released, and tell her to make some changes. Because she knows darned well that going back in always has unintended effects. Object orientation helps make going back in a lot less painful, by partitioning off chunks of code.

Here's what we cover in this appendix.

- *What Object Orientation Is*
- *Some of Antoine's Objects*
- *Good Object-Oriented Design*
- *Objects and Classes*
- *Why Object Orientation Is Good*
- *The Importance of Being Separate*

What Object Orientation Is

Writing code without using object orientation means that you've got long lines of code running processes in your application.

then bake the pizza and get the name of the pizza and put it here and a great deal more complicated code adjusting the oven and getting the name from wherever it is and anyway all the instructions are spelled out explicitly when anything needs to be done

Object orientation means you write the code as if the real life things that the application deals with were sentient and knew about what they were and what they could do. Then you just give those things orders to do the processing, to simulate what real objects do in real life. You create code representations of the pizzas, the toppings, the customers, and so on. You write code so that they know about themselves (the pizzas know that they include dough and toppings and cost $14.99 for a large), and you write about them so that they can do stuff (the pizzas can be sold, they can be baked, they can be delivered). Then when you need to get or change data about an object, or you need an object to do something, you just tell it to do it.

You say this:

```
Pizza mypizza = new Pizza();  // create a new Pizza object and call it myPizza
redsauce = true;  // use red sauce
mypizza.bake(450,22);  // bake the new pizza at 450 for 22 minutes)
```

and it works because you've got code like this that those two lines hook up to.

```
public class Pizza
{
  boolean redsauce;  // there's a boolean, i.e. true/false value variable, for whether
                     // red sauce will be used on a given pizza

  void bake {int temperature, int time};  // to tell a pizza to bake, use this method and pass it
                                          // values for the temperature and the time
}
```

Some of Antoine's Objects

You've got the Pizza object, the Customer object, possibly a Toppings object, an Order object, and so on. Those objects sit around waiting to be called to do their thing. And all the objects are written with the name of the object, of course, plus the things they know about themselves, and the things they can do.

Figure B-1 shows a possible partial design for a Pizza object and an Order object.

Pizza
size toppings price
getSize() setSize() getPrice() setToppings()

Some of the things the pizza knows about itself.

Some of the things the pizza can do.

Some of the things the order knows about itself

Some of the things the order can do.

Order
orderID custID items date
getID() getDate() computeTotal() save() computeTaxes()

Figure B-1 Two possible objects in Antoine's object-oriented pizza application

The things an object knows about itself are *attributes* (or variables), and the things an object can do are *methods*, also called behavior.

What's With the Diagrams?

If you
really want
to know

The diagrams in Figure B-1 are UML class diagrams, which you'll see a lot on the white boards in meeting rooms and cubes wherever programming is going on. We've also got a whole section on it in this book so you can go there for a little more background. UML means Unified Modeling Language, and it's just a standard notation for planning application designs, just like notes and staffs are standard for writing down music. The words at the top of the rectangle are the object or class (kind of the same thing, don't worry about that for now); the words at the next level are its characteristics or attributes, and the words at the bottom are the things it can do, or methods.

Good Object-Oriented Design

Objects are designed, or should be, so that they only keep track of stuff about themselves, and not about anything else. Or as little else as possible. In the Order object in Figure 1, for instance, the Order doesn't know the Pizza price. An order isn't an Item, so it follows good OO rules and keeps track of as few Item things as it can get away with. It just knows the IDs of the items that are on it. When it needs to know the item price in order to compute the total, it *asks* the Pizza object, and the Pizza object uses its own getPrice method to tell the Order.

If the Order object and the Pizza object both kept track of the Pizza price, that would be double the code, double the maintenance, and almost undoubtedly result in some errors with two different prices.

Objects and Classes

We've been talking about two different things, actually, both covered by the word objects. There are two different concepts, object and classes, in object orientation and the code you write for it.

Objects and classes are both representations of the things in the application: customers, items, orders.

Classes are the code you write to describe the things in the application.

```
public class Pizza
{
   private String topping1;
   private String topping2;
   private boolean redsauce;

   public Pizza(boolean redsauce, String topping1, String topping2) {...}
   public void bake (int temperature, int time) {...}
   public void deliver(String Customer;String Address) {...}
}
```

But classes don't generally do anything. Mostly they're a blueprint for what you get when you create a real "object." So the class Pizza describes how a pizza is made, how it behaves when it gets cooked, and so on, but it's the actual Pizza objects that do these things.

Objects are individual items. You can have a Pizza class, but you would have an object for the pizza ordered at 4:20 PM by Simon Roberts with mushroom and Marmite toppings.

Here's the new pizza object for Simon. You could call it myPizza or simonsPizza or pizza420, but it's called myPizza here.

```
Pizza mypizza = new Pizza(true, "mushroom", "Marmite");
mypizza.bake (450, 25);
mypizza.deliver(Simon, 1209 Main Street)
```

People often talk about objects when they mean classes. "What objects ya got in that design of yours, Gus?" echoes in the halls of countless development departments around the world. Even the ones where there's no one named Gus, which we think is kind of creepy.

Why Object Orientation Is Good

Countless books, articles, and epic Icelandic poems have been written on this subject.

The Main Benefits

Object orientation is good for many reasons, including these:

- It's easier to find the code to fix. If you've got long dribbling code that defines pizzas in 11,093 places, finding and fixing the code for your pizzas is going to be a pain.
- You're less likely to break other stuff. You're going to break other stuff if you have to go hunting furiously through all those lines of code to find what needs fixing. If all you have to do is go into the one pizza class, you're not going to have to touch the order class or anything else.
- It keeps the hot things hot, and the cold things cold. If your pizzas are over in this code corner, and interact very carefully and in a limited manner with the code that makes sure your transactions work, then neither can affect the other, i.e. break it. And that's a good thing.
- It enhances *encapsulation*. Encapsulation is basically just objects being polite and asking for each other to pass the salt instead of reaching for it. It's what you always wanted on a long car trip with your brothers and sisters—for them to stay on their side of the car and not reach over and just poke you or take your toys. They can ask for your toys or to stop singing, but they can't make you do anything you don't want to do.

More on Encapsulation

Imagine an elevator in a 12-story department store and the programs that run it. In a well encapsulated system, the elevator object has its own GoUp method, and the GoUp method won't run without checking the FloorsInTheBuilding and FloorNumberYoureOn attributes. The FloorNumberYoureOn attribute is *private*, meaning that no one but the Elevator object can change it.

Other pieces of code can't reach in and change the FloorNumberYoureOn, and the GoUp and GoDown methods won't take you past the FloorsInTheBuilding. The methods are written to always check FloorsInTheBuilding and, if there is one basement and twelve floors, will never ever take you three floors below the basement where the bargains are or up to the mythical 15th floor where there's nothing to buy at all.

Encapsulation is good judgment, put into methods, and made safe from outside influences.

The Importance of Being Separate

We're going to talk about object orientation, and the separation principles underlying it, on a larger scale.

Imagine All the Logic...in One Big Ball of Code From Hell

Imagine one big piece of code that first defines your products, then what tax to apply when you sell two for the price of one. So there's a big honkin' piece of code doing that. Not only does that code cover allllll the tax stuff and how it relates to your business, but on top of everything else it defines how your Web pages look and work.

go get some SQL code and then some HTML code and oh yeah make sure that the firewall is running and oh yes, make sure that the pizza toppings are all in inventory oh they're not? agh! OK,wait, what about this color scheme, it sucks! EXCEPTION 40566 CANNOT RUN, this obviously isn't working...getting sleepy...

The Application From Hell

This is in fact the application from hell.

That would be awful to write, since your HTML GUI people would need to check out the same code file that the programmer and the business analyst need to be updating. And since your Web designer Cilantro and your grumpy programmer Gus don't get along at the best of times, fighting over access to the same code is only going to make things worse.

It also means that as you're thinking about and designing and coding the interface, you have to be thinking about everything else too. All of which is hard enough to think about separately.

Separating Unrelated Functions

One of the main issues with code maintenance is that anytime you update something, you run the risk of breaking whatever's near it. So how do you reduce the risk of breaking code? You isolate code, sorting it by function and what it deals with (*separation by concern* in tech talk) as much as possible. You put the code for computing taxes over there, and you put the code for validating credit cards over there, and you keep everything that's not related as far apart as possible.

If the furnace guy came over to fix your furnace, and your furnace and ducts were tangled up with the plumbing, it's entirely likely that pretty soon you'd have more problems than just your furnace not working. Worse problems. However, the furnace is usually down in the basement, by itself, and the only thing the furnace guy has to deal with that's not related to the furnace is picking his way through boxes of old croquet sets and your high school basketball trophies.

Object Orientation Analogy: Houses

Think about how your house is set up. It's got the kitchen with a sink and stove, a furnace in the basement, some phone lines, an electrical system, a plumbing system, and so on. When you need to fix one thing, you fix that one thing and you don't usually have to fiddle with other systems in your house.

Houses are great examples of object orientation.

To bring the object orientation thing into focus, let's think about what a non-object-oriented house would be like. (It would be pretty much one big room and really messy, kind of like that old barn your geeky uncle Alfred was renting in Montana, the summer he was experimenting with massive doses of nutmeg.) It would have wiring running all over the place. The phone line might run straight through some of the furnace ductwork. Your closet probably wouldn't exist, and you'd be keeping your socks in the top kitchen drawer. (If you were lucky enough to have drawers.) None of the wires or pipes are labeled. You try to unplug the phone and it turns out to not be the phone, and you electrocute yourself.

That way madness lies, with houses as well as with applications.

appendix 

It's All About Communication: RMI

"Is anybody at home? There was a sudden scuffling noise from inside the hole and then silence. "What I said was, 'Is anybody at home?'" called out Pooh very loudly. "No!" said a voice; and then added, "you needn't shout so loud. I heard you quite well the first time." "Bother!" said Pooh. "Isn't there anybody here at all?" "Nobody."

A. A. Milne, Winnie-the-Pooh

We've talked a lot about talking to different pieces of code on different machines. Cool, huh? But how exactly do you make code A, on machine X, talk to code B, on machine Y? Or how does code A in Los Angeles, talk to code B, in Dublin? Especially when code A never actually knows where code B is? Think about a system with distributed code and data all over the world and having to write down, absolutely accurately, absolutely always up to date, where every bit of the system is at any given time. As a programmer, how would you handle this?

The Appendix in Brief

All code isn't local to each other, and since they still need to communicate with each other, they need special powers to do so remotely. RMI lets pieces of code that aren't right next to each other in the same JVM or on the same machine locate and communicate with each other. This is essential in a distributed system.

RMI is really complicated to do right. That's plain RMI, that is. With the RMI you get as part of J2EE, using RMI is easier.

RMI isn't unique to J2EE. And you don't actually need to know much RMI with J2EE which is a huge plus. But it's such a huge part of distributed communication that we decided the book would be incomplete without an RMI appendix.

- *The Reason for RMI, Quick and Dirty*
- *Why Applications Even Need Help Communicating Remotely in the First Place*
- *Basic Explanation of How RMI Works*
- *A Few Geeky Things About RMI*

The Reason for RMI, Quick and Dirty

Communication among pieces of local code is easy. Communication among pieces of code that are remote from other code is harder. This section covers what this local and remote hoohah is all about, what makes things local or remote.

Normal Java Code Needs Everything to Be Local

For your application to work, regular Java objects and anything else participating in the application have to be able to talk to each other.

Otherwise nothing happens and there are just a bunch of lonely session beans sitting there thinking "Why didn't he call me back? Did I seem to eager when I asked for his handle?"

To communicate with normal Java powers, the bits of code all have to be *local* to each other. If some of the code in your application isn't local, then it's *remote*, and in that case it needs special powers.

What Makes Code Local or Remote?

So how do you know if all of your code is all local or some of it's remote?

How a JVM Makes Code Local or Remote

Bits of code are local to each other if they're running in the same JVM. (See *The Gist of Java in General* on page 257 for more on Java.) Sun makes a JVM and lots of other companies do too. You can have your application running in one JVM or you can have a whole bunch of JVMs running for one application. (You'd do this for a bunch of possible reasons including performance).

But only the bits of code inside the same JVM are local to each other; the code inside the other JVMs are remote. If code inside Bob's JVM wants to talk to code in Jane's JVM, it needs to do Something Else besides use normal Java powers.

So Java code needs special powers to communicate with code in another JVM. Code in another JVM is *remote*, even if it's on the same machine. Code in the same JVM is *local*. Code on the same machine might be local or remote.

Your Code Might Be Physically Elsewhere

Another reason that some code in an application would be remote from another is if it's off on another machine. That's a clearer distinction.

You can increase performance significantly by installing your J2EE server as well as your application on multiple machines so you can get some load balancing during the holidays, Valentine's Day, Saint Antoine's Day of Holy Pizza, or whenever your rush season is. Which means in essence that you've got code all over the place, on different machines.

And Of Course Being in a Different Container Means Code is Remote Too

As we mentioned in the last section you might install the server once on multiple machines. Or you might install the server two or more times on a really powerful machine. In which case some of your code might all be on the same machine but inside different containers. And still remote because different containers make things remote, too. Whether you've got multiple EJB containers, or code in an EJB container that wants to talk to code in a Web container on the same machine, anything separated by container is remote.

Life is So Uncertain

Given all the potential for remoteness, and given that your system administrator has way too much power and might decide to redistribute some of your beans, and, OK, due to the EJB rules, you have to assume all the time that your code is always remote. (We took you through all that just to say that the code's always presumed remote. Sorry about that.) So because of that required assumption, you always have to use the Special Powers Beyond Normal Java Powers to make the bits of code in your application community.

If you
really want
to know

If Your Code Is Really, Truly Local, You Don't Have to Assume Remoteness and You Can Use Local Interfaces

Local interfaces in the 2.0 release of EJBs have changed the necessity of assuming this. If you know absolutely for sure that the code you're calling is going to be right there next to you, then you can bypass RMI.

You can read about local interfaces in Talking to Session Beans and Entity Beans With Local Interfaces on page 141.

RMI Gives Java Applications the Ability to Communicate Remotely

RMI, a.k.a. Remote Method Invocation, is the Special Power that your Java application (and others) can use to communicate Outside the JVM, Outside the Container, and of course Outside the Box (the computer). That's why you care about RMI. Now that you care deeply about RMI, here's some information on how it actually works.

Why Applications Even Need Help Communicating Remotely in the First Place

This is good to mention at geek cocktail parties, if you ever find yourself at one and at a loss for a good RMI anecdote.

You might be wondering, since we certainly did, why applications are so lame that they can't just communicate remotely too. After all, we can send a man to the moon and make velcro; why can't code just communicate remotely without any help from us?

Object-oriented applications (see *All About Object Orientation* on page 271) are about objects. Objects have state (things they know) and behavior (things they do). State could be a pizza's size or its price; behavior could be the bake and deliver methods.

When you've got a *distributed* object-oriented application with objects all over the place, like a typical J2EE application, you need to move things across the network in order to run your application.

That's where the trouble starts. You can move *state* around on a network but not *behavior*. That's just how networks are. It's not really Java's fault; it's the darned network.

Well, that's inconvenient. You can know about a pizza just fine but you can't make one. That's bad for business.

Enter RMI. RMI lets you move behavior around on a network. You might say RMI gives you back true object orientation when there's a network involved.

RMI also lets programmers write their applications without actually thinking much about the code that will make the objects whiz around the network.

And RMI lets you take advantage of the key advantage of object orientation, which is that when you need to rewrite some code, you just rewrite the bit that needs it, without doing a huge song and dance and impacting a bazillion other pieces of code.

Basic Explanation of How RMI Works

Finally, huh? But the other stuff was fascinating. Admit it.

Here's a very high level look at the mechanics.With RMI, what you get is a couple copies, or *stubs*, of the remote object. One comes over to hang out with your local object, and the other sits on the other side of the great divide with the remote object. The stubs are created by the application server when you start it up using a lovely little application by the name rmic.

Let's Take a Look at some Remote Communication Action

Let's say Jeannie wants to find out what the pizza specials are in Boulder, Colorado. She goes to Anthony's Web site. The code that does the special-figuring-out process is remote, yet she gets the answer back anyway, as shown in Figure C-1.

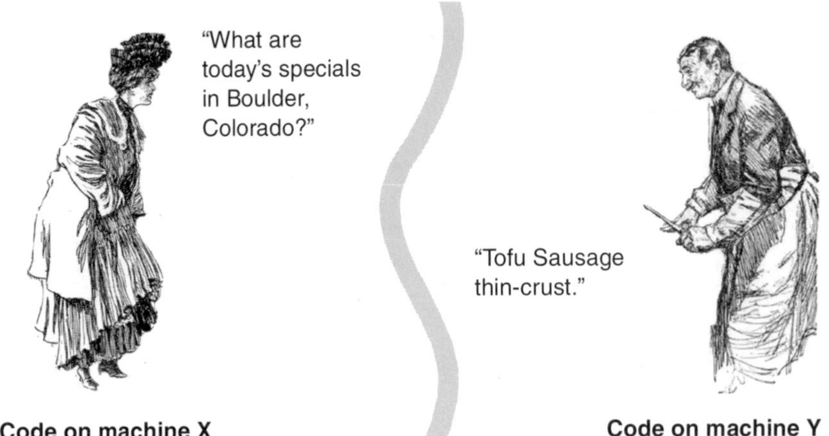

Figure C-1 Remote conversation between chunks of code

How did the code communicate with the remote code? Here's approximately what happens, in Figure C-2. It's all about the *stubs*.

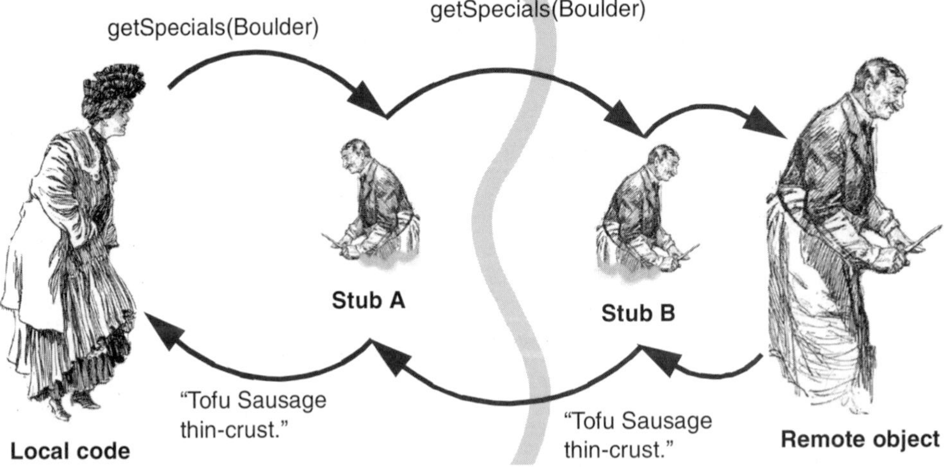

Figure C-2 Basic RMI process

The magic in RMI that makes it all happen is the stub. The rmic application, kind of a magic little application itself, creates stubs from the object that you want to be able to get to even though it's off doing its remote thing. The stubs are kind of a copy, or alternate version, or proxy, for the remote object.

The remote object's *stubs* usually just sit out there on the remote machine, and a phone-book-type application called the rmiregistry keeps track of the stubs.

When the local code needs the remote object to do something, the code actually calls the rmiregistry and says, hey, I need xyz. The rmiregistry sends a copy of the requested stub off to that local object and keeps the original copy.

Figure C-3 illustrates the local object looking for the remote object.

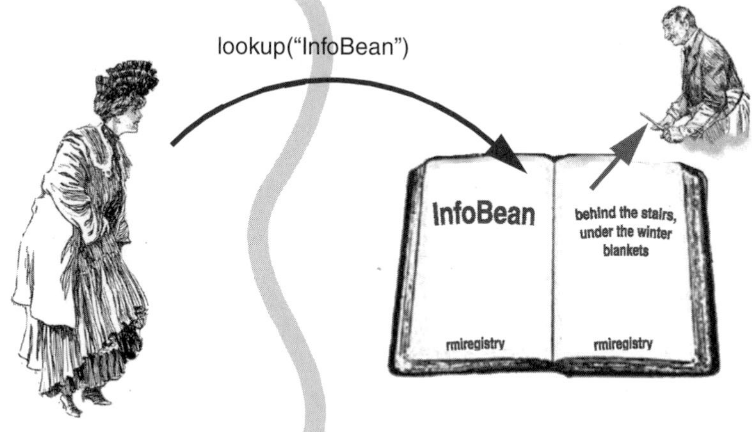

Figure C-3 Asking the rmiregistry for help locating that pesky remote object

Figure C-4 illustrates the rmiregistry sending the stub where it's needed.

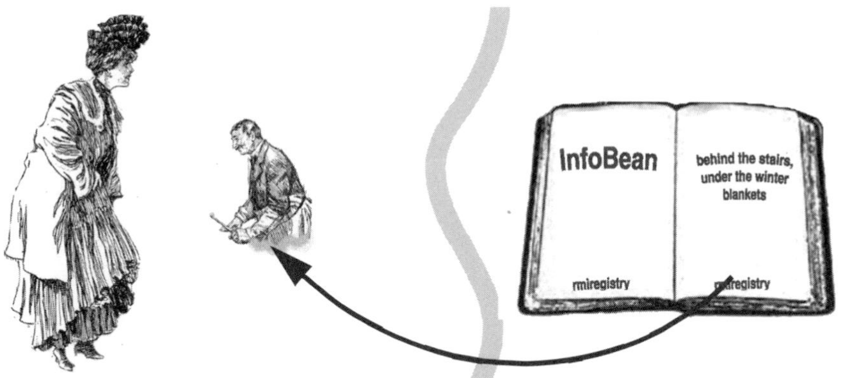

Figure C-4 rmiregistry sends the stub for that bean to the requesting object

There's just one more vocabulary word/concept that you need to know, and that's that the stub when it's sent over is *serialized*. Sometimes called being *marshalled*. Basically it means the stub is squished down flat, like an air mattress when you're done using it and want to store it, so that the stub can travel light over the network. This is shown in Figure C-5. It's the same thing that we showed in Figure

C-4; it's just that this time we're showing what we left out last time, the serialization.

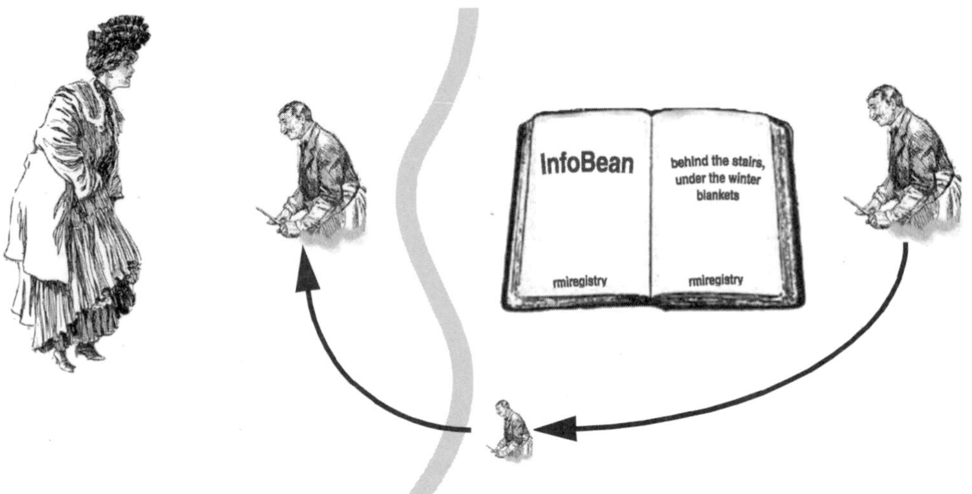

Figure C-5 Same as Figure 4, but this time with the serialization showing

The stub gets automatically serialized (deflated/dehydrated), goes through the special stub transportation portal, and falls out on its head next to the New Jersey Turnpike. Or alternately and more commonly, plops down next to the client object that wants its services. WHUMP! the stub gets deserialized automatically again (inflated/rehydrated).

What About the Skeleton?

You might have heard about stubs and skeletons. *Wherever there's one, there's the other, right? Well, kind of. A stub is a thing that participates in all that remote communication with the object. It's right in the thick of it. The skeleton is more like the laws of physics that make it all possible. The skeleton creates the stubs. There's skeleton code in the application server that makes the stubs. Skeletons are more of a function than a thing.*

More on the Stub

A stub does a few things that make it special and very useful:

- It knows how to get remote. It can go where no object has gone before. It has built-in long distance phone lines, which another book would refer to as networking code and sockets and streams and stuff like that.
- It knows the methods in the remote object. It's like a special objectbot, kind of like the remote object on the outside but with special powers on the inside. It can't actually implement the remote object's methods. But it knows about'em and knows how to pass the requests for those methods off across the Chasm of Remoteness to the remote object, who then takes care of things.
- It's available. It hangs out locally to whoever needs to call the remote object. So the stub is local even though its object isn't. You want to call the remote object? You actually call the stub. Sometimes you don't even know you're calling the stub.
- It can travel light. Regular object behavior can't get to a remote place because networks just don't do that. It's not because of visa issues; it's just the way things are. However stubs have a special attributes that lets them travel all over the place to go where they're needed: they're serializable.

A Few Geeky Things About RMI

When you start the J2EE server, it starts the naming service (rmiregistry or whatever naming service the J2EE server uses) and the Web server. J2EE uses the JNDI (Java Naming and Directory Interfaces) API for the naming service. The JNDI API makes it very easy to change from one naming service (i.e. LDAP, NIS+, COSnaming) to another. Don't worry about these names. The point is that rmiregistry isn't the only naming service, a.k.a. yellow pages, that you could use, and you or your IT person or application architect might want a particular one for various reasons. You might already be using one naming service for un-J2EE purposes. (Again, J2EE makes changing vendors easy.) The deployment tool also creates and utilizes a security manager and policy so you don't have to do that either.

Another difference between regular RMI and J2EE RMI is the protocol. Regular RMI uses JRMP as the protocol for sending messages across the network. J2EE RMI (or RMI/IIOP or RMI over IIOP) can use IIOP (the Internet Inter-Object Protocol).

Who cares? Why would you care? Well, IIOP is the protocol that CORBA (Common Object Request Broker Architecture) uses. CORBA is another communication system. Using IIOP in J2EE allows CORBA and J2EE to get along nicely. And that means that if you want to connect your system to something that uses CORBA instead of RMI, then it's easier.

CORBA??? IIOP? Is This Slow Death By Acronym?

If you
really want
to know

IIOP is actually the protocol that CORBA uses to talk over the network. CORBA is the Common Object Request Broker Architecture, it's been around for years, and is used in general by lots of applications to communicate over a network. CORBA is just another way to talk over the network, like SOAP. (More on SOAP and Web services later.)

So you've got CORBA, a commonly used architecture, or system, for getting stuff back and forth over a network, and it uses IIOP as the protocol for doing so. Basically, CORBA speaks IIOP, just like French is the language spoken by people in France. CORBA is the guidelines and structure for how communication is done. IIOP is what it speaks.

appendix D

J2EE Products

"You can do such a lot with a Wompom, you can use every part of it too. For work or for pleasure, it's a triumph, it's a treasure, oh there's nothing that a Wompom cannot do."

Swann and Flanders, The Wompom

The J2EE standards resulted, after an appropriate time development, in a bunch of companies who sell J2EE application servers. These companies, usually referred to as vendors in techtalk, include Sun's iPlanet, now the Java Enterprise System, and BEA's WebLogic. J2EE servers have to be endorsed by Sun before they're officially considered J2EE compliant.

Some companies also sell J2EE toolkits that you can make J2EE applications with. BEA's WebLogic Portal product is a set of page templates and other tools that let you roll your own portal. Your portal then interacts with BEA's J2EE server or another J2EE server.

Then the rest of the world buys these application servers and writes J2EE applications to work with them.

Note: This was presumed correct at the time this book was published, but is of course subject to change.

J2EE Products

The following table lists the products, vendors, and their version compatibility. *Compatible* means that the server has passed Sun's compatibility test suite. Compliant means that the server follows the spec but has not been submitted for compatibility testing.

J2EE 1.4 had only just came out when we were writing this book. Also note that it takes a while for these vendors to update their servers to 1.4. Typically at least six months, sometimes longer.

Table 1-1 J2EE vendors and products

Company	Product	Description
IBM	WebSphere Application Server 5.0	A J2EE 1.3 compatible server
BEA	WebLogic Server 7.0 and 8.1	A J2EE 1.3 compatible server
Sun	Sun ONE Application Server Sun ONE Studio 5	A J2EE 1.3 compatible server
Macromedia	JRun 4	A J2EE 1.3 compatible server
Oracle	Oracle 9i Application Server	A J2EE 1.3 compatible server
ATG	Dynamo Application Server	A J2EE 1.3 compatible server
Borland	Enterprise Server	A J2EE 1.3 compatible server
Hitachi	Cosminexus	A J2EE 1.3 compatible server
Fujitsu	Interstage Application Server	A J2EE 1.3 compatible server
Iona	Orbix E2A Application Server 5	A J2EE 1.3 compatible server
NEC	WebOTX 5	A J2EE 1.3 compatible server
Novell	exteNd Application Server	A J2EE 1.3 compatible server
Pramati	Pramati Server and Studio 3.0	A J2EE 1.3 compatible server
SAS	AppDev Studio 2.0.2 Preview release	A J2EE 1.3 compatible server

Table 1-1 J2EE vendors and products (Continued)

Company	Product	Description
See Beyond	SeeBeyond ICAN	A J2EE 1.3 compatible server
SpiritSoft	SpiritSoft	A J2EE 1.3 compatible server
Tmax Soft	JEUS 4.0	A J2EE 1.3 compatible server
Sybase	EAServer 4.1	A J2EE 1.3 compatible server
Trifork	Trifork Application Server 3.1	A J2EE 1.3 compatible server
Apache	Tomcat	A servlet and JSP container
JBoss	JBoss	A J2EE 1.3 compliant server
IronFlare	Orion 2.0	A J2EE 1.3 compliant server

appendix E

J2EE-to-English Dictionary

"Alice felt dreadfully puzzled. The Hatter's remark seemed to have no meaning in it, and yet it was certainly English."

Lewis Carroll, Through the Looking-Glass

This chapter is meant to give you a reference for meetings, documents, and other situations where you think that if you just knew what people were talking about, you'd know what they meant. Where possible, we give you a cross-reference to one of the pages where we discuss the concept.

A

abstraction — An object-orientation term meaning to stop thinking about the specific details of an item and think about its salient characteristics, sometimes combining it conceptually with other similar objects. For instance, if you abstract Lassie, you realize that she's just a collie, and if you abstract out further, you get to Dog, then to Pet, and now she's in the same group with your sister's cat and Michael Jackson's giraffes. You could also abstract out in a different direction, from Lassie to Things That Rescue You and pretty soon Lassie is in the same group with the Jaws of Life and First Aid.

access object	An access object is also referred to as a DAO, database access object, and is typically part of a pattern such as MVC where different parts of the application have different roles. The role of the access object is very specialized: simply to get data in and out of the database.
application server	Software that provides services such as security or transaction handling to an application, so that the application can contain primarily business logic.
architecture	The structure of an application concerned with the number of application servers, the hardware, the security functions, the network, qualities of services such as availability and scalability, and other features. The architecture should be sufficient so that a designer, concerned with the APIs that will be used to write the application, can use the architecture as a resource to do all his or her work.
atomicity	Atomicity refers to the concept in transactions of being made up of several nondivisible tasks. An ATM transaction is made up of several steps such as entering a PIN and receiving cash. See also *Three Aspects of Transactions* on page 200.
attribute	In terms of object orientation, something that the object knows about itself, such as its name, size, or price.
authentication	In terms of security, the process of determining who a user is.
authorization	In terms of security, the process of determining what an authenticated user has rights to access.
availability	Your application is highly available because it is always, always up and running. This is important for air traffic control, not so crucial for www.PezDispensersRUs.com. Availability can be obtained by having multiple servers which "brain-share" and when one fails, another takes over. It's also linked to performance; if people have to wait a minute to get a response, that's not really available, in a practical sense, though it is in a literal sense. For more information, see *Qualities of Service (QOS): What's Most Important in an Application* on page 227.

B

bean — A bean is a piece of Java code which is meant for reuse with little or no rework. A JavaBean is standard Java code that is required to have a specific set of methods to read and change its attributes. An Enterprise JavaBean is Java code written in a very specific way so that an EJB container can manipulate and provide services to it. JavaBeans and Enterprise JavaBeans have nothing to do with each other.

BMP and CMP — BMP, or bean-managed persistence, means that a programmer writes the code himself. CMP, or container-managed persistence, means that the EJB container handles getting data in and out of the database.

business logic — The programming in an application that deals with the primary part of the application, rather than logistical issues like security or transaction control, database access, or the user interface.

business to business — Commerce or other business-related tasks performed over the Internet between businesses, rather than between a customer and a business. Business to business or B-to-B actions might be a salesperson for retailer X going to the Web site for wholesaler Y to order more parts for the items that retailer X sells.

business to customer — B-to-C, or business to customer, is pretty much your normal ecommerce. You shopping at Amazon is B to C. Amazon sending you emails about the latest Harry Potter book is B to C.

C

cell — In database context, see *field*.

CGI — Common Gateway Interface is a set of rules for how to write a program, in any programming language, that will run over the Internet and interact with a Web server. CGI replaced standard application programming languages when vendors began rewriting their applications to be browser-based.

class — In a programming language, a template for creating objects. A class could be a piece of code defining the attributes and methods for a Customer in an application, an Item, or a non-concrete concept such as a Shape.

class diagram A UML diagram showing classes, interfaces, and relationships in an application, or part of an application. You can see one in Figure 20-2 on page -240. See also *UML*.

client The part of an application, typically on a separate computer, that the user interacts with to place orders, make inquiries, or whatever the intended functions of the application are. Sometimes referred to more loosely as the user or customer.

client-server An architecture for an application in which there are at least two parts, a client and a server, in which the client is the part that the customer interacts with to perform the intended functions of the application, and the server contains the rest of the application. The division of code between client and server can vary; a client can have only a browser and nothing else, or the client can contain both presentation and business logic, and the server can contain the database.

client container A client container is a substitute for a browser. The client container gives the services of a container, in the front-end application that customers use. Application server vendors provide tools for application developers to use to developer client containers. Once developed, you can send the client containers to your customers who install them and use them when they run your application.

Client containers are convenient if you want to have the services of a container but not the EJBs. Client containers let the client application interact directly with the database, without giving up services.

commit and rollback In database transactions, the ability to wait until a series of related tasks that make up an entire transaction are completed correctly, and commit the completed results to the database; or if the tasks were not all completed correctly, to roll back the tasks that were completed so that none of them took place and it is as if the tasks were never begun.

component

A component is a fairly vague phrase, but refers to an EJB, a servlet, a JSP, or any other piece of code that is written by itself but interacts with the container and other components. A component is written using a specific API for that type of component.

component interface

In previous versions of the EJB specification, this was called the remote interface. Because it had to be a remote interface. You had to assume that the bean might be right next door or in Poughkeepsie or St. Petersburg so you had to give it a remote interface. (We talked about this in the Chapter 1, "It's All About Communication: RMI," on page 269. Skip back for a few minutes if you'd like a review.)

However, now with local interfaces, it ain't necessarily so. That is, the interface formerly known as remote might be local or remote. So the EJB folks came up with another term for it, a component interface. So your component interface is either a remote interface or a local interface. Got it? Good. Heck, if it were easy to understand, everyone would be doing EJBs, right?

We discuss local interfaces more in *Talking to Session Beans and Entity Beans With Local Interfaces* on page 141.

component provider

A role in Enterprise JavaBeans development and deployment. A component provider writes the EJB code.

concurrency control

Concurrency control just means controlling how many clients or processes can get at the same data in a database. If you're changing Marge Hickenlooper's address, is someone else allowed to look at or change her name at the same time, as long as they don't change her address also, or is everyone else totally locked out, even of just reading the data? Concurrency control, particularly optimistic and pessimistic concurrency control, determine this. See also optimistic concurrency control and pessimistic concurrency control.

connection pooling

Creating a connection to a database takes a considerable amount of time and resources such as memory, so performance is considerably improved if connection pooling is used. Connection pooling means that several connections are created ahead of time, when the container is started, and are used when necessary.

connector architecture — A standard defined by the J2EE specification to integrate a J2EE application server with an Enterprise information Systems.

container — The heart of an application server is the container. The container program handles requests from the clients and relaying the appropriate messages to the application, provides services such as security and transactions, and typically handles getting data in and out of the database. A container handles all external requests, coming and going, and the application interacts only with the container.

conversational state — See state.

cookie — A cookie is a small text file that a Web server places on a client computer to store information about the browser's actions. For instance, the cookie can contain the user's login so that returning to Amazon or the Gap means the user is automatically recognized and logged in.

custom tag libraries — *See* tag libraries.

"'I never knew words could be so confusing,' Milo said to Tock as he bent down to scratch the dog's ear.

'Only when you use a lot to say a little,' answered Tock."

The Phantom Tollbooth, Norton Juster

D

DAO, data access object — The Data Access Object (DAO) pattern makes code written for accessing data easier to reuse or modify.

See also *The Data Access Object Pattern* on page 164.

data integrity — Data integrity is a term we're using to apply to transactions and related topics. Transactions means making sure that all the things that make up a task, like Jeannie's pizza order, get done, or not at all. (So she either gets her pizza and pays for it, or at least if she doesn't get her pizza, she doesn't have to pay for it.) Data integrity also means making sure that Jeannie gets the pizza she ordered, not Victor's calzones instead, and that Jeannie's Extra Mushrooms request doesn't get muddled up with Victor's order.

DBMS — A database management system, or a relational database management system, and the database it manages is like a librarian's relationship to the books in the library. The DBMS handles requests to read, remove, and change information in the database. An RDBMS is the same thing, simply for a relational database. Most databases used with J2EE are relational databases.

declarative — With declarative security, the programmer states exactly how to do it; with programmatic security, the Web container takes care of security with its builtin security features.

deployment — The process of preparing a Web or EJB application to be run. Deployment includes many steps and can be somewhat complex. Steps include using ANT or another program to copy the files to the correct directory structure for deployment and updating the deployment descriptor.

deployment descriptor — A deployment descriptor is an XML file that functions as a powerful configuration file for an EJB or Web container. The descriptor specifies among other things how many database connections to create, where each EJB is located, how security should be implemented, and many other settings.

deploy-time — When the application is deployed, as opposed to runtime, when the application is run.

distributed — A distributed application has essential components that are in separate containers or on separate computers. This is distinct from a standalone, nondistributed application such as a standard text editor which has all its essential components in one location on one computer.

Code isn't the only thing that's distributed. The code might all be on the same computer, but if the data is on a different computer, then the application is distributed.

Data is sometimes what makes an application distributed, because a separate computer or computers are required to store all the data for all the users. If you have 10 users and each requires 2 MB for their data, that's not a big deal. If you're a bank or a credit card company or Amazon and you have millions of users, you're going to need a lot of machines to store all that data.

distributed transaction — A transaction that can span across multiple, separate containers.

domain — A group of related items within a hierarchy. Keyboards, monitors and hard drives are part of the computer domain, but domains can be in software as well. Domain is one of those annoying vague words that comes up just about anywhere meaning anything. If someone's talking about a domain and you don't know what they're talking about, it's very possible they don't either. It's OK to ask for more information.

driver — Generally, a driver is a piece of software that allows a program to communicate with another program or piece o hardware without knowing the second program's idiosyncrasies and variations. Thus, a printer driver lets your text editor say "Go, print" to several different printers even though the printers have different syntax for running the Print command.

A database driver allows a container or a programmer to communicate with a Sybase, Oracle, or other DBMS in the same way, simply by using the Sybase, Oracle, or other database driver.

dynamic content — Dynamic content is part of a Web page that does something besides standard HTTP functions like hyperlinks, animated GIFs, and forms. Dynamic content is achieved by using JSPs instead of HTML pages, or servlets. You can get dynamic content by having latestinfo.jsp check the database and serve up the latest information; a static page would just have the same information no matter how out of date.

E

EAR file — An EJB archive file. EAR files are no different from JAR files (Java archive files similar to ZIP files) except that their file extensions are different. Certain components must be put into EAR files before an EJB application can be deployed. See also WAR file.

EJB container — The container that handles EJBs. (Not that you couldn't have guessed that.) See also EJBs and container.

EJBs (Enterprise JavaBeans) — Enterprise JavaBeans are just pieces of Java code that, controlled by the EJB container, form the heart of an application. EJBs do things like calculating taxes and making sure orders get sent, and checking whether you're out of mozzarella. EJBs are pretty much your application; everything else is less central. They're called *beans* because they're separate pieces of *Java* code that work together to form a Greater Good (a nice big application).

For more information, see *Introduction to Enterprise JavaBeans* on page 117.

encapsulated

To be well encapsulated is to be good code. Well encapsulated code means other code can't get at your private stuff like your name or price or other things that shouldn't be changed without making sure they're changed right. They can ask to see your private stuff, and ask to change your private stuff, but whether it's done and how it's done is up to you.

For more information, see *Why Object Orientation Is Good* on page 266.

enterprise

A fancy-sounding term that just means a company that's on the big side. Hence "Java 2, Enterprise Edition" since J2EE is generally for big companies with big applications. Generally. However, small companies or organizations use J2EE too. Enterprise is mostly a buzzword to make any Enterprise Product sound big and cool.

entity bean

An Enterprise JavaBean that sits around holding data. They think they're the database. They stand there very proudly, holding the data like Mrs. Hickenlooper's address, and when a process is done the container gently plucks the data out of the entity bean's arms (without it noticing) and sends it over to the DBMS and says "here, put this in the right row, would you? that's a dear." See also session bean.

For more information, see *Introduction to Enterprise JavaBeans* on page 117.

environment

It's hard to get a vaguer word that *environment*, unless it's *thing*. Environment can mean many things, and if you're not sure what someone's talking about regarding environment, ask'em. They probably don't know either. But in general, environment means the system an application exists within. Is it a heterogeneous environment? That means there are computers with lots of different operating systems all working together. A J2EE environment means you've got servers and beans and stuff.

extensibility

If you can add new features to the system without rewriting a lot of the application, that's extensibility. Not merely the ability to add features, but to add features relatively easily. A house with the plumbing and electric running through logical, easily accessible spots means that the house is easily extensible if you wanted to put on an addition.

For more information, see *Qualities of Service (QOS): What's Most Important in an Application* on page 227.

See also *XML*, which stands for eXtensible Markup Language.

F

field

In a database table, a field is one distinct piece of information, like Mrs. Hickenlooper's postal code or her last name. Or, if her first name and last name are stored in the same column, a field could be her entire name. A field is the intersection of a column and a row, in a table.

firewall

A piece of hardware or software the limits network traffic.

"I don't know what you mean by 'Glory', Alice said.

Humpty Dumpty smiled. 'I meant 'there's a nice knock-down argument for you.'

"But 'Glory' doesn't mean 'a nice knock-down argument,'" Alice objected.

"When I use a word," Humpty Dumpty said, "It means exactly what I choose it to mean, neither more nor less."

"The question is," said Alice, "whether you can make words mean so many different things."

"The question is," said Humpty Dumpty, "which is to be master, that's all.'

Lewis Carroll, Through the Looking-Glass

G

garbage collector

The garbage collector goes around all the time looking for bits of memory that nobody's using anymore. This is a Java feature, not just J2EE. The garbage collector decides that nobody's using an object anymore if no other object has a reference to it.

Garbage collection's whole point is to recycle memory. If you had to buy new memory all the time, it would be as stupid and expensive as if you bought new clothes every time you'd worn all your current ones. Garbage collecting memory is like doing laundry and putting the clean clothes back in your closet.

granularity

It refers to the size of the chunks making up an item. A high number of small chunks means high granularity. A crowd of 10,000 has high granularity if it's composed of individuals; it has low granularity if it's composed of a bunch of Republicans and a bunch of Democrats.

H

handle

Handles are just another word for a reference. What's a reference? It's how object A in regular ol' Java gets ahold of object B and tells it to do something. You can't do nothin' without references. Handles are the word for it when the reference is to an EJB, who have slightly different physiognomies than regular objects. For more information, see *A New Concept: Handles* on page 72.

Home interface

The Home interface contains methods for getting ahold of a bean. One of the things that the container needs to be able to do is to create a new instance of the bean. One of the methods a Home interface contains is a create method. For more information, see *The Home Interface* on page 147.

HTTP

HTTP is the language of the Web. It stands for HyperText Transfer Protocol, but you don't need to remember that. Stuff people do on the Web is sent across in an HTTP request, and an answer is returned in an HTTP response.

I

IIOP

See RMI/IIOP.

implements

If you say that your application server implements transactions, that means, yes, that your application server makes sure that transactions are handled correctly. It's a little bit beyond just *uses*; with *implements* there's the assumption that there are a bunch of things you could implement and you're choosing whether to implement them or not. There are some required features which application servers must implement, and some optional ones they don't have to. *Implements* comes up more often referring to the second group, since people want to know whether an application server implements certain features.

instance

An instance is pretty much in programming what it is in English. An instance is kind of like an object—you have a class file, and when you create a real thing based on it, that's an instance. When you make cookies, there are about 24 instances of the cookie recipe. Unless you've eaten too much of the dough first.

interface

An interface is a piece of code that defines the "what" but not the "how" for something. J2EE relies heavily on interfaces to make sure that the code programmers write is right.

When you apply for a job, you have to send in a cover letter and a resume (what) but you can send them in using PDF or text or HTML, you might have multiple pages for the resume (or cover letter, though we don't advise it), and so on. But you do those two things. The rigid, protocol-oriented HR person receiving your information is going to be expecting those two things, and if you don't send'em in, she's going to freak, and start saying "Does not compute!"

Here's how interfaces can apply in programming. A programmer is told to create a method called `bakePizza` but exactly how he or she writes that code is up to the individual. The server needs this method because it's going to call a method called `bakePizza` at some point when it does its server business, and it's going to need that method to be there and baking the pizza. There's more to the code than just that, though, and all that extra stuff is up to the programmer. A smaller pizza might need less time; a pizza with fresh basil spread on top might need a lower temperature; and so on.

For more information, see *How Interfaces Make It All Work* on page 36.

internationalization

Making an application or other product usable by people who speak other languages than the one spoken and used by the people coding the project. *Internationalization* implies some techniques and tools used to do this more easily than just going through every line of code one by one and making the appropriate changes.

For more information, see *Internationalization* on page 219.

J

J2EE

J2EE is Java 2, Enterprise Edition. It's the set of tools in the Java programming language that let you do distributed applications. It's also the set of guidelines for doing it. In J2EE you have a J2EE application server, which provides services like security and help making sure the transactions don't get goofed up, and a J2EE application, running inside the server. It's kind of like workers inside a factory, just doing their business, and letting the factory take care of things like locking the doors at night and running the assembly lines.

J2EE runs on top of J2SE, kind of like a big trailer full of tools towed behind an SUV.

J2ME

J2ME is Java 2, Micro Edition. It's tools for things like cell phones and smart cards. It runs without J2SE.

J2SE

J2SE is Java 2, Standard Edition. It's regular Java, just the stuff you need if you're writing a regular application that runs on one computer and doesn't need to worry about doing complicated transactions on computers all over the world.

JAR file

Java Archive file. For all intents and purposes, it's a ZIP file, just a bunch of files all tied up together into one. Sometimes your Java code needs to be tied up in a JAR file because that's just what the rules are.

Java Beans

Not EJBs. Not even close. The marketing people goofed up the naming on this bigtime.

Java Beans are really just very clearly, predictably written Java code. See also *What's up With This "Bean" Name, Anyway?* on page 51.

JAX

This is just an acronym for the Java XML tools, or Java API for XML.

JAXM

JAXM is the Java messaging service API that you can use with Web services. It's not in the J2EE 1.4 release but it's been talked about a lot.

JAXR

The Java API for XML Registries lets you get at standard business registries over the Internet. Business registries are basically just online yellow pages. You can get at the information in them, as well as register a business, using JAXR. It gives developers a uniform way to use business registries that are based on open standards like ebXML or semi open industry-led specifications like UDDI.

JDK — See SDK.

JMS — JMS is the means by which message-driven beans deliver their little asynchronous messages. It's just a way within Java to send messages around.

JNDI — What RMI/IIOP looks at, for a J2EE application, to figure out where a requested part of the application is. JNDI keeps track of where all the beans are. When you deploy a bean, you have to specify a set of information that gets rolled into JDNI. So when RMI needs to find a bean, there it already is, in the JNDI lookup mechanism. Techies will always tell you, "Oh, JNDI, it just works, don't worry about it," and they're right.

JRE — The bare essentials of what it takes to run a Java program: the JVM plus the prewritten code classes.

For more information, see *JRE, JDK, and More Acronym Soup* on page 270.

JSP — JSPs are basically HTML on a bit of steroids; you can slip in various kinds of extra codes, plus actual Java code. They go on the Web tier and the Web server sends them to the client tier so users can see the pages.

For more information, see *Overview of JSPs* on page 103.

JVM — The program that takes bytecode (a compiled Java program) and translates it appropriately for the operating system the Java program is running on. There's at least one JVM for every operating system.

For more information, see *More on the Compiler and the Java Virtual Machine* on page 268.

"You keep saying that word. I do not think it means what you think it means."

Inigo Montoya, The Princess Bride

L

legacy application Rather than a Legacy brand application, it's an old application, one's legacy, that one is trying to integrate with something modern like J2EE.

life cycle One often hears about an EJB life cycle or a servlet life cycle. Both are created, used, and killed off heartlessly by the EJB or Web container. However, it's all part of the circle of life, and none of them truly suffers.

local interface This is a new thing in the latest EJB release.

In previous versions of the EJB specification, you had to write a remote interface as part of any EJB. So that the container could get ahold of it and so that other beans could get ahold of it in case they were in Fargo and this bean was in Sheffield. You had to assume that the bean might be right next door or in Poughkeepsie or St. Petersburg so you had to give it a remote interface.

See also *Talking to Session Beans and Entity Beans With Local Interfaces* on page 141 and *It's All About Communication: RMI* on page 269.

localization A general term including or equating to internationalization. Localization can mean translation as well as anything else to adapt an application to run for a different culture or different location.

M

maintainability This covers a variety of characteristics. Can you just go into one part of the system and fix it without breaking the entire system? Is it easy to figure out which part of the application to go to, to fix a feature, and can you go to just one or two places, or do you have to hunt and peck through thousands of lines of code? That's maintainability.

See also *Qualities of Service (QOS): What's Most Important in an Application* on page 227.

manageability This is more accurately thought of as *monitorability*, but nobody calls it that. It means, can your system administrator keep an eye on its CPU usage, memory usage, etc., and accurately add memory, machines, extra servers, or whatever else is necessary when the system needs better performance, scalability, etc.

For more information, see *Qualities of Service (QOS): What's Most Important in an Application* on page 227.

many to many

Many to many is a term used in databases and in UML. It means, for every one of the Poozixes, there can be many Lummoxes, and for every one Lummox there can also be many Poozixes. Many to many. Kind of like you and your friends. You all have many other friends, they have friends, and so on.

Many to one is a little more strict. You can have many Poozixes but they relate to only one Lummox. Like phone lines to phones; you have 7 lines coming out of your phone, all relating to only one phone. You can't get at any of those lines with any other phone. Or there can be multiple orders placed by one particular person.

One to many is just the opposite. For every one Poozix there are can be many Lummoxes. For every one phone you can have many phone lines; for every single person there can be multiple orders.

One to one is the simplest. For every one Poozix there can be only one Lummox and vice versa. Theoretically, at any one moment in time for every wife there can be only one husband and vice versa.

method

A synonym for behavior, in Java. Methods are what Java code does, just as attributes (synonym for state) are what they know about themselves.

For more information, see *What Object Orientation Is* on page 262.

modular

Modular is kind of like granular, kind of like atomicity, and kind of like componentized. It means made up of a bunch of littler bits that work together, and if you want to change one thing, you just have to change one of the modules, rather than the whole thing. Good J2EE applications are modular.

multitier model

Also called the n-tier model or four-tier model. This just means, a structure where you've got the browser, and the Web tier, and the business logic or EJB tier or middle tier, and the database tier. See also *tier*.

MVC

MVC stands for Model-View-Controller. Basically, MVC is a way to represent the parts of an application. It's a complicated techy way of dividing up how the Web part of the application looks, how it acts, and where it stores the information. Which is just the same old separation of presentation, business, and persistence logic we've been blabbing on about pretty much since the beginning of the book.

O

object

In programming, an individual instance, like the red shirt you bought yesterday, or your oldest sister. Objects are made from classes, like Shirt or Relatives or Clothing or Men.

For more information, see *Objects and Classes* on page 265.

object orientation

Object orientation essentially means that programmers write code that starts with the name of a thing that will be used in the program, like socks or customers. The programmer writes a little code, called a class file, about what the thing is; what it knows about itself such as a color and size or address and customer number; and what it can do such as change its color or size, be sold, shrink; or change its address and order things. Then the object can be asked to get or change the things it knows about itself (attributes), and to run the things it can do (methods). This is in contrast to other programs where the programmer is responsible for writing the code, every time, for changing a sock color, rather than just asking the sock to change its own damn color.

Advantages of object orientation mean that changing code for one part of the program means you're less likely to break code in another part. Objects are also able to have private attributes, which is kind of like a secretary having a locked file cabinet. You can ask him to shred the Enron file, but unless his Shred method is set up to allow that, it's not going to happen.

For more information, see *The Attributes of Object Orientation* on page 261.

one to many, one to one

See many to many.

optimistic concurrency control — This is related to but the opposite of pessimistic concurrency control. Optimistic control means that you have kind of a free and easy, optimistic approach to the idea of multiple people accessing the same row in a database.

Let's say you and some guy named Bob halfway across the country are both trying to book a seat on the same flight at the same time. Now, if you both try to book the same seat on the same flight at the same time, one of you is going to lose. There'll be tears and recriminations, or at least annoyances. On the other hand, if you wanted to prevent the possibility of that happening, you'd have to only let one person at a time book a ticket on a particular flight. That too would be annoying, and for more people. So given the number of people who book flights online, the low odds of two people booking exactly the same seat at the same time, and the fact that it's really not a life-threatening issue if that happens, optimistic concurrency is a good choice for this. Optimistic concurrency control means you let multiple people have access to the same records at the same time, and hope for the best. In the event that wackiness ensues, you go back through whatever steps you need to do to fix the situation, like offering Bob a seat on a later flight.

Pessimistic concurrency control is what you'd use if the results of two people accessing the same record at the same time were worse than the fuss you'd have to go through to fix the situation. For instance, let's say instead of booking flights, this is an air traffic control system. If two guys book the same seat at the same time, well, not a huge deal. If two airplanes try to occupy the same space at the same time, that's a huge bad big deal. Pessimistic concurrency control would be a better choice for things where lives are on the line.

P

package — A group of several related pieces of Java code. Java comes with packages of related prewritten classes, and programmers can package up their own classes, as well. Packages are what you refer to when you want to use some prewritten code—you write at the top of your Java code a package import statement, which starts logically enough with the word import, and then just list the packages.

pattern — A design pattern is a common solution to a common problem encountered in software development. There are patterns for shopping carts, for situations where you need to be able to change information frequently and want the application to reflect it quickly, and so on.

For more information, see *Design Patterns* on page 236.

performance — Application processing speed. When a user clicks "Show me the last ten pizza orders I placed," is there a response in two seconds or two minutes?

For more information, see *Qualities of Service (QOS): What's Most Important in an Application* on page 227.

persistence — An unnecessary fancy word for "not floating around in memory, but written down somewhere in the computer." That's what databases are for: persistence.

pessimistic concurrency control — See optimistic concurrency control.

portal — A portal is a specially designed Web page, roughly. A portal is a Web page composed of several different components, such as a Web service that gives you stock quotes; a portlet that contains weather, and plain HTML content sucked in from your company intranet main page.

presentation logic — Presentation logic is a complicated way of saying "the GUI" or "the interface" or "the part of an application you see when you run it." The presentation logic in a 4-tier J2EE application is the Web pages and JSPs.

For more information, see *The Importance of Separating the Presentation Logic* on page 59.

primary key — In databases, a primary key is the main piece of information used to sort the rows in a table and to find data in the first place. The primary key might be a customer ID, or vendor ID, and really really should be unique for every row in the table. First name is not a good primary key.

programmatic — Programmatic means, you're doing it on purpose and writing the code yourself. Programmatic security means you've written up some programming code and you're telling the whole application exactly what and how to do it. Now, isn't this normal? Aren't applications by nature programmatic? Not necessarily, and not for everything. Not when you've got containers that are ready, willing, and able to do certain services for you. Programmatic is the opposite of declarative, which means you just let the container knock itself out doing it for you, its own way. BMP or bean-managed persistence is programmatic.

protocol

A vague word that just means "the way you do it." Any two things in the computer world might or might not know how to talk to each other, so they need to decide ahead of time on a protocol to use for communication. Just as you and your friends have a protocol of English (or Dutch or Spanish) as a means of communication, bits of the application have various protocols for communication. IIOP is a protocol used in RMI to let bits of applications whiz around all over a network.

"I've been very lonely in my isolated tower of indecipherable speech."

Dr. Lester, Being John Malkovich

Q

qualities of service

Also called service requirements, qualities of service refer to application performance goals such as availability, security, extensibility, and so on. These are not features of the J2EE application but characteristics. Many qualities of service require tradeoffs: if you want absolute reliability, then performance will not be as good. An architect should consider qualities of service when developing the application architecture.

For more information, see *Qualities of Service (QOS): What's Most Important in an Application* on page 227.

R

RDBMS

See DBMS.

realm

You get a security realm in J2EE with the J2EE toolkit, often a simple text file listing authentication and authorization information. Application server vendors like BEA and IBM provide their own security realms, which are pretty good and highly recommended over the included security realm.

Security realm is a pretty poor term for it. Realm is used to mean about ten different things, from the completely conceptual to the very physical. It's not a realm, it's a list of logins and passwords.

reference implementation

The reference implementation is an obscure way of saying a sample application server. People writing J2EE servers use it as an example of how things work and to copy code from; people writing sample applications use it as a stopgap, free application server. It's not meant to be used for commercial purposes, and is a bit on the slow side.

referential integrity

This is an extremely fancy way of saying "Making sure a table doesn't get screwed up." Referential integrity means doing things like locking a table row so that while one part of the application is changing Mrs. Hickenlooper's address, no other part of the application can get to any information about Mrs. Hickenlooper in that row. There are other less strict ways of trying to have referential integrity, as well. See also *optimistic concurrency control* and *pessimistic concurrency control*.

Databases and these referential issues are covered in the chapter titled *The Database* on page 157.

relational database

All the databases you'd use with J2EE are relational. Relational just means that the data is grouped logically in tables, with customers here and inventory over there and orders up there, behind the cool air duct. Sometimes the tables contain the relationships between the tables, so that you can tell which orders contain which inventory items, and which customers placed which orders.

Databases and these referential issues are covered in the chapter titled *The Database* on page 157.

remote interface

A remote interface is the code you write as part of an Enterprise JavaBean so that the container can grab onto it, and so that other beans can locate it using RMI. After all, the bean could be anywhere.

A remote interface is one kind of component interface. That is, you need a component interface, and it can either be a remote interface or a local interface. We discuss local interfaces more in *Talking to Session Beans and Entity Beans With Local Interfaces* on page 141.

reliability

Without reliability, your application will gack on you or your customers periodically. Pure reliability means that your application never ever messes up, or if it does no one can tell. This is important for air traffic control, not so crucial for www.PezRUs.com. Reliability can be obtained by having multiple servers which "brain-share" and when one fails, another takes over.

For more information, see *Qualities of Service (QOS): What's Most Important in an Application* on page 227.

remote services Interestingly, this does not mean services that are remote. It means services that are run by remote clients. Let's say there's a guy shopping on Amazon in Turkjebistan, when the EJB container and all the session beans that provide services are in Fargo, North Dakota. Those Amazon session bean services are remote services, even if you're standing there in Fargo right next to the server computer. Yet another example of why the whole darned tech naming system needs to be overhauled.

resource management An application server takes care of *resource management*, so that memory used by one part of the application gets freed up and available for use by other parts. And the application server can create copies of bits of the application when it needs more help completing tasks. However, it's a balancing act. Just as it can be expensive and destructive to go out and buy 2500 new sewing machines for a beanbag factory, since now there's all this equipment but no money for anything else, the server has to be careful not to create too many connections to the database, or there'll be no resources left for anything else.

See Chapter 15, "Resource Management," on page 185.

RMI RMI is *remote method invocation*. Which is actually a reasonably clear acronym. When bit A wants bit B to do something, do they just yell at each other and say, "Hey, Gus, bring me that order from the ORDERS database!" Nope. For one thing, one part of the application has no clue where the other part is even stored, or where the order would be in the database, and no clue about all of the networking code that's required on order to do these cross-network tasks.

So you need RMI. RMI is Java's way of providing a connection between computing power on one machine and computing power on another machine, or a different container.

See *It's All About Communication: RMI* on page 269.

RMI/IIOP

RMI/IIOP is the kind of RMI used in J2EE. It's easier. A lot easier.

IIOP is actually the protocol that CORBA uses to talk over the network. CORBA is the Common Object Request Broker Architecture, it's been around for years, and is used in general by lots of applications to communicate over a network. CORBA is just another way to talk over the network, like SOAP.

So you've got CORBA, a commonly used architecture, or system, for getting stuff back and forth over a network, and it uses IIOP as the protocol for doing so. Basically, CORBA speaks IIOP, just like French is the language spoken by people in France. CORBA is the guidelines and structure for how communication is done. IIOP is what it speaks.

robust

This is one of the all-time best buzzwords. It just means "big with lots of features." Notepad is not robust; OpenOffice.org Writer is robust.

roles

Roles might mean in some contexts something like who gets to wear the lion suit, and who gets to be the lion tamer. However, in J2EE it means who writes the beans, versus who takes the beans and puts them in the right directory so they'll run, versus who creates the Web pages that link up to the beans and let users get at the bean functions. The whole EJB specification is very much into the whole Roles idea. Roles are include bean deployer or bean developer.

For more information, see *The Development Process Is Supported by Blueprints and J2EE Patterns* on page 119.

row

A row is one item's record in a database table, like Mrs. Hickenlooper's name and address, or one item in the PRODUCTS table.

For more information, see *So, Just to Be Absolutely Clear, What's a Database?* on page 159.

runtime

When the application is running. A runtime debugger means a debugger that works while the application is running. Being updated at runtime means, yep, once the application starts running again, it gets updated. You will also occasionally hear *compile time* and *deploy time*.

S

scalability

The ability to handle increased load without affecting the application. If you go from 100 orders a week to 10,000 orders a week, you don't want to have to rewrite parts of your application. You want to be able to just throw more servers and hardware at it.

For more information, see *Qualities of Service (QOS): What's Most Important in an Application* on page 227.

schema

You can create a file called a *schema* to describe the structure of a particular type of XML document. For example, you can write a schema for a price list that specifies which tags can be used and where they can occur. This is useful because an XML document can rapidly get big and disorganized and ugly without some rules for how to use the tags. Schemas, of course, are written in their own language, and the most common type is the Document Type Definition (DTD) schema language. It's part of the XML 1.0 specification, which is just the rules for how to write XML in general.

A schema written in this language is usually referred to as a DTD, which makes things kind of confusing. You've got a schema, a.k.a. a schema written in the Document Type Definition schema language, a.k.a. a DTD. DTD is actually a language for schemas but it's used as a synonym for the schemas. It's like referring to a newspaper as an English or as a *Croatian*. However, DTD is the most common schema language, so while the naming is confusing, it's not as confusing as it could be.

scriptlets

Scriptlets are bits of Java code inserted in a JSP, rather than kept separate in their own Java code files and referenced. Scriptlets are generally nasty since they are not compilable, so finding errors is very difficult. Likewise if you use common scriptlet code in multiple JSP pages you must cut-and-paste to keep the code identical. This is a maintenance nightmare if you need to change all of that scriptlet code in all of the pages that use it. See *Scriptlets* on page 105 for more information.

SDK

The Java SDK is the same as the JDK. It's the essentials of what it takes to develop a Java program. The JVM, the compiler, and a bunch of other tools and prewritten code. It also has the Java source code the classes are made from—the source is the blueprint of the prewritten code classes.

security — Preventing code with Inappropriate Intentions from getting in and do nasty things. For instance, your security system should ensure Susie Peon can't get to the changeAllPrices method in your EJBs.

For more information, see *Qualities of Service (QOS): What's Most Important in an Application* on page 227, and the chapter titled *J2EE Security* on page 207.

security realm — A system of authorization, specifying what users there are, their passwords, and what roles they have. LDAP is a type of security realm.

security role — Security is based on two things: making sure you are who you are (authentication) and then making sure that you can go only where you're supposed to go. Where you're supposed to go is based on your *security role*. Are you a Peon, a Manager, a Superuser, a Grunt, or a small white fox typically found in northern Peru? All of those are security roles, which then are mapped to things like "everything" or "only the login page" or "only the pages in the **public** directory."

For more information, see *J2EE Security* on page 207.

server — A *server* has many possible meanings. A server can be just a computer of any sort, a *Web server*, or an *application server* which of course is what we spent most of this book talking about. Additionally, there is the meaning of server in *client-server*. See the appropriate definition in this chapter.

servlet — Servlets are for processing on the Web tier, pumping up what you can do in response to Web page requests, and what you can send back to Web pages. Servlets can speak HTTP, which is the Language of the World Wide Web, so that means they understand the commands that come across from the Web server.

Servlets are just Java code, but they use and extend classes like HttpServlet which are specifically designed to deal with Web stuff and interact with JSPs.

session — *Sessions* just means that when you enter information in window 1 of 3, by window 3 the application still remembers who you are and the information you entered. Because, as many many people are fond of saying, HTTP is a stateless protocol. HTTP, the native language of the World Wide Web, is great at passing information back and forth in a carefree way but has no longterm memory and will not remember you the second time no matter how memorable you were the first time. Stateless session beans are the same way; they don't carry on conversations with other objects by building on the first step.

session bean

Session beans represent the stuff your business needs to do, like letting customers buy and return beanbags. When you register as a new customer, session beans check the database (well, the entity bean) to see if you're already in the database, before they send your new registration to the database.

Stateful session beans are faithful to one client for their lifetime, and store all the information that the client sends it. Stateless session beans will service any client's request, with no regard to who they've just been with, and don't remember a thing from the last client. Both are useful, depending on what you want done.

For more information, see *Introduction to Enterprise JavaBeans* on page 117.

specification

The instructions for how to do something, namely how to write an application server, or how to write an application that works with an application server. The specification is the English counterpart to the JDK prewritten code (classes, interfaces, etc.) that you get with something like J2EE. The specification tells you the rules for how to do it (must have XYZ implement PDQ in order to instantiate LMNO), and just generally a cryptic but accurate description of what the whole thing is about. Reading a specification is an excellent way to get to sleep, and an excellent thing to keep on your desk, bristling with sticky notes, to scare the techies into thinking you've read it and understand it.

SSL

SSL stands for secure sockets layer. It's a protocol developed by Netscape for transmitting private documents via the Internet. SSL works by using a private key to encrypt data that's transferred over the SSL connection. Both Netscape Navigator and Internet Explorer support SSL, and many Web sites use the protocol to obtain confidential user information, such as credit card numbers. By convention, URLs that require an SSL connection start with https: instead of http: It's all kind of complicated, since encryption is freakin' complicated. Just accept it on faith.

state

State is a slightly fuzzy concept if you're not familiar with the way most business processes are coded. State is the data that's exchanged between object A and object B as they interact to complete a given business process. State is the means to the end, and the end is the completion of the business process. The business process might be a customer buying a pair of red suede pumps, or the results to a personality quiz that reveals you are most like the dark-haired Power Puff girl. The point of the whole process is receiving red suede pumps in exchange for money, or discovering your true nature. All the state collected along the way, like your credit card and shoe size and favorite scent, are just incidental to the main goal.

State is information gathered in a conversation, a series of requests and responses, between objects. Why not just give all the information at once, though—why have the conversation? Why ask all those questions back and forth? Because neither party knows ahead of time what information to provide or request. Let's say you're filling in a tax program, like Quicken. It asks you if you have any dependents. If you do, then the next window tells you to give information about them; if you don't have any, there's no point in providing information about them. Conversational state is a good way of asking for the right information. And state, just plain state, is the information that is accumulated during that conversation.

State is not any data that an object carries around. State is data specific to a conversation, several requests and responses.

state and behavior

State and *behavior* are alternate terms for attributes and operations, or variables and methods. The first word refers to the object's values, such as red or $12.95 or Mary, and the second word refers to what it can do: delete things, order things, print things, and so on.

For more information, see *What Object Orientation Is* on page 262.

This kind of state is distinct from the state in the context of conversational state.

static content — Standard HTML content, rather than dynamic content. See also dynamic content.

support — *Support* means more or less "has the capability to do." So if WebLogic Server supports transactions, that means that the WebLogic Server application server has the ability to do transactions.

"Some people have a way with words. Some people...not have way."

Steve Martin, Wild and Crazy Guy.

T

table — In a database, a table is a set of related data composed of rows, columns, and fields where the row and column intersect. A list of customer names and addresses, with information about each customer in a different row and a different piece of data in each column, is an example of a table.

For more information, see *There's the Database, and the DBMS* on page 159.

tag libraries — A tag library is Java code written in a specific way so as to be usable from a JSP (JavaServer Page). Tag libraries are a powerful way to enable a JSP to trigger nearly any programming function.

See *Custom Tag Libraries* on page 106 for more information.

tier — A distinct set of software that works together, and interacts with other tiers through one designated function or piece of software. For instance, a database tier is the DBMS and its associated database and tables. Anything that wants to get at those tables goes through the DBMS, and if the tables need anything, the DBMS goes and gets it.

Tiers are sometimes kept on separate computers, so that there is only one tier on each computer. However, there is no limit to the number of tiers that can be on the same computer together. It's probably not practical from a performance standpoint to do this, of course.

For more information about all the tiers, see *Why Bother With Tiers?* on page 55.

tool provider

A J2EE development role. A tool provider writes software to facilitate development, assembly, or deployment of a J2EE application.

transactions

A transaction is a set of tasks that go together, and that really should be all completed together or not at all can happen. Getting money out of an ATM is a transaction, since if the money is taken out of your account at the bank but never spit out of the machine at you, that's bad. Likewise if you take money off a customer's credit card but never ship him or her the product ordered, that's bad too. Application servers typically have services that make sure that, if a set of tasks like these gets started, that they're completed successfully or else everything is *rolled back* so that it's as if the first task was never even started.

See Chapter 16, "Data Integrity, Transactions, and Concurrency," on page 197.

transparent

Transparent to the user is an oft-used phrase meaning that the users won't notice. A transparent login might mean that the program takes information gathered elsewhere and automatically logs in the user without him or her having to type a user name and password. *Transparent* is usually used to refer to features that are important, but not visible. This is to reassure people that complicated sounding features won't be a hassle for the users.

two-phase commit

Not engagement followed by marriage; rather, it's the way a J2EE transaction is processed. The first phase queries each player in the transaction to see if they are ready to commit. The second phase tells each player to commit if everyone voted commit in the first phase or rollback if any one voted rollback in the first phase. (Commit and rollback, likewise, sounds like marriage followed by divorce.)

U

UDDI

Universal Description, Discovery, and Integration (UDDI) is the standard for registering Web services in a central location. The UDDI registry receives queries about what Web services are available and sends back information about the Web services available.

UML

The Unified Modeling Language is a standardized notation, like musical notation for composition, for describing designs. It is used for application design but can be used for other designs, as well. UML has a variety of diagrams including class diagrams, sequence diagrams, and deployment diagrams. A designer creates the diagrams, from which programmers can start coding. See *Meeting Room Wallpaper: UML Diagrams* on page 239 for more information.

URL rewriting HTTP is a stateless protocol; it doesn't have a way of connecting one request, like your filling in a form and clicking Submit, to a related request. URL rewriting is one way of creating this link, referred to as a session. Web containers support URL rewriting. To do this, the programmer attaches a session ID to the URL that's sent from the browser with a request. That ID is used to keep track of all the related requests.

---

vendor Anyone who creates a database, application server, component, or other product that they sell as a product. Database vendors include Sybase and Oracle; application server vendors include BEA and Sun Microsystems.

WAR file A Web archive file, similar to an EAR file or a JAR file but with a different file extension. Certain components need to be put into WAR files to be deployed in Web applications. See also EAR file.

Web component Any component code created for the Web, typically a JSP or a servlet.

Web container A container that handles Web components such as Web services, servlets, and JSPs. The Web server sends requests for these components to the Web container, which passes on the requests to the appropriate component, then sends the responses back to the Web server. See *There's a Web Container Too* on page 28.

Web server A simple program that understands HTTP and can respond to HTTP requests from a browser such as asking for the page at a particular URL. A Web server takes care of requests for pages with static content and passes requests for dynamic content to the Web container. See also *Just to Confuse Things, There's a Web Server Involved Too* on page 29.

Web services

A Web service is just a way of making a function, like getting a stock quote or finding people to supply pizza toppings, available over the Internet. The most useful way to implement them is to combine related tasks that a user would have to do separately and put them together in one task. Web services are often used between businesses. See Chapter 14, "Web Services and SOAP," on page 167 for more information.

WSDL

Web Services Description Language (WSDL). A WSDL description is an XML document that gives all the important information about a Web service, like its name, the operations that can be called on it (like getWholesalers or computeAveragePrice), the parameters for those operations (do you have to send it the name of the company whose stock you want to check, the four-letter abbreviation like BEAS, or both?), and the location of where to send requests (the URL where the Web service is located).

Think of it as the Web service's online personal ad. Anyone who wants to can then just read it, see what it's like, and see how to access it. See Chapter 14, "Web Services and SOAP," on page 167 for more information.

X

XML

eXtensible Markup Language is a standard way of writing up information by indicating what type of information is enclosed in it with tags. It's similar to HTML, except that HTML tags are used to indicate content that should be displayed differently, while XML indicates content that should be evaluated differently. *Extensible* in this case means that instead of having a preset list of tags like HTML, you can create any set of tags you want to express the data used in your application.

index

A

B

C

E

F

G

H

I

J

N

O

P

Q

R

S

T

U

V

W

X

Prentice Hall Professional Technical Reference
http://www.phptr.com/
Prentice Hall PTR InformIT InformIT Online Books Financial Times Prentice Hall ft.com PTG Interactive Reuters
Tomorrow's Solutions for Today's Professionals
Prentice Hall Professional Technical Reference
Browse
Book Series
What's New
User Groups
Alliances
Special Sales
Contact Us
Search | Help | Home
Quick Search
PTR Favorites
Find a Bookstore
Book Series
Special Interests
Newsletters
Press Room
International
Best Sellers
Solutions Beyond the Book
Shopping Bag
Keep Up to Date with
PH PTR Online
We strive to stay on the cutting edge of what's happening in professional computer science and engineering. Here's a bit of what you'll find when you stop by www.phptr.com:
What's new at PHPTR? We don't just publish books for the professional community, we're a part of it. Check out our convention schedule, keep up with your favorite authors, and get the latest reviews and press releases on topics of interest to you.
Special interest areas offering our latest books, book series, features of the month, related links, and other useful information to help you get the job done.
User Groups Prentice Hall Professional Technical Reference's User Group Program helps volunteer, not-for-profit user groups provide their members with training and information about cutting-edge technology.
Companion Websites Our Companion Websites provide valuable solutions beyond the book. Here you can download the source code, get updates and corrections, chat with other users and the author about the book, or discover links to other websites on this topic.
Need to find a bookstore? Chances are, there's a bookseller near you that carries a broad selection of PTR titles. Locate a Magnet bookstore near you at www.phptr.com.
Subscribe today! Join PHPTR's monthly email newsletter!
Want to be kept up-to-date on your area of interest? Choose a targeted category on our website, and we'll keep you informed of the latest PHPTR products, author events, reviews and conferences in your interest area.
Visit our mailroom to subscribe today! http://www.phptr.com/mail_lists